The Oxfordian

Volume 18

October 2016

ISSN 1521-3641

The Oxfordian is an annual journal dedicated to publishing scholarship and informed opinion relating to the authorship and production of important literary works in Early Modern English. It is a publication of the Shakespeare Oxford Fellowship.

Writers interested in being published in **The Oxfordian** should review our publication guidelines at the Shakespeare Oxford Fellowship website:

http://shakespeareoxfordfellowship.org/the-oxfordian/

Our postal mailing address is:

> The Shakespeare Oxford Fellowship
> PO Box 66083
> Auburndale, Massachusetts
> 02466
> USA

Queries may be directed to the editor, **Chris Pannell** at cpannell3@cogeco.ca

Back issues of **The Oxfordian** may be obtained by writing to newsletter@shakespeareoxfordfellowship.org

Cover Photograph: Janice Jackson

The front cover is an interior view of the balcony at the restored Globe Theatre in London (circa 2013).

Acknowledgments

This volume of The Oxfordian owes it existence to the continuous support of the journal's editorial board, which has reviewed submitted articles, advised the editor, and provided much supplementary support and enthusiasm.

Bob Meyers	Don Rubin	Lynne Kositsky
Tom Regnier	Ron Hess	Richard Waugaman
Linda Theil	Ramon Jiménez	Jim Boyd
Justin Borrow	Wally Hurst	

+ + +

Proofreading: Jim Boyd, Ramon Jiménez, Rick Waugaman, Janice Jackson, Michael Kositsky.

Graphics Design, Software Support: Caitlin Pannell-Evans.

The editor thanks everyone listed above for their ongoing support. Additionally he thanks the contributors to this journal, and its readers, without whom it would not thrive.

The OXFORDIAN Volume 18 2016

Table of Contents

1. An Evening at the Cockpit: Further Evidence of an Early Date for *Henry V*

by Ramon Jiménez 9

A better explanation of the performance and printing history of *Henry V* is that lines 22-34 of the Act 5 Chorus do not refer to Essex at all, and were not written in 1599, but at least fifteen years earlier, when the Folio version of [the play] was first seen by an Elizabethan audience. . . . This passage . . . is much more appropriate to events earlier in Elizabeth's reign – before the Irish revolt of the 1590s – when there were two serious uprisings in Ireland known as the First and the Second Desmond Rebellions.

2. Reconsidering the Jephthah Allusion in *Hamlet*

by Connie J. Beane. 23

While Hamlet is talking to Rosencrantz and Guildenstern in the second act, prior to the arrival onstage of the visiting Players, Polonius enters to deliver news of their coming. Hamlet then taunts Polonius, calling the old man "Jephthah" and referring to his "one faire daughter and no more, the which he loued passing well" (2.2.349-350). The incident occupies less than a dozen lines and on the surface, appears trivial. However, in Shakespeare's plays, what appears to be trivial is sometimes significant. Who was Jephthah, and why would Hamlet compare Polonius to him?

3. Sc(e)acan, Shack, and Shakespeare

by Eddi Jolly. 41

Changes in semantics, pronunciation, and spelling during the period of Early Modern English (1500-1650) are of particular interest to those interested in 'Shakspere' and 'Shakespeare' . . . . One of the changes in Middle English was that some short vowels were lengthened. Baugh gives the example of the Old English infinitive *bacan*, which became Middle English *baken*, modern *to bake*. Other words which shared the sound change of *bacan* include *tacan*, modern *to take*; *sc(e)acan*, *to shake*; and the noun *nama, name*. Part of the change to modern pronunciations took place during what is called the Great Vowel Shift, generally seen as occurring between 1400 and 1600, but there were later vowel changes too.

4. *Twelfth Night*: How Much Did deVere Know of Dubrovnik?

by Richard Malim 55

We know that Oxford incurred an injury to his knee on a Venetian galley in 1575 during his stay in Italy. In September 1575, an Italian banker wrote from Venice: "God be thanked, for now last [lately] coming from Genoa his lordship found himself somewhat altered by reason of the extreme heats: and before [earlier] his Lordship hurt his knee in one of the Venetian galleys . . . " A Venetian galley would only have been used on a sea voyage, not a canal or river journey. Possibly, de Vere made a trip to the free city state of Ragusa (its Italian name) or Dubrovnik (its Croatian name). If so, he could have seen for himself a culture and location that he would later use as background for *Twelfth Night*.

5. Evermore in Subjection: Wardship and Edward de Vere

by Bonner Miller Cutting 65

One might feel for the plight of the youth who entered Cecil's magnificent London house in 1562. Even the brightest of twelve-year-olds would be no match for . . . William Cecil, a man who commanded the Privy Council, the Court of Wards, and the Treasury. Because of wardship, Edward de Vere accrued backbreaking debts and entered into a disastrous marriage. In the end, he lost everything: property, children, and his reputation. . . . Burghley himself wrote "The greatest possession that any man can have is honor, good name, and good will of many and of the best sort" – sentiments that Shakespeare ascribes to Iago.

6. The Sycamore Grove, Revisited

by Catherine Hatinguais. 85

[In] Verona, our bus stopped briefly near Porta Palio to allow us to see Romeo's sycamore grove. I asked our Italian guide – just to be sure – if those trees . . . through the bus windows were the famous sycamore trees. She answered bluntly: "No, those are plane trees. Sycamores are a different species." Once I recovered from my surprise, I started thinking . . . Are there really two different tree species, each with its own unique name? Or is there only one species of tree, but with two different names, depending on the region or the era? . . . To get to the root of this problem, we first had to get to the leaves. . . . Little did I know how far this modest inquiry would lead.

7. The Great Reckoning -- Who Killed Christopher Marlowe and Why?

by Stephanie Hopkins Hughes 101

The Oxfordian thesis has forced us into areas of psychology, biography and history – English, continental, and literary . . . [because of] the issue of Shakespeare's identity . . . . Seeking the truth about the author of the western world's most important and influential literary canon has required that we examine the facts surrounding the production of other literary works at the time, facts that demonstrate that the Stratford biography is not the only one rife with anomalies. Although Christopher Marlowe's biography holds together far better than most, his death remains as much a mystery as Shakespeare's identity. Could these two mysteries be related?

8. Essex, The Rival Poet of Shakespeare's *Sonnets*

by Peter Moore. 133

[Some] principal questions about the Sonnets are the identities of the fair youth, the dark lady, and the rival poet . . . The most often proposed rival poets are George Chapman and Christopher Marlowe, but the arguments for them are thin; even weaker cases have been offered for virtually every other contemporary professional poet. . . . Robert Devereux, the second Earl of Essex, was . . . intelligent, handsome, athletic, improvident, charming, a generous patron of writers . . . He was also the best friend and hero of the youthful third Earl of Southampton. He was also a poet whose talent was admired by his contemporaries.

9. The Rival Poet in *Shake-speare's Sonnets*

by Hank Whittemore 141

The Oxfordian model opens the door to an entirely new way of looking at the nine sonnets in the rival series, resulting in a view . . . that the rival was not a person at all, but a *persona*. . . . The rival series contains Oxford's own testimony about the authorship – a grand, poetic, profoundly emotional statement of his identity as the author being erased for all time and being replaced by the printed name known since 1593 as William Shakespeare. In this context, the sonnets about the so-called rival refer not to Oxford's original use of the pseudonym in 1593, but rather to the need several years later for his real name – his authorship – to be permanently *buried*.

10. A Psychiatrist's View of the *Sonnets*

by Eliot Slater 155

Shakespeare's preoccupation with his own aging, a physical decay destined to end in death, gives by itself an impression of such melancholy that we are bound to consider whether he may have had a depressive illness. Scholars have repeatedly emphasized the world-weariness, the despair of human kind and the self-contempt that inspire so much of the poetry and the action of such plays as *Hamlet*, *King Lear*, and *Timon of Athens*. Some (Chambers, for instance) think of the possibility of a nervous breakdown. The *Sonnets* are a record which can help us to a partial answer of whether the poet was ever in worse case than merely very miserable, or whether, in fact, he had a mental illness.

11. Review of Quentin Skinner's book, *Forensic Shakespeare*

by Richard Waugaman 175

12. Review of Robert Bearman's book, *Shakespeare's Money*

by Richard Waugaman 183

An Evening at the Cockpit
Further Evidence of an Early Date for Henry V

by Ramon Jiménez

Aside from the identity of the author of the Shakespeare canon, the most important question facing revisionist scholars, those who reject the Stratfordian theory, is an accurate dating of the plays. An accurate date for the composition of almost any play in the canon would be a valuable starting point for dating a good percentage of those remaining. For many decades now, orthodox scholars have almost unanimously asserted that a passage in the fifth act Chorus of *Henry V* fixes the composition date of that play to the spring of 1599, when Robert Devereux, second Earl of Essex, departed London with a substantial army to put down a major rebellion in Ireland.

In this passage, just preceding the fifth act, the Chorus describes the crowds coming out to meet King Henry in London on his return from his signal victory at Agincourt. The Chorus compares the crowds to those who must have turned out to greet Julius Caesar when he returned in triumph from Spain:

> But now behold,
> In the quick forge and working-house of thought,
> How London doth pour out her citizens!
> The Mayor and all his brethren in best sort,
> Like to the senators of th'antique Rome,
> With the plebeians swarming at their heels,
> Go forth and fetch their conqu'ring Caesar in;
> (5. Chorus. 22-28)[1]

The Chorus then introduces another comparison, one that might be similar, but that has not yet taken place:

> As by a lower but by loving likelihood,
> Were now the general of our gracious Empress,
> As in good time he may, from Ireland coming,
> Bringing rebellion broached on his sword,
> How many would the peaceful city quit,
> To welcome him!   (5. Chorus. 29-34)

"Nearly everyone agrees that in these lines 'the General' is Robert Devereaux, Earl of Essex," whom Queen Elizabeth had sent to Ireland in March 1599 to put down a protracted revolt (Craik 1-2). Another scholar writes that "The likening of Essex to Henry V by Shakespeare himself in the chorus of the Folio version is indisputable" (Albright 729). Even the maverick scholar Eric Sams agrees that the line refers to Essex, and adds that he was "the only living person to whom Shakespeare ever alluded anywhere in his work" (112). He overlooks the woman in the same line – Queen Elizabeth.

The outcome of the Earl's expedition is well known. He failed at his mission entirely and returned in disrepute to London in September. Orthodox scholars therefore claim that the fifth act Chorus, and the entire play itself, were written, and the play performed in the spring of 1599, before this outcome became known.

The play was registered in August 1600, then published three times in Quarto form (1600, 1602, and 1619) and then in the Folio in 1623. The title page of Q1 bore the phrase "As it hath bene sundry times playd by the Right honorable the Lord Chamberlaine his servants." But the three Quartos contained less than half the lines of the Folio text. The entire Prologue, Chorus, and Epilogue apparatus, several entire scenes, hundreds of lines, and eleven small speaking parts were cut from the play text that ultimately appeared in the Folio.

Orthodox scholars are divided about the process that resulted in the foreshortened Quartos, some favoring memorial reconstruction, and others deliberate cutting for performance. But they cannot explain the odd, if not improbable, scenario in which the Folio text was written and performed in 1599, then literally cut in half, performed, and the truncated text then printed three times before the complete text reappeared in the First Folio more than two decades after it was allegedly written. The claimed reference in the Folio text to the Earl of Essex in 1599 does not make sense in the light of the subsequent performance and printing of the play. It cannot be claimed that the Earl's loss of face (he was beheaded for treason only a year-and-a-half later) required that the play be cut in half. A deletion or replacement of four lines in the fifth act Chorus would have excised the reference to him sufficiently.

A better explanation of the performance and printing history of *Henry V* is that the

---

Ramon Jiménez *has a degree in English from U.C.L.A. and lives in Berkeley, California. He is the author of two books on Julius Caesar and the Roman Republic,* Caesar Against the Celts *and* Caesar Against Rome, *both book club selections. A lifelong Oxfordian since reading* This Star of England *in his last year of high school, Jiménez has published more than twenty articles and reviews in* The Shakespeare Oxford Newsletter *and* The Oxfordian. *His particular interest has been to demonstrate that several anonymous plays, none attributed to Shakespeare, were actually Oxford's earliest versions of canonical plays.*

passage does not refer to Essex at all, and was not written in 1599, but at least fifteen years earlier, when the Folio version of *Henry V* was first seen by an Elizabethan audience. The *harey the v* that Philip Henslowe mounted at his Rose theater more than a dozen times in 1595-6 was most likely the severely abridged version that appeared in the Quartos. For printing in the Folio, the publishers obtained the author's original text.

Background

In 2001 and 2002 I published three papers in the *The Shakespeare Oxford Newsletter* describing the seventeenth Earl of Oxford's transformation of his early prose play *The Famous Victories of Henry the Fifth* into the three Prince Hal plays, *1* and *2 Henry IV* and *Henry V*. In "Rebellion broachéd on his sword: New Evidence of an Early Date for *Henry V*" (v. 37:3 Fall 2001), I presented evidence that the orthodox date of spring 1599 for the composition of *Henry V* is incorrect on several counts, and that Oxford wrote the fifth act Chorus of the play during the six-month period after November 1583.

To begin with, Oxford's profound dislike for the Earl of Essex by the late 1590s would have precluded the favorable reference to him in the fifth act Chorus in 1599. In his October 1595 letter to Robert Cecil, Oxford rejected a suggestion that he approach the Earl for a favor, writing that it was "a thing I cannot do in honour, sith I have already received diverse injuries and wrongs from him, which bar me from all such base courses" (Chiljan 53). Oxford may have been referring to the rumors circulating as early as May 1595 that his newly-married daughter, Elizabeth, Countess of Derby, was having an affair with Essex.[2] But regardless of the particular reason, Oxford's statement makes it most improbable that less than four years later he would refer to the "loving likelihood" that Robert Devereaux "the general of our gracious Empress" may soon be coming from Ireland, "Bringing rebellion broached on his sword." Other reasons for rejecting a 1599 date include the political climate at the time, the Queen's own suspicions of Essex, and the Earl's actual failure to accomplish his mission in Ireland (Jiménez 8-10).

The passage in the fifth act Chorus is much more appropriate to events earlier in Elizabeth's reign – before the Irish revolt of the 1590s – when there were two serious uprisings in Ireland known as the First and the Second Desmond Rebellions. The first took place in the 1560s, and the second developed in the late 1570s under the brothers James, John, and Gerald Fitzgerald, the leaders of the House of Desmond, an ancient Irish earldom in the southern province of Munster. The Second Desmond Rebellion, also called the Munster Rebellion, was a major conflict that threatened the crown's authority and possessions in Ireland, and required a substantial mobilization of England's military apparatus. It attracted foreign intervention in the summer of 1579 and again a year later, when small armies of continental troops, described as primarily "Italian swordsmen," landed on the southwestern Irish coast, having been dispatched by Pope Gregory XIII in support of the rebellion against Elizabeth (Lennon 222-24).

In November 1579, after several years of fighting and unsuccessful attempts at negotiation, the English administrators of colonial Ireland finally lost patience with the leader of the rebellion, the forty-six-year-old Gerald Fitzgerald, fourteenth Earl of Desmond, and declared him a traitor (Bagwell 3:30-1). In her attempts to settle her Irish wars with as little expense as possible, Queen Elizabeth routinely offered pardons to even the most persistent rebels if they would lay down their arms and pledge their loyalty. But the Earl of Desmond had deceived and betrayed her too often. She had pardoned him once before, and had sent him to the Tower and then released him twice. Finally conceding that he was an unreclaimable rebel, she declared him ineligible for a pardon and offered "head money," £1000 for his head.

Over the next three years, several different English commanders led armies into Munster with varying degrees of success, gradually killing or capturing hundreds of the Desmond rebels. In the summer of 1580, James Fitzgerald was captured, hanged, drawn and quartered (Bagwell 3:55). By May 1581, the English army in Ireland numbered more than 6400 men, and in early January 1582 the youngest brother, Sir John of Desmond, was ambushed and killed. His turquoise and gold ring was sent to Elizabeth, and his head to the Governor of Ireland, Lord Grey of Wilton, as "a New Year's gift." Grey displayed it on a pole on a wall of Dublin castle (Bagwell 3:94).

Nevertheless, the rebellion dragged on and in December 1582, on the advice of Sir Walter Raleigh, Elizabeth appointed Sir Thomas Butler, tenth Earl of Ormond, her commanding general in Ireland. Known as "Black Tom" because of his dark hair and complexion, Butler was the scion of one of the oldest and most prominent families in Ireland and a major figure in Anglo-Irish relations throughout Elizabeth's reign. Butler was a distant cousin of Elizabeth Tudor on the Boleyn side – the eighth Earl of Ormond, Thomas Boleyn, was Anne Boleyn's father. They had been raised in close proximity at the court of Henry VIII; Butler, being born in 1531, was two years older.

As a staunch supporter of the English colonial presence in Ireland, Butler carried out a variety of diplomatic and military missions there for Queen Elizabeth during the 1560s and 1570s. According to Sidney Lee, she was so fond of him during the 1560s that "the attentions she paid him . . . gave rise to no little scandal, and induced him to linger at court for the next five years."[3] Elizabeth is said to have called him her "black husband."[4] He was active in court politics, being favored by the Cecils and aligned with the Sussex faction against the Earl of Leicester, whom he despised. In this context, he would have become acquainted with the young Edward de Vere, who came to London in 1562. Both of them were among the dozen diplomats and courtiers receiving Master of Arts degrees at Oxford University in September 1566, and they were admitted to Gray's Inn within weeks of each other the following year (Edwards *ODNB*, Thomas Butler).

When Sir Thomas Butler arrived in Ireland in January 1583 to deal with the Desmond Rebellion, the situation in Munster had deteriorated badly. But a vigorous campaign by Butler during the spring and summer forced most of the individual rebel leaders to surrender and reduced the rebellion to a small band of men loyal to the last of the three rebel Desmond brothers, Gerald Fitzgerald. In November he was cornered, killed, and beheaded in County Kerry by Ormond's troops, effectively ending the rebellion. Desmond's head was taken to Thomas Cheston, constable of Castlemaine, "who brought it on his sword point to the Earl of Ormond in Cork" (Sheehan 108). In his letter of November 15th to Lord Burghley recounting the death, Butler wrote "So now is this traytor come to the ende I have longe looked for, appointed by God to dye by the sword to ende his rebellion . . . " The summary of Ormond's letter contains the brief sentence: "Sends Desmond's head by the bearer."[5]

According to tradition, Queen Elizabeth "would not believe the news of the earl's death until she saw his head, and when it was brought to her, she stared at it for hours" (Sheehan 108). In mid-December 1583 she had it mounted on a pole and placed on London Bridge (Holinshed 6:454). As we know, the heads of criminals on London Bridge were nothing unusual, but this rebel's head was sent from Ireland to London by a general who had been dispatched there to put down a rebellion. Oxford's striking image, "Rebellion broached on his sword" conveyed perfectly the circumstances of Desmond's death and the transportation of his head. (The *OED* cites the use of the verb "broach" in this specific passage to support the definition "To stick (something) on a spit or pointed weapon").[6] When Ormond had not returned to London by January 1584, Elizabeth wrote him in her own hand on the 31st, congratulating him on his success and urging him to come to England to receive her thanks.[7]

The lines of the key passage:

> As by a lower but by loving likelihood,
> Were now the general of our gracious Empress,
> As in good time he may, from Ireland coming,
> Bringing rebellion broached on his sword,
>
> (5. Chorus. 29-34)

are precisely appropriate to the period November 1583 to May 1584, that is, between the date that the last Desmond rebel, Gerald Fitzgerald, was killed and the date that Butler actually returned to London. Oxford and Butler were not only long-time friends, they were distantly related by marriage, and had remained in contact during the 1570s. In a letter from Butler to Lord Burghley in May 1575, while Oxford was traveling in Europe, Butler comments on Anne's pregnancy and compliments Oxford on "tokens and letters" he had sent her.[8] What more gracious compliment could Oxford have paid to a fellow earl, whom he had known since boyhood, than to allude to his service to Queen Elizabeth in connection with Henry V's conquest of France?

Thus, all the phrases in the famous passage are identified and associated with actual events and people. The "general of our gracious Empress" being Sir Thomas Butler, tenth Earl of Ormond, a favorite of the Queen, who appointed him general of her forces in Ireland in 1582; "As in good time he may, from Ireland coming," referring to his mission in Ireland, and suggesting that he may yet come to London in triumph, as did Henry V from France; "Bringing rebellion broached on his sword," referring to the transportation of the rebel earl's head to Butler, and then to Queen Elizabeth.

This scenario places the composition of the Act 5 Chorus in the six month period between mid-November 1583 and mid-May 1584, just a few months after Oxford had regained the favor of the Queen and returned to court. Since the fifth act Chorus occurs with only fifteen per cent of the play remaining, it is likely that by November *Henry V* was nearly completed, and that the reference to Butler's return could be easily inserted before the final act. A patriotic play about an English king's victory in France would have pleased the Queen – and a reference to the recent conclusion of a lengthy rebellion in Ireland by one of her favorite generals would have been doubly satisfying.

An additional detail supporting a 1583/4 date for *Henry V* is Pistol's response to the French soldier's question in Act 4, Scene 4 – "calen o custure me." The phrase is an English corruption of a popular Irish song, *cailín óg a stór*, "maiden, my treasure" (Taylor 234). The song was registered in March 1582 (Arber 2:407) and was issued on a single sheet, a "broadside," between that date and 1584, when it was included in the ballad collection *A Handful of Pleasant Delights* (Rollins viii, 38-9, 99). Frequent references to it suggest that it was popular at that time; it was clearly more topical in the early 1580s than in 1599.

The entire body of evidence for a date of 1583/4 for *Henry V* is set out in my 2001 paper.[9] What follows is evidence of the location and audience for the performance.

Further Evidence -- The Audience and the Venue

Certain other lines in the Prologue and Chorus supply clues about the audience and the venue for a performance of the play written during the six-month period described above. Several scholars have proposed that the use of the Chorus, and certain language in the Chorus, imply a court or private performance, rather than one in a public playhouse. In a 1978 article, G. P. Jones wrote that "the Chorus of *Henry V* is fundamentally incompatible with the public theatre and is fully comprehensible only in terms of performance under more specialised conditions" (95). He pointed out that language alluding to "the spatial inadequacies of the theatre" and "the discrepancy between the size of the real events and the size of their theatrical representation" suggests that the manuscript for the Folio text was prepared for a performance "under more cramped conditions," such as at court or at a private residence.

Another aspect of the Chorus's language suggests the same thing. Such facetious solicitations as "Piece out our imperfections with your thoughts" (Prologue. 23), "Play with your fancies" (3. Chorus. 7), "eche [eke] out our performance with your mind" (3. Chorus. 35), and "Heave him away upon your winged thoughts" (5. Chorus. 8) all suggest that the audience is "confidential and personal," rather than "collective and public." As Jones remarks, such requests "might have met with ribald counter-suggestions in a public forum." Jones also cites such language as "But pardon, gentles all" (Prologue. 8) and "the scene / Is now transported, gentles, to Southampton" (2. Chorus. 34-5) as evidence that the Chorus is addressing a royal or, at least, an aristocratic audience (96-8). The complimentary, even affectionate, reference to Queen Elizabeth – "our gracious Empress" – strongly suggests that she was in the theater.

If it were a royal or an aristocratic audience, it would not be an unusual venue for a Shakespeare play. In his 2004 paper, "Shakespeare's Audience," Richard Whalen presented substantial evidence that Shakespeare wrote primarily for "royalty, the nobility, educated aristocrats, their retainers and court officialdom." The admittedly scanty records that survive list more performances at court or aristocratic homes than in public theaters. These facts comport with the view that the Folio text of the play was derived from a prompt copy that the author prepared for use at a court or private performance. Considering the author's relationship to such an audience, they also suggest that the Chorus's remarks were personal and that he may have been the person delivering them. In the opening lines of the Epilogue, he may well have been referring to himself:

> Thus far, with rough and all-unable pen,
> Our bending author hath pursued the story,
> In little room confining mighty men,
> Mangling by starts the full course of their glory.
> (Epilogue 1-4)

It is easy to imagine the Earl of Oxford, perhaps clad in the hooded, black cloak typical of the role, speaking the lines of the Chorus, carefully introducing each act to his Queen and fellow courtiers.[10]

Other phrases in the Prologue to *Henry V* – "this unworthy scaffold," "Can this cockpit hold / The vasty fields of France?," "Or may we cram / Within this wooden O," "the girdle of these walls" – have been cited by editors as indications that the author was anticipating a performance by the Lord Chamberlain's Men at either the Curtain theater or the newly-constructed Globe in 1599 (Craik 3-4; Gurr, *Henry V* 5-6; Wilson xiv). But these lines, and another in the Epilogue – "In little room confining mighty men" – suggest a much smaller space than either the Globe or the Curtain. The Globe was an open-air amphitheater with a yard about one hundred feet in diameter, and a capacity of over 3000 spectators (Gurr, *Stage* 128; Egan, *Globe* 1). Nor does the Curtain seem a likely venue for the theater described by the Chorus. Although theater historians have long maintained that the Curtain was an amphitheater of about seventy-two feet in diameter (Bowsher 64-7), excavations of the site in the spring of 2016 revealed the foundation of a rectangular building of approximately one hundred by seventy-two feet that could hold about 1000 spectators.[11]

Reacting to this discovery, Heather Knight, a senior archeologist at the London Museum of Archaeology, suggested that the play may still have premiered at the Curtain in 1599, but without the prologue. "There's a school of thought now that says prologues were actually a later addition," she said. This school of thought would, of course, invalidate the claim that "the general of our gracious Empress" refers to the Earl of Essex in the spring of 1599. Any reference after July or August 1599 to the triumphal return of Essex from Ireland would have been met with disbelief or laughter, or both. What seems more likely is that the performance, perhaps the first of *Henry V*, took place at Elizabeth's Whitehall palace, her principal residence during the 1580s, and one of only two containing a "cockpit."

The history of the complex of buildings known as Whitehall confirms that such a performance could have taken place. In the 1530s, Henry VIII undertook a major redesign of York Place, Cardinal Wolsey's former residence, later called "Whitehall." According to John Stow, there were "divers fayre Tennis courtes, bowling allies, and a Cocke-pit, al built by King Henry eight" on the west side of the roadway that bisected the palace grounds (Stow 2:102; quoted in Chambers, *Elizabethan Stage* 1:216, n.2). Henry VIII's Cockpit was a square two-story building, within which a quasi-circular space was constructed with tiered seating to enable spectators to witness cock-fighting.[12] On occasion it was modified to accommodate the performance of plays and masques. With temporary alterations, such as "added curtains for a tiring-house and scaffold planking for a stage" the space could be easily "turned to use as a simple, intimate theatre protected from wind and weather" (Wickham v. 2, pt. 2: 47). The Revels Accounts clearly record that in the early years of his reign, James I witnessed plays performed in the Cockpit at Whitehall (Streitberger 5, 7, 25, 30, 31, 36; Wickham v. 2, pt. 2: 78-81). Although there is no surviving record, modern stage historians agree with Edmond Malone that Queen Elizabeth also witnessed plays performed in Henry VIII's Cockpit (Malone 3:166; Ordish 258-9; Gurr, *Stage* 121; Kernan 18, 53).

It was not until about 1630 that Inigo Jones transformed the interior of the Whitehall Cockpit for Charles I to create a permanent theater. It would serve as such until

1698, when it and nearly all of the surrounding palace were destroyed by fire. The word "Cockpit" evolved to denote a complex of buildings on the same site that were used for various purposes, including residences of the nobility and, in later times, government offices (*ODNB* 1.c.(b)). Considering the importance of the Cockpit at Whitehall to the accurate dating of *Henry V*, and to the authorship question in general, it is fitting to note that the site retains some importance in the modern era. "Its site is now occupied by the Prime Minister's London residence, No. 10 Downing Street" (Wickham v. 2, pt. 2: 45).

Surviving records of entertainments at court, fragmentary as they are, also support the observations detailed above about the audience and the venue for a performance of *Henry V* at the Cockpit at Whitehall in late 1583 or early 1584. One of the thirteen appendices that E. K. Chambers included in his *The Elizabethan Stage* was "A Court Calendar," in which he summarized all the information he could obtain about the monarch's location between 1558 and 1616, and about "the plays, masks and quasi-dramatic entertainments at court" (4: 75). The Court Calendar appendix indicates that Queen Elizabeth arrived at Whitehall on December 20, 1583 and remained there, except for visits to Heneage House and Tower Hill, until April 20, 1584 (4: 100). The Calendar also records that the newly-formed Queen's Men played at court on December 26 and 29, 1583 and on March 3, 1584; that the Children of the Chapel performed at court on January 6 and February 2, 1584; and that the Earl of Oxford's Men performed on January 1 and March 3, 1584.

In another appendix, "Court Payments," Chambers listed the information available about "the expenditures on plays or masks at court" (4: 131). This appendix lists a payment of £20 made at Westminster to the Queen's Men on May 9, 1584 for their performances in the previous December and March. The plays listed for this payment were "vj histories, one Comedie" (4:159). The Court Payments appendix also lists payments to the Children of the Chapel and to the Earl of Oxford's Men for their performances during the same period, but does not indicate what plays were performed.

Thus, it appears that the Queen's Men performed one or more history plays before the Queen at Whitehall on several occasions during the winter of 1583-4 and that two other companies, both controlled by the Earl of Oxford, performed there several times during the same period.[13] As Jones noted, the words of the Chorus referring to a confined circular space and to a "cockpit" suggest that *Henry V* was performed at the Cockpit at Whitehall, rather than at the Great Chamber or the large Banqueting Hall, which were rectangular rooms also used for theatrical performances (96-7). The words of the Chorus also suggest that the audience was an aristocratic one, very likely a royal one, with the Queen present. This internal evidence comports with the external evidence and topical references already described, and in my 2001 paper, that place the composition of the Chorus during the six-month period ending in May 1584, when Sir Thomas Butler returned to London.

A secure date for the composition of *Henry V* in 1583 serves as a benchmark for an accurate dating of the first half of the Shakespeare canon. In the forty-year writing career of the Earl of Oxford, the play falls naturally at about the mid-point, just as it falls at the mid-point of the career of the author alleged in the Stratfordian theory. The fifteen-year difference between the two theories — Stratfordian and Oxfordian — reflects the nearly fifteen-year difference in their birth dates.

Moreover, in the orthodox sequence of composition, *Henry V* is the eighteenth or nineteenth play and the last history play that Shakespeare wrote, except for *Henry VIII* (Chambers, *William Shakespeare* 1:246-50; Wentersdorf 164). There is a consensus that Shakespeare wrote the *Henry IV* plays in the two or three years just prior to writing *Henry V*. It is reasonable to assume that during the five years after 1575 Oxford was occupied with writing the half-dozen early Italian plays in the canon. It is likely, then, that he wrote the six earlier history plays, at least the *Henry VI – Richard III* tetralogy, before beginning his European tour in 1575.

Works Cited

Albright, Evelyn M. "The Folio Version of *Henry V* in Relation to Shakespeare's Times." *PMLA* v. 43 (1928) pp. 722-56.

Anderson, Mark K. *"Shakespeare" by another Name, The Life of Edward de Vere, Earl of Oxford, the Man Who Was Shakespeare.* Gotham Books, 2005.

Arber, Edward, ed. *A Transcript of the Registers of the Company of Stationers of London: 1554-1640, A. D.* 5 v. Birmingham: Privately printed, 1875-77.

Astington, John H. "Inigo Jones and the Whitehall Cockpit." in G. R. Hibbard, ed. *The Elizabethan Theatre* 1980. pp. 46-64.

Bagwell, Richard. *Ireland Under the Tudors.* 3 vol. Longmans Green & Co., 1909-16.

Bowsher, Julian. *Shakespeare's London Theatreland, Archaeology, History and Drama.* Museum of London Archaeology, 2012.

Calendar of the State Papers Relating to Ireland, of the Reign of Elizabeth, 1574—1585. London. Longmans, Green, Reader & Dyer, 1867.

Carte, Thomas. *An History of the Life of James, Duke of Ormond.* 6 vol. Oxford University Press, new ed. 1851.

Chambers, Edmund K. *The Elizabethan Stage.* 4 vol. Oxford, Clarendon Press, 1923.

------- *William Shakespeare. A Study of Facts and Problems.* 2 vol. Clarendon Press, 1930.

Chiljan, Katherine, ed. *Letters and Poems of Edward, Earl of Oxford.* San Francisco, 1998.

Craik, T. W., ed. *King Henry V.* The Arden Shakespeare, Third Series. Routledge, 1994.

Creizenach, Wilhelm. *The English Drama in the Age of Shakespeare.* New York, Russell & Russell. 1916.

Edwards, David. "Butler, Thomas, tenth earl of Ormond and third earl of Ossory (1531–1614)", *Oxford Dictionary of National Biography*, Oxford University Press, 2004; online edition, May 2012. //www.oxforddnb.com/view/article/4209 (Accessed 18 June 2016.)

Egan, Gabriel. "The 1599 Globe and its modern replica: Virtual Reality modelling of the archaeological and pictorial evidence." *Early Modern Literary Studies*. Special

Issue v. 13:5 (2004) pp. 1–22. //purl.oclc.org/emls/si-13/egan

Evans, G. Blakemore, ed. *The Riverside Shakespeare*. Houghton Mifflin, 2nd ed. 1997.

Gurr, Andrew. *The Shakespearean Stage, 1574-1642*. Cambridge University Press, 3rd ed. 1994.

-------, ed. *The First Quarto of King Henry V*. Cambridge University Press, 2000.

Hammer, Paul E. J. *The Polarisation of Elizabethan Politics: The Political Career of Robert Devereux, 2nd Earl of Essex, 1585-1597*. Cambridge University Press, 1999.

Hibbard, G. R., ed. *The Elizabethan Theatre VII*. Port Credit, Ontario: P. D. Meany, 1980.

Holinshed, Raphael. *Holinshed's Chronicles of England, Scotland, and Ireland*. Henry Ellis, ed. 6 vol. London: J. Johnson, 1807-08.

Jiménez, Ramon. "Rebellion broachéd on his Sword": New Evidence of an Early Date for *Henry V*." *The Shakespeare Oxford Newsletter* v. 37:3 (Fall 2001) pp. 8-11, 21.

------- "*The Famous Victories of Henry the Fifth* – Key to the Authorship Question?" *The Shakespeare Oxford Newsletter*. vol. 37:2 (Summer 2001) pp. 7-10.

------- "Edward de Vere, Sir Philip Sidney, and the Battle of Agincourt, '. . .In brawl ridiculous.' " *The Shakespeare Oxford Newsletter*. vol. 38:2 (Spring 2002) pp. 1, 12-15.

Jones, G. P. "*Henry V*: the Chorus and the Audience." *Shakespeare Survey*. vol. 31 (1978) pp. 93-104.

Kernan, Alvin B. *Shakespeare, The King's Playwright: Theater in the Stuart Court, 1603-1613*. Yale University Press, 1995.

Lee, Sidney. Biography of Thomas Butler. *Dictionary of National Biography*. 66 vol. London, Smith, Elder & Co., 1885-1901.

Lennon, Colm. *Sixteenth Century Ireland: The Incomplete Conquest*. St. Martin's Press, 1995.

"London's theater dig's surprise." Associated Press story in the *San Francisco Chronicle*. (May 23, 2016) p. E3. //www.sfgate.com/entertainment/article/Dig-at-theater-where-Shakespeare-worked-uncovers-7929431.php

Malone, Edmond. *The Plays and Poems of William Shakespeare*. 21 vol. James Boswell, ed. London: F.C. and J. Rivington, et al. 1821.

Ordish, T. F. *Shakespeare's London*. London: J. M. Dent, 2nd ed. 1904.

Rollins, Hyder E., ed. *The Paradise of Dainty Devices*. (1576) Harvard University Press, 1927.

Sams, Eric. *The Real Shakespeare*. Yale University Press, 1995.

Sheehan, Anthony J. "The Killing of the Earl of Desmond." *Cork Archaeological and Historical Society Journal*. Ser. 2, v. 88 (1983) pp. 106-110.

Stow, John. *A Survey of London*. (1603) C. L. Kingsford, ed. 1908. 2 vols. Oxford University Press, 1971 ed.

Streitberger, W. R., ed. *Jacobean and Caroline Revels Accounts 1603-1642*. Oxford, Malone Society, 1986.

Taylor, Gary, ed. *Henry V*. Oxford University Press, 1982.

Wentersdorf, Karl P. "Shakespearean Chronology and the Metrical Tests." *Shakespeare-Studien: Festschrift fur Heinrich Mutschmann*. Walther Fischer & Karl Wentersdorf, eds. Marburg: Elwert, 1951. pp. 161-93.

Whalen, Richard. "Shakespeare's Audience: A Reassessment of the Stratfordian View." *The Shakespeare Oxford Newsletter*. vol. 40:4 (Fall 2004), pp. 1, 7-9.

Wickham, Glynne. *Early English Stages: 1300—1660*. 3 vol. Columbia University Press, 1972.

Wilson, J. Dover, ed. *King Henry V*. Cambridge University Press, 1947.

Notes

1 Quotations from the Shakespeare canon are taken from *The Riverside Shakespeare*. G. B. Evans, ed.

2 The documents attesting to the affair are cited in Hammer at 320-1. See also Anderson pp. 297, 538.

3 *Dictionary of National Biography*. v. 8, p. 80.

4 David Edwards, 'Butler, Thomas, tenth earl of Ormond and third earl of Ossory (1531–1614),' *Oxford Dictionary of National Biography*.

5 Calendar of State Papers, Ireland. 2: 478, 480.

6 "broach, v.1 3b." *OED* Online. Oxford University Press, September 2015.

7 Carte 1: cv-cvi.

8 The letter can be seen at //www.oxford-shakespeare.com/StatePapersOther/SP_63-51-3_%20ff_92-3.pdf

9 "The Famous Victories of Henry the Fifth – Key to the Authorship Question?" *Shakespeare-Oxford Newsletter*, Vol. 37, N. 3 (2001).Available online at //shakespeareoxfordfellowship.org/wp-content/uploads/2014/03/SOSNL_2001_4.pdf

10 Wilson 122. Creizenach describes the customary garb of the Prologue/Chorus, and comments further that the *Henry V* Chorus "occupies a place apart. Its services . . . could well have been spared; it seems rather as if the author's object had been to give direct expression to his patriotic enthusiasm for the glorious deeds of his favorite hero by breaking through the dramatic form" (275-6).

11 "London's theater dig's surprise." Associated Press story in the *San Francisco Chronicle*. (May 23, 2016) p. E3.

12 Astington 46-56. On p. 49 the square Cockpit building with a pitched polygonal roof can be seen in the detail of the painting, "Whitehall from St James's Park," done in 1674 by Hendrick Danckerts (c. 1625-1680).

13 According to Chambers, the Children of the Chapel were under the patronage of the Earl of Oxford in 1583-4 (*Elizabethan Stage 2*: 37, 101, 497).

Reconsidering the Jephthah Allusion in Hamlet

by Connie J. Beane

> O Jephthah, judge of Israel, what a treasure hadst thou!
> *(Hamlet* 2. 2. 345)[1]

While Hamlet is talking to Rosencrantz and Guildenstern in Act 2, prior to the arrival onstage of the visiting players, Polonius enters to deliver news of their coming. Hamlet then taunts Polonius/Corambis,[2] calling the old man "Jephthah" and referring to his "one faire daughter and no more, the which he loued passing well" (2.2.349-350). The incident occupies less than a dozen lines and on the surface, appears trivial. However, in Shakespeare's plays, what appears to be trivial is sometimes significant.

Who was Jephthah, and why would Hamlet compare Polonius to him?

The Biblical Jephthah

Scholars have long recognized that "Jephthah" is a reference to a story found in the eleventh and twelfth chapters of the biblical Book of Judges. Hamlet's remarks allude specifically to the last ten lines of chapter eleven, which detail how Jephthah, going into battle against the Ammonites on behalf of Israel, makes a solemn vow to God that if he returns victorious, "that thing that commeth out of the doores of my house to meete me…shall be the Lordes, and I will offer it for a burnt offering" (Judges 11:31, Geneva Bible (1587)). Tragically, the first "thing" to come out of Jephthah's house upon his return is his only child, an unmarried daughter, whom he duly sacrifices in obedience to his vow: "…for I haue opened my mouth vnto the Lorde, and can not goe backe" (Judges 11:35).

The story of Jephthah was familiar to Elizabethans. Judges 11 was read on April 1st as the first lesson at Morning Prayers, per the calender established in the Book of Common Prayer, 1559. Therfore literate households would probably have read it, or would have heard it read regularly in their personal devotions as well. Hamlet's reference at 2.2.361 to "the pious chanson"[3] has led researchers to search for contemporary ballads on the subject of the biblical Jephthah. They found one listed in the Registers of the Stationers' Company for 1567-8 entitled the "songe of Jefphas dowgter at his [her] death" (Collier 169). Unfortunately, no copy of this ballad has survived. The copyright to another ballad, entitled "Jeffa, Judge of Israel," was transferred in 1624, but its date of composition is unknown (Arber 93).

Research also turned up references to three contemporary dramas based on the biblical story. George Buchanan's neo-Latin school play, *Jephthes sive votum tragoedia* [The Tragedy of Jephthah's Vow], was probably written some time between 1540 and 1547 and published in 1554; Roger Ascham praised it in *The Scholemaster* (1570) (Shugar 135). A second play on the subject, written in Greek by John Christopherson around 1544, was so obscure as to be virtually unknown, even to university graduates. Finally, entries in Philip Henslowe's *Diary* in 1602 indicate that he laid out money for costumes, licensing, and payments to authors Anthony Munday and Thomas Dekker, for a play entitled *Jephthah Judge of Israel* (Wiggins and Richardson, IV, 388-89). The play appears to have been performed in July 1602, but it does not seem to have ever been printed, and there is no contemporary mention of it, other than in Henslowe's *Diary*.

Commentary by Shakespeare scholars on Hamlet's Jephthah allusion has been sparse. They identify the biblical reference in Judges 11:37-38, delve into Hamlet's reference to a "godly Ballet" or "pious chanson,"[4] and note the existence of the three more-or-less contemporary English plays on the subject.

The majority of commentary has focused on the allusion's supposed foreshadowing of the death of Ophelia and on the parallels between Jephthah and Polonius in their "sacrifice" of their respective daughters to their ambitions.

While these readings can be supported by the scant handful of lines in Act 2, Scene 2, we should remember that in Shakespeare the plain meaning of the text does not always constitute the only possible interpretation. Most commentators,[5] because their focus has been largely on the biblical text and the associated ballad, have neglected to

---

Connie J. Beane *graduated from college in 1970 with a Bachelor of Arts degree with a dual major in English and Library Science. Following graduation, she was employed by the Florida State Archives, leaving in 1984 to establish Florida Information Associates, Inc., a service providing research and information retrieval from the records of the Florida Legislature, Florida government agencies, and state and county courts located in Tallahassee. She was introduced to Shakespeare in college, but it was the discovery of the authorship question and the work of Charlton Ogburn which sustained and deepened her interest not only in Shakespeare but the history and culture of Elizabethan England generally. She particularly enjoys exploring the origins of obscure references in the plays of Shakespeare.*

explore the possibility that other contemporary references to Jephthah existed that would have been known to Elizabethans.

Jephthah and the Seventh Homily Against Swearing

Following the schedule mandated in the Book of Common Prayer, Judges 11 was read in church once a year, but it was not the only time Jephthah was mentioned in a liturgical context. He also makes an appearance in the seventh homily of *Certain Sermons or Homilies* (1547),[6] written by Archbishop Thomas Cranmer, which would have been read in many churches as part of the Anglican service.

The seventh homily is entitled "Against Swearing and Perjury," and the second part, in which Jephthah is mentioned, is sub-headed "Unlawful oaths and promises are not to be kept." Here Jephthah is linked with Herod (Mark 6:14-29, Matthew 14:6-11) and the "wicked Jews" of Acts 23, as examples of those who "make wicked promises by an oath, and will perform the same." The homily goes on to say that "the promise, which [Jephthah] made most foolishly to God, against God's everlasting will and the law of nature most cruelly he performed, so committing against God double offence...." (Griffiths 78).

Jephthah and An Invective Against Swearing

> To keep that oath were more impiety
> Than Jephthah's, when he sacrific'd his daughter.
> *(3 Henry VI 5.1.93-94)*

Contemporaneous with the First Book of Homilies was a treatise written by Cranmer's chaplain, Thomas Becon,[7] entitled *An Invective Written Against the Most Wicked and Detestable Vice of Swearing* (115-78). Whether Becon's work was an expansion of the seventh homily, or the homily was based on Becon's *Invective* – the matter has been debated (Griffiths xxviii, and Wright and Neil 266) – the two share a similar structure and references. Becon's *Invective* however, was a detailed, scholarly work suitable for a more educated audience than the Homilies, citing many commentaries – including those of Solomon, the Venerable Bede, and saints Isidorus, Jerome, Augustine, and Ambrose – at some length (Ayre 350-92).[8]

> Some man will say, peradventure, Are all oaths to be observed? Shall a man fall into the sin of perjury, if he performeth not whatsoever he hath promised? I answer, Nay, not so. God forbid, that all oaths promised and vows should be performed: for many are foolish, wicked, and ungodly. ...For "an unfaithful and foolish promise," saith Salomon, "displeaseth God." "In evil promises, break thy faith," saith Isidorus; "...That thou has vowed unadvisedly, look thou do it not. For that is a wicked promise, which is fulfilled in

> sin." ...St. Jerome also saith" "Thous shalt do better, O brother, if thou dost abstain from the ungodly act, then if thou dost stiffly perform foolish words and perilous vows." Hereto agreeth the saying of St. Austin: "It is a point of great wisdom for a man to call that again, which he hath evil spoken." St Ambrose also saith: "It is against all godly honesty many times to perform the oath that is made . . ."
>
> *In concilio Toletano* it was decreed, "it is better not to fulfil the vows of a foolish promise, than by the observance of them to commit any wickedness" . . .
>
> Such an oath, promise, or vow made Jephte . . . .
> (Ayre 372)

Becon's works, which numbered over forty, were highly popular in the latter half of the sixteenth century. Most were originally printed as separate tracts and widely circulated in that form. The printer John Day, who specialized in Protestant literature and pamphlets, and was the publisher of Foxe's *Actes and Monuments*, was granted a license in 1549 to reprint all of Becon's writings, indicating that the demand for them was considerable (Becon 13). A three-volume folio edition was published in 1564.

Between the homily and Becon's treatise, an Elizabethan with the standard Protestant religious education was probably familiar with the unlawful oath aspect of the Jephthah story, beyond the bare bones of the story in Judges 11 and its balladic incarnation.

Jephthah in Drama

It was just prior to the publication of the Homilies and *Invective* that the two academic dramas mentioned above were written: Christopherson's Greek tragedy and Buchanan's *Jephthes sive votum tragoedia*. Although Christopherson's play is frequently mentioned by modern scholars in connection with Jephthah, it was probably unknown to the vast majority of Elizabethans[9] and should not be considered part of the cultural landscape of *Hamlet*. Buchanan's play, on the other hand, was popular both on the Continent and in England, and was readily available in both the original Latin and in French translation, although it was not translated into English until the eighteenth century.

Buchanan's play was consciously modeled on Euripides' tragedy of *Iphigenia at Aulis* and its classical themes predominated. As in the homily and Becon's treatise, the morality of Jephthah's oath was considered, but the tragic events were Buchanan's primary focus (Ephraim 23). It has been suggested Buchanan's play may have been the source for Anthony Munday's and Thomas Dekker's lost play of 1602 (Shugar 239, note 40). There is no manuscript or printed text of the latter, so there is no way to be certain of the nature or extent of any parallels. However, both Munday and Dekker were probably familiar with the homily and Becon's *Invective* as well as Buchanan's play. Anthony Munday's poem on Jephthah (see below) appears to be unknown to commentators on Shakespeare's *Hamlet*, but it may provide some indication of how he and Dekker handled the subject in dramatic form.

Jephthah in Poetry

Anthony Munday published a series of metrical tragedies entitled *The Mirrour of Mutabilitie* in 1579, "Describing the Fall of divers famous Princes and other memorable Personages. Selected out of the Sacred Scriptures." It was modeled on the pattern of the highly popular *Mirror for Magistrates* and dedicated to "the right honourable the Earle of Oxenford."

Mutabilitie was laid out in two parts, the first dealing with the seven deadly sins represented by various biblical characters such as David, Herod, Pharaoh, and Nebuchadnezzar. The second part illustrated other sins and virtues such as *Cruelty*, *Magnaminity*, *Vain-glory*, etc. Under the heading of *Rashnes* we find Jephthah. The induction recites a brief prose version of the biblical story, ending with a summary whose wording is not found in the scriptures: "A right and rare example for all men to take heed of vaine oaths." Then comes a seven-line rhymed acrostic spelling out "r-a-s-h-n-e-s," followed by eleven six-line stanzas of poetry in which "Jephta sometime Judge of Israel" utters a "complaint...for his so rash vow, in the sacrificing of his Daughter...." The first nine stanzas review the familiar details from Judges 11, but in the tenth and eleventh, the moral is cast in terms of vows and rash oaths:

> The time expirde, the Mayden turnd agayne,
> Then offered I to God my Sacrifice:
> Thus my *rash vow*, returned to my payne,
> To hunt for praise, which did me moste despise.
> When Man will make *a vow without respect*:
> It God offends, his soule it doth detest.
>
> You yunger peeres therefore be warnd by me,
> Unto your vowes always have good regard:
> Respect in time the daunger for to flee,
> Least unto you do happen like reward.
> *Stil vow no more than well perfourme you may*:
> And to be sure you cannot goe astray.
>   (emphasis added)

Jephthah in Chaucer

Another allusion to Jephthah overlooked by commentators on *Hamlet* is in the Physician's Tale in Geoffrey Chaucer's *Canterbury Tales*. That it was overlooked is perhaps not surprising, since the tale is not one of the better-known ones, and some modern editions of the *Tales* omit it entirely (Harley 1). Richard L. Hoffman says "the Physician's Tale has called for very little literary criticism, even of the appreciative variety; less, perhaps than any other complete tale in the book …" (21).

The Jephthah reference in Chaucer is even more fleeting than the one in *Hamlet*. The doomed Virginia requests that her father "yif me leyser… / My deeth for to compleyne a litle space; / For, pardee, Jepte yaf his doghter grace / For to compleyne, er he did hir slow, allas! (328-44)" (Hoffman 23). Sadly for Virginia, her father did not give her the two-month reprieve that Jephthah allowed his daughter, but "slow" [slew] her almost immediately.

In Chaucer, Jephthah's daughter is mentioned, but his vow is not, "…[it] is presumably to be inferred by readers who know the story of Jephthah" (Beidler 276). In *Hamlet* the vow also goes unmentioned, presumably also to be inferred by those who know the story.

The Franklin's Tale precedes the Physician's Tale[10] and is traditionally considered its companion (Beidler 178). While it makes no specific reference to Jephthah, his daughter, or his vow, it explicitly explores the making of a rash vow to commit an unlawful act – just like Jephthah. In some ways these two tales are mirrors, because in the Franklin's Tale the vow is not kept and everyone survives; in the Physician's Tale, Virginius, who hasn't made any vow at all, commits the same horrific murder as Jephthah.

Chaucer's *Canterbury Tales* was published in nine editions between 1477-78 and in 1561. New editions in 1598 (dedicated to Sir Robert Cecil) and in 1602 made it available to an even wider readership. We know that Shakespeare was familiar with the "Doctor of Physik's Tale" because he makes at least one direct reference to it when Titus, in *Titus Andronicus*, compares himself to Virginius when he kills his daughter Lavinia after she is raped and mutilated.

Scott Hollifield finds extensive evidence of Shakespeare's knowledge of Chaucer in many of the plays, but specifically sees "strong tonal echoes" of the Physician's Tale in *The Rape of Lucrece* (36). Sherron Kopp, as well as a number of other scholars, sees the magician in the Franklin's Tale as the pattern for Prospero in *The Tempest*. We are justified, therefore, in concluding that Shakespeare would have known the Jephthah parallels in both tales.

Jephthah and John Foxe's Actes and Monuments

The author of *The First Book of Homilies*, Thomas Cranmer, Archbishop of Canterbury, suffered martyrdom under Queen Mary (and King Philip) on March 21, 1556. The story of his martyrdom was included in the 1570, 1576, and 1583 editions of John Foxe's *Actes and Monuments* and would therefore be part of the cultural landscape of Elizabethan England.[11] During his trial for heresy on September 12, 1555, Cranmer was interrogated by Dr. Thomas Martin on the subject of the oaths he had taken:

> Master Cranmer, ye have told here a long glorious talke, pretending some matter of conscience in apparaunce, but in verity you have no conscience at all. You say that you have sworne once to King Henry the eight against the Popes jurisdiction, and therefore ye may never forsweare the same, and so ye make a great matter of conscience in the breach of the sayd oath. Here will I aske you a question or two. What if you made an oath to an harlot to live with her in continuall adultery? Ought you to keepe it?
>
> *Cranmer*. I thinke no.
>
> *Martin*. What if you did sweare never to lend a poore man one penny, ought you to keep it?
>
> *Cranmer*. I thinke not.
>
> *Martin*. Herode did sweare what soeuer his harlot asked of him, he would geue her, and he gave her John Baptistes head: did he well in keeping his oath? [Marginalia: Unadvised oathes are not to be kept.]
>
> *Cranmer*. I thinke not.
>
> *Martin*. Jehpthe, one of þe Iudges of Israel, did sweare unto God, that if he would give him victory over his enemies, he would offer unto God the first soul that came forth of his house: it happened that his owne daughter came first, and he slue her to saue his oath. Did he well? [Marginalia: Jephthes oath.]
>
> *Cranmer*. I thinke not.
>
> *Martin*. So sayth S. Ambrose de officijs. ***miserabilis** necessitas quæ soluitur parricidio.
>
> Then M. Cranmer, you can no less confesse by þe premisses but that you ought not to have conscience of every oath, but if it be just, lawfull, and aduisely taken. [Marginalia: That is, it is a miserable [*sic*] which is payd with parricide.] (Foxe 2091)

Dr. Martin was probably familiar with the homily *Against Swearing and Perjury* authored by Cranmer, and he may have deliberately repeated two of the references – Herod and Jephthah – the archbishop had used, seeking to expose Cranmer's failings in regard to the oaths he had sworn variously to the Church and to the King.

Polonius and Oaths

The homily *Against Swearing*, Becon's *Invective*, Munday's poem "Rashnes" in *Mirrour of Mutabilitie*, Foxe's *Actes*, and Chaucer's Physician's Tale clearly indicate that Jephthah's oath would have been recognized by most Elizabethans as at least as significant as the sacrifice of his daughter.

Does Shakespeare, when Hamlet compares Polonius to Jephthah, merely intend to foreshadow Ophelia's death and draw a parallel between the destructive ambitions of the two men, as most commentators conclude – or is he intimating that the King's councilor was a party to some sort of unlawful oath?

Based on his actions in the play, Polonius is not given to oaths. He utters a few mild ones such as "by the mass" and "Marry [Mary]," a pervasive social habit criticized in the first part of the homily *Against Swearing*.[12] In this regard, Polonius is practically a Puritan in comparison to some of Shakespeare's other characters. He does tell Queen Gertrude that "I swear I use no art at all" (2.2.96), when she accuses him of embroidering his account of Hamlet's behavior, but this also falls into the first category mentioned by the homily, being intended only "to bring himself in credence with his neighbours."[13]

Other than this, Polonius's remarks on the subject actually suggest a cynical attitude toward the keeping of vows, oaths, and solemn promises. Early in the play he remarks "how prodigal the soul / Lends the tongue vows" (1.3.115-116) and a few lines later he warns Ophelia, "Believe not his [Hamlet's] vows, for they are brokers,… / Breathing like sanctified and pious bawds / The better to beguile…" (1.3.126,129-130). There is little evidence in the play to indicate that Polonius the character has sworn any oath that was rash, unlawful, or ill-advised. Was Shakespeare using him as a proxy to represent someone who had?

In 1869 George Russell French suggested that Polonius was based at least in part on Queen Elizabeth's chief minister and close confidante, William Cecil, Lord Burghley (French 301-2). This idea was followed up in 1921 by Lilian Winstanley. If Polonius was intended to represent Burghley, is there any incident in the latter's life which connects to the theme of an unlawful oath? There is, indeed, such an incident – a highly politicized one, which would account for the oblique and abbreviated nature of the allusion.

The Bond of Association

In the late fall of 1583 England was shaken by the revelation of the abortive Throckmorton plot to assassinate Queen Elizabeth. On the heels of this came the assassination in July 1584 of William of Orange, the leader of the Dutch revolt against the Spaniards in the Netherlands. Within weeks of the Dutch leader's assassination, on October 19th, Burghley and Walsingham drafted and presented to the Privy Council an unusual document entitled *The Instrument of an Association for the Preservation of Her Majesty's Royal Person*,[14] more commonly known as the *Bond of Association*:

> And to that end, we and every of us, first calling to witness the Name of Almighty God, do voluntarily and most willingly bind our selves, every one of us to the other, jointly and severally in the band of one firm and loyal society; and do hereby vow and promise by the Majesty of Almighty God, that with our whole powers, bodies, lives and goods, and with our children and servants, we and every of us will faithfully serve, and humbly obey our said sovereign lady Queen Elizabeth, against all states, dignities and earthly powers whatsoever; and will as well with our joint and particular forces during our lives withstand, pursue and offend, as well by force of arms, as by all other means of revenge, all manner of persons, of whatsoever state they shall be, and their abettors, that shall attempt any act, or counsel or consent to any thing that shall tend to the harm of Her Majesty's royal person; and will never desist from all manner of forcible pursuit against such persons, to the utter extermination of them, their counsellors, aiders and abettors….
>
> But do also further vow and protest, as we are most bound, and that in the Presence of the eternal and everlasting God, to prosecute such person or persons to death, with our joint and several forces, and to act the utmost revenge upon them, that by any means we or any of us can devise and do, or cause to be devised and done for their utter overthrow and extirpation.
>
> And to the better corroboration of this our Loyal Bond and Association, we do also testify by this writing, that we do confirm the contents hereof by our oaths corporally taken upon the Holy Evangelists, with this express condition, that no one of us shall for any respect of person or causes, or for fear or reward, separate ourselves from this Association, or fail in the prosecution thereof during our lives, upon pain of being by the rest of us prosecuted and supprest as perjured persons, and as public enemies to God, our Queen, and to our native country; to which punishment and pains we do voluntarily submit ourselves, and every of us, without benefit of colour and pretence.
>
> In witness of all which premises to be inviolably kept, we do to this writing put our hands and seals….
>
> (*Bond of Association*, spelling modernized)

Although her name was not specifically mentioned, it is believed that Mary, Queen of Scots was its target (Lyon 194).

The heavy religious emphasis in the instrument—"calling to witness the name of Almighty God," "vow and promise," "our oaths corporally taken upon the Holy Evangelists"[15] – is striking, as is the fact that the language implicitly authorizes the signatories to act extra-judicially "to prosecute such person or persons to death… and to act the *utmost revenge upon them…by any means we or any of us can devise or do…for their utter overthrow and extirpation";* indeed, it obligated them to do so *"upon the pain of being by the rest of us prosecuted and supprest as perjured persons"* (emphasis added).

This "assassins' charter," as it has been called (De Lisle), was signed by all the members of the Privy Council within days of its being presented to them. In the weeks afterward Burghley and Walsingham worked to persuade other peers and prominent men to sign. Although there was an initial rush to subscribe, there were some who held back, uneasy over the vigilante features of the "instrument." To ease these fears, in December a "Bill for the Queen's Safety" was drafted which more or less replicated the provisions of the Bond, but provided for issuance of formal warrants against the accused and a trial by a commission prior to imposition of punishment. After some revision it was eventually passed (27 Eliz. I. c. 1) in March. However, there was still a lingering question whether or not the Bill superseded the Bond and thereby abrogated the oath the signatories had sworn therein (Cressy 225; Dean 64). Elizabeth herself seemed to think not, because after Mary, Queen of Scots was tried and condemned in connection with the Babington plot, she attempted to evade the public opprobrium of ordering Mary's formal execution by persuading one of the Bond signatories (Guy 480-1) to fulfill his oath and commit a private assassination.

Burghley's Unlawful Oath and Its Fulfillment

Burghley, as one of the primary architects of the 1584 *Bond of Association* and probably one of its first signatories, can be seen as a contemporary Jephthah: a man who swore a solemn, conditional oath to God, the fulfillment of which obligated him to commit an unlawful act – murder – against a person or persons yet unnamed. Not only did Burghley swear to the oath himself, but he used his considerable influence to have other members of the Privy Council and dozens, if not hundreds, of others around England to do likewise.

With the private "Instrument of an Association for the Preservation of Her Majesty's Royal Person" and its companion parliamentary law – "An act for provision to be made for the surety of the Queen's most royal person" (27 Elizabeth I, c. 1, 1585) (Cobbett, vol. 1, p. 1642)[16] – at hand, Burghley and Walsingham waited patiently for the fly to walk into their net, which she soon did, probably with some help from Walsingham's network of spies and provocateurs. The law passed in March 1585, and by January 1586, the Babington plot[17] was "discovered." Mary was arrested on August 11, moved to Fotheringay Castle, and tried for treason. She was convicted on October 25 and sentenced to death. Burghley was one of the noblemen who served on the commission appointed to try her, and although he was nominally ranked low in the peerage, his office as Lord Treasurer made him one of the four top-ranking members of the Commission. From accounts of the trial, it is clear that he took an active part in the proceedings.[18]

Despite the Commission's verdict and sentence, however, Queen Elizabeth refused to issue an order of execution. Over the next several weeks, Burghley and other members of the Privy Council put great pressure on her. There was a major debate in Parliament on November 3. On November 12 a joint petition drafted by the Speaker of the House of Commons, John Pickering – carefully amended by Burghley – was presented to her, requesting her to give directions for proceeding against Mary. Elizabeth declined to act. On November 24 a Parliamentary delegation visited her to urge action, but again she evaded them. She eventually consented to a public proclamation of the verdict on December 6, but allowed things to drag on for several more weeks until she finally signed the warrant of execution on February 1, 1587.

Although Elizabeth gave her secretary, William Davison, strict instructions not to send the warrant until she gave him leave, Burghley somehow gained possession of it, and on February 3 he called the Privy Council together and convinced them to act, as a group, to order the dispatch of the document to Fotheringay, on the grounds that the Queen having done all that was necessary under the law, it was now their duty to carry out her orders without bothering her with the details (Hosack 457-8). The Clerk of the Privy Council was hastily sent off to Fotheringay, and on February 8, 1587, Mary was beheaded. Burghley did not, like Jephthah, do the deed with his own hands, but it is abundantly clear from the record that he did everything in his power short of wielding the ax himself, to fulfill the oath he and others had sworn.

The Bond of Association and the Date of Hamlet

The orthodox date assigned to *Hamlet* by strict constructionists[19] is after the publication of Meres' *Palladis Tamia* in 1598 and before the publication of the 1602 quarto of *Hamlet*. However, as early as 1796, James Plumptre (or Plumtree) argued in his *Observations on Hamlet* that many details in the play reflected events of the life of Mary, Queen of Scots, and in 1921 Lilian Winstanley covered much of the same ground in *Hamlet and the Scottish Succession*. If this thesis is correct, the play would have been topical between 1584-1589. A number of scholars have admitted – without mentioning the theories of Plumptre or Winstanley – that the existence of a handful of anecdotal references to a *Hamlet* play dating back to 1589 suggest that a date of 1586-1589 for a first version is possible.

Several nineteenth-century scholars, disinclined to ascribe this early version of the play to Shakespeare himself, postulated the existence of an *Ur-Hamlet*,[20] supposedly written by Thomas Kyd or some unknown playwright. More recent commentators have concluded that it is possible that Shakespeare himself was the author of the version of the play noticed in 1589.

> ...Andrew Cairncross, who devoted a book to *The Problem of Hamlet*, dated it 1589 (182). ...Harold Bloom believes that "Shakespeare himself wrote the *Ur-Hamlet* no later than 1589" (383). Charles Knight assumes its existence in 1587 (329). Carl Elze suggests around 1585-6 (xvi). And there is the scholars' bible, *Narrative and Dramatic Sources of Shakespeare* by Geoffrey Bullough, who would see *Hamlet* as highly topical around 1587, but speculates on a 1597 to 1600 date for Shakespeare's first version of it (VII 18).
>
> (Jolly 11)

If the Jephthah allusion is linked to the *Bond of Association*, the case for a pre-1598 Hamlet is strengthened. Like the details in the play supposedly reproduced from the life of Mary, Queen of Scots, references to the Bond and its unlawful oaths would have been a white-hot topic a year or two either side of her death in 1587, but not a decade later.

Edward de Vere and the Jephthah Allusion

In James Black's 1978 article, "Hamlet's Vows," he says, "*Hamlet* itself...is a play in which there is special emphasis on promises and vows" (33), but he points out that many of these – such as Gertrude's marriage vow to her first husband, Hamlet's father – have either been broken, or are brushed aside as likely to be broken – as Polonius brushes aside Ophelia's account of Hamlet's vows of love for her (36). Hamlet's vow to revenge his father is a contravention of an admonition in the Sermon on the Mount (Matthew 5), but "whatever pattern of imagery we may detect in Hamlet's speech, there can be no doubt that Hamlet has taken . . . a vow of the most profound nature" (Black 37). Not only has he sworn an unwise oath, but he has also disregarded the Sermon's admonition not to exact an eye for an eye (38).

This situation in *Hamlet* is eerily reminiscent of what we have seen of the events surrounding the signing of the *Bond of Association*, but the resemblance becomes even more pointed when Black goes on, "His appalling doubts about the task he has undertaken are voiced chiefly in the soliloquies. But what also appears to surface in at least one of Hamlet's speeches is an uneasiness in his mind concerning swearing itself." Black then brings forward the Jephthah allusion and describes its connection with the ballad, the biblical story, and the homily *Against Swearing* (40-1).

> But if we accept this exchange only as Hamlet "harping on [Polonius's] daughter...and baiting Polonius, we get no more from the business than Polonius himself understands. ...as Polonius talks...perhaps Polonius momen-

tarily becomes for Hamlet the nearest convenient mirror, a glass in which Hamlet sees not just Polonius, the prating fool and ruthless intriguer, but also himself, a Jephthah. …Hamlet may be harping not just upon Polonius and his daughter, but also upon his own rash vow. For in terms of that vow, Hamlet is a Jephthah too.

(Black 41-2)

This is where Black stops short. Either he was unaware of the old research connecting *Hamlet* to events in the life of Mary, Queen of Scots, or he did not consider it relevant to his thesis. But in ignoring this possible connection to historical events, he missed the connection between the *Bond of Association* and *Hamlet's* "especial emphasis on promises and vows" (33).

As one of the highest-ranking members of the Elizabethan peerage, Edward de Vere was at the epicenter of the events of 1584-1587 surrounding the Bond of Association. As the earl of Oxford he would have been under pressure to sign the Bond. As Burghley's son-in-law, he would have been under even greater pressure. There is no definitive record whether or not he signed, but it seems likely that he would have.

If we consider that Polonius is in part a reflection of Lord Burghley, then Hamlet's fleeting mention of the biblical Jephthah becomes far more than a simple reference to a man with a daughter whom he sacrificed to his own ambitions, and becomes an oblique commentary on one of the most dangerous political issues of the time – the execution of an anointed queen.

The Stratford man, a 26-year-old provincial with (as yet) no documented connection to London, is unlikely to have dared to pen a play dealing with such potentially explosive subject matter. If, on the other hand, Edward de Vere was Shakespeare, the portrayal of Hamlet's famous "irresolution" may be an accurate, and highly personal, depiction of the state of mind of a signatory to the Bond who subsequently began to question whether it would be lawful or moral to carry out its provisions.

Conclusion

It is impossible to know for certain how closely the text of the hypothetical 1589 *Hamlet* may have resembled the texts of the first and second quartos, or whether this version contained the Jephthah reference. However, given the play's "special emphasis on promises and vows," and the Elizabethan understanding of the Jephthah story with its emphasis on "unlawful vows," it is difficult to believe that the reference to Jephthah and his daughter was intended merely as a casual analogy to Polonius and Ophelia.

Works Cited

Arber, Edward A., ed. *Transcript of the Registers of the Company of Stationers of London, 1554-1640,* vol. 4. London, Privately printed, 1877.

Ayre, John, ed. *The Early Works of Thomas Becon.* 1843.

Becon, Thomas. *Writings of the Reverend Thomas Becon.* London: Religious Tract Society, 1829.

Beidler, Peter G. "The Pairing of the Franklin's Tale and the Physician's Tale." *The Chaucer Review* (vol. 2, no. 4), Spring 1969. pp. 279-285

Black, James. "Hamlet's Vows." *Renaissance and Reformation,* (vol. 2, no. 1 new series) 1978.

Bond of Association. Tudorplace.com.ar. Accessed 24 September 2016.

Calendar of State Papers (Domestic).

Cobbett's Parliamentary History of England, vol. I, London, Hansard et al, 1806.

Collier, John, P., ed. *Extracts from the Registers of the Stationers' Company of Works Entered for Publication Between the Years of 1559 and 1570.* London, Shakespeare Society, 1848.

Cressy, David. "Binding the Nation: The Bonds of Association, 1584 and 1696." Delloyd J. Gurth and John W. McKenna, eds. *Tudor Rule and Revolution: Essays for G. R. Elton from His American Friends.* Cambridge University Press, 1982. 217-34.

De Lisle, Leandra. *Tudor: The Family Story.* Chatto and Windus. 2014.

Dean, David. *Law-Making and Society in Late Elizabethan England: The Parliament of England, 1584-1601.* Cambridge University Press, 1996.

Ephraim, Michelle. *Reading the Jewish Woman on the Elizabethan Stage.* Ashgate, 2013.

Foxe, John. *Actes and Monuments.* 1570.

French, George Russell. *Shakespeareana Genealogica.* London, Macmillan and Company, 1869.

Geneva Bible. 1587.

Griffiths, John, ed. *Two Books of Homilies Appointed to be Read in Churches.* Oxford University Press, 1859.

Guy, John. *Queen of Scots: The True Life of Mary Stuart*. Houghton Mifflin, 2005.

Harley, Marta Powell. "Last Things First in Chaucer's Physician's Tale: Finale Judgment and the Worm of Conscience." *Journal of English and Germanic Philology*, vol. 91, no. 1, 1992.

Hoffman, Richard L. "Jephthah's Daughter and Chaucer's Virginia." *The Chaucer Review*, vol. 2, no. 1 (Summer, 1967), pp. 20-31.

Hollifield, Scott A. "Shakespeare Adapting Chaucer: 'Myn auctour shal I folwen, if I konne' " (PhD dissertation). University of Nevada, August 2010. //digitalscholarship.unlv.edu/cgi/ viewcontent.cgi?article=1892&context=thesesdissertations

Hosack, John. *Mary, Queen of Scots and Her Accusers, . . .*, vol. 2. London, William Blackwood and Sons, 1870.

Jolly, Eddy. "Dating Shakespeare's Hamlet." *The Oxfordian*, vol. 2. Shakespeare Oxford Society, 1999, pp. 11-22.

Kopp, Sherron. "Poetry as Conjuring Act: The Franklin's Tale and *The Tempest*." *The Chaucer Review*, vol. 38, no. 4. 2004.

Larson, Kenneth J. *Essays on Shakespeare's Sonnets* "Sonnet 152" (www.williamshakespeare-sonnets.com). Accessed 13 February 2015.

Lyon, Ann. *Constitutional History of the United Kingdom*. London, Cavendish, 2003.

Munday, Anthony. *The Mirrour of Mutabilitie, or principal part iv of the Mirrour for Magistrates....* London, John Allde, 1579.

Plumtree, James. *Observations on Hamlet*. Cambridge, J. Burges, 1796.

Shugar, Debora K. *The Renaissance Bible: Scholarship, Sacrifice and Subjectivity*. University of California Press, 1994.

Wiggins, Martin and Richardson, Catherine T. *British Drama 1533-1642*, vol. 4: 1598-1602. Oxford University Press, 2014.

Winstanley, Lilian. *Hamlet and the Scottish Succession*. Cambridge University Press, 1921.

Wright, Charles H.H. and Neil, Charles, eds. "The Homilies." *A Protestant Dictionary, Containing Articles on the History, Doctrines, and Practices of the Christian Church*. Hodder and Stoughton, 1904.

Notes

1. All quotes are from *William Shakespeare: The Complete Works*, Stephen Orgel and A. R. Braunmuller, eds. Penguin Books, 2002 ed. Most modern editions use the spelling "Jephthah," although the sixteenth-century spellings varied considerably – Jeptha, Jeffa, Jephthes, Jepthes, etc. The first and second quartos of Hamlet and the First Folio used the spelling "Jepha" consistently.

2. The first quarto calls the character "Corambis." The second quarto and the First Folio call him "Polonius." There is considerable scholarly commentary on the change.

3. In the first quarto it was "the godly Ballet."

4. "[Jephthah had] One fair daughter, and no more, The which he lovéd passing well" (2.2.349-350). These lines are printed as a quotation in most modern editions; some editors have suggested that Hamlet sings the lines. However, in Q1, Q2 and F1 there is nothing to distinguish them from ordinary text. The earliest known ballad on the subject – "The Song of Jephthah's Daughter at her Death" – was entered in the Stationers' Registers for 1567-8. There is no surviving text, so there is no way to know if there were similarities in phrasing between it and the *Hamlet* text.

   There are similarities between the *Hamlet* text and the first stanza of a ballad (which exists in several variants) known from printed texts, all extant copies of which date from more than a century after the First Folio. What appears to be a transcript of a very early printed copy turned up in the Shirburn MS in the library of the Earl of Macclesfield. The part of the manuscript containing the Jephthah ballad was dated 1601-1603, based on the handwriting and other factors (Andrew Clark, ed., *The Shirburn Ballads*, 1585-1616. Oxford: Clarendon Press, 1907). It may have been the same ballad entitled "Jepha Judge of Israel" whose change of ownership was registered – along with 127 others – with the Stationers on 14 December 1624.

5. I have found only two significant exceptions. James Black, in his 1978 essay, "Hamlet's Vows," noticed the homiletic reference to Jephthah, and makes a very cogent argument that Jephthah's vow, rather than his daughter, is central to the understanding of the play. Kenneth J. Larsen, in an essay on Sonnet 152, notes the Jephthah reference in the homilies, but does not make the Hamlet connection.

6. This book, first published in 1547, contained twelve homilies. A second book,

containing 21 additional homilies, was prepared, but the death of Edward VI intervened before it could be published, and it was not until Queen Elizabeth succeeded in 1559 that it eventually reached print. The two books were republished frequently until combined into one volume late in James I's reign. (*The Two Books of Homilies Appointed to be Read in Churches*, ed. John Griffiths. Oxford: University Press, 1859). By royal command, the entire group of 33 homilies were read each Sunday in constant rotation in every church in England during Elizabeth's reign.

7   Thomas Becon (c.1511-1567) was a Protestant reformer who at one time served as Edward Seymour's chaplain. He was certainly known to Sir William Cecil, as he dedicated his "Principles of Christian Religion" to "the most gentle and godly disposed child, Master Thomas Cecil," who was Cecil's eldest son (*The Catechism of Thomas Becon*, edited for the Parker Society by the Rev. John Ayre, Cambridge University Press, 1844), p. 480.

8   The Ayre edition, unlike the Religious Tract Society's edition of *The Writings of the Rev. Thomas Becon* (1829), includes Becon's marginal notes, which give specific references to the various religious commentators he cited.

9   It was originally written in Greek – a language familiar to only a handful of Englishmen at the time – and although it appears to have been completed by 1544, there is no definitive record of when or even if it was ever performed. Christopherson apparently made a Latin translation of the play, which would have been more accessible to an academic audience, but it has disappeared. Given that he was a devout Roman Catholic who died in prison shortly after Elizabeth's accession in 1558, the play would have had scant attraction for a Protestant audience, even an academic one. There are only two extant manuscripts of the Greek version of the play, one each held by St. John's College and Trinity College, Cambridge.

10 The Franklin's Tale is the last in what is known as "Fragment V," and the Physician's Tale is the first in "Fragment VI."

11 "…In April 1571 the upper house of the convocation ordered that [the Actes] should be set up alongside the bible in all cathedral churches, and in the homes of senior and cathedral clergy. A less formal . . . archepiscopal instruction also required parish churches to provide copies . . . Most copies were probably donated. These orders provide at least a partial explanation for the scale and rapidity with which Foxe's stories and images penetrated the public conscience." – David Loades, "The Early Reception," John Foxe's *The Acts and Monuments Online*, www.johnfoxe.org. (Accessed, February 22, 2015).

12 "But when men do swear of custom, in reasoning, buying and selling, or other daily communications, . . . such kind of swearing is ungodly, unlawful, and forbidden

by the commandment of God: for such swearing is nothing but taking of God's holy name in vain..." – *Certain Sermones or Homilies, Appointed to be Read in Churches* ... (1852), p. 65.

13 *Certain Sermones and Homilies*, p. 76.

14 *Calendar of State Papers* (Domestic), vol. 174 (October 1584), item 1.

15 Meaning that the oath was sworn by placing one's hand physically on the Book of the Gospels, the form today termed a "solemn oath" – that is, the kind of oath one swore in the context of legal proceedings, which could subject one to prosecution if violated.

16 This is the accepted form of citation for Acts of Parliament. In this reference, statutes enacted before 1962 are cited by regnal year, chapter number, section, common name or a description of its subject matter, and year" (New York University School of Law, *Guide to Foreign and International Legal Citations* (2006) p. 208)

17 The Babington Plot, as it was called, was a scheme to assassinate Elizabeth and place Mary, Queen of Scots on the English throne. Anthony Babington, a young recusant, was recruited by John Ballard, a Jesuit priest, to organize the attempt. Unfortunately for Babington, one of his fellow conspirators was a spy for Sir Francis Walsingham and the group was tried, convicted and executed in September 1586.

18 *Cobbett's State Trials*, vol. 1, pp. 1431 ff.

19 Strict constructionists are scholars who adhere strictly to the documentary evidence of dating, discounting anecdotal references to a possible pre-1598 version of the play.

20 This appellation appears to have been first used by Gregor Sarrazin in his 1892 study of Thomas Kyd.

Sc(e)acan, Shack, and Shakespeare

by Eddi Jolly

Our English language has been growing and evolving steadily for the past 1500 years. Those who study it tend to divide it into three periods: Old English, from 450 to 1100, Middle English up to 1500, and Modern English, from 1500 to the present day. The latter is often subdivided into the Renaissance or Early Modern English (1500-1650), the Appeal to Authority (1650-1800), and Modern English.[1] Early Modern English is the time span of particular interest here. There are six principal areas in which the development of the language is evident: letters or graphology, grammar, vocabulary, semantics, pronunciation, and orthography. We might look very briefly at a feature or two in the first four of these areas, just to have some idea of the details and differences. Most people who study the language will also touch upon the rise of Standard English, the effects of printing, and the issue of spelling reform.

For example, by the beginning of Early Modern English the **letters or graphs** are those we expect today. The old letter thorn, <þ>, representing <th> today, is still present; it was gradually written with the top open, so that it looked like a <y>, as we find in texts from around 1500, for instance. Early printers, who were seeking to justify lines, sometimes abbreviated words like *the* (three letter spaces) by printing <y> with an <e> over the top, to represent *the* (taking up one letter space). Sometimes an ampersand, <&> (one letter space), was used instead of *and* for the same reason. Occasionally ād, with a horizontal line over the <a> to indicate the predictable letter <n>, was used, to take up just two letter spaces. The horizontal line over a letter to show that a predictable letter followed was not uncommon.

Grammar, loosely denoting the rules which govern language, has changed considerably. Old English was a highly inflected language, where word endings on nouns signified subject or object (or dative or genitive) and adjectives agreed with the case and gender of the noun they modified, for example. Word order therefore wasn't as critical as it is today. By Middle English these inflected endings had largely been eroded, and meaning was dependent on word order, as it still is today. Verbs in Early Modern English still used <eth> as the third person singular present tense inflection, but by the end of that period it had been replaced by <(e)s> almost completely. So while at the beginning of the period *he speaketh* would have been found, by the end *he speaks* would have been the norm. Speeches like Portia's 'The quality of mercy

. . .' in *The Merchant of Venice* use both <eth> and <(e)s> inflections, showing the playwright was writing in this transition period. Q1 *Hamlet* has proportionally more <eth> and fewer <(e)s> endings on third person singular present tense verbs than Q2 *Hamlet*, which contributes to suggesting that Q1 is earlier than Q2 (Jolly 26-29).

As for **vocabulary**, our post-Conquest lexis was already supplemented extensively by words which speakers had borrowed from French, like *parliament*, and *petticoat*. In Shakespeare's time writers delighted in coining more words, and particularly in deriving them from Latin and Greek. Some people complained about these 'inkhorn' terms, but generally the opinion was that to have splendour and magnificence in our language, we needed to borrow. There was a practical reason for some of the loan words, for they provided labels we lacked.

A number of the words used in earlier times have changed their **semantics**. Caxton uses *mete* to denote *food* generally (Bolton 2), whereas today *meat* denotes edible *dead flesh*. Shakespeare uses *enlargement* to denote freedom, whereas we are more likely to use it to mean a *bigger photograph*, or similar. The biggest change in meaning is probably *nice*, which originates from the Latin *nescius*, and originally meant *ignorant*, or *silly*, later meant *fastidious* (retained in legal *niceties*), and now means a rather bland *pleasant*. A good dictionary offers a fuller history of this quite fascinating change of semantics for *nice* over the centuries.

Those are the briefest of examples to hint at some of the significant changes over the 1500-year history of the English language. Two changes across this time span are particularly relevant to those interested in 'Shakspere' and 'Shakespeare,' namely pronunciation and spelling. These are best understood with some additional background information about late Middle English.

The **rise of Standard (written) English** comes towards the end of the fourteenth century; it was then that the East Midlands dialect began to be the preferred version. This was partly because

> [the] men of the east with the men of the west . . . accordeth more in sounding of speech than the men of the north with the men of the south; therefore it is that Mercia, that beeth the men of middle England . . . understandeth better the side languages, Northern and Southern, than Northern and

---

Eddi Jolly *is a retired lecturer in English Literature and Language; presently she is an independent researcher. She is particularly keen to return to primary sources in all areas of Shakespearean studies, hence her research on the priority of the first two quartos of* Hamlet, *and more recently on* Romeo and Juliet. *She is very pleased to have been awarded a research grant by the Shakespeare Oxford Fellowship, to investigate any records in Paris relating to the visits there of the Earl of Oxford in 1575 and 1576.*

Southern understandeth each other (Baugh 287).²

It also had to do with the region being relatively wealthy and influential, thanks to the success of sheep-farming and the resulting wool for the cloth trade in this part of the country. Above all it was the presence of London with all its trade and the power of government, and it may owe something to the presence of the two universities. It is usually roughly the triangle between the universities and London which is seen as giving rise to the standard.

Consequently, this area, especially London, tended to see the first stages of language change, which then radiated out to the rest of the country. The **accents** which survive today still show that not all changes reached the furthest parts of the British Isles. For example, in Chaucer's time the velar fricative <gh> (/x/³) in *knight* was pronounced, but gradually that sound has been dropped from the speech of the English, although it is retained in Scotland in words like *loch*. Another example might be rhotic <r>.⁴ This too was country-wide in Chaucer's day, but from the eighteenth century was gradually dropped in, for example, the word-final position in much of England; it is retained in Scotland on words such as *beer*. Its retention in Scotland goes alongside a tendency for Scots not to have changed their vowels quite so much as has happened further south in Britain.

One of the changes in Middle English was that some short vowels were lengthened. Baugh gives the example of the Old English infinitive *bacan*, which became Middle English *baken*, modern *to bake* (Baugh 287). Other words which shared the sound change of *bacan* include *tacan*, modern *to take*; *sc(e)acan, to shake;* and the noun *nama, name*. Part of the change to modern pronunciations took place during what is called the Great Vowel Shift, generally seen as occurring between 1400 and 1600, but there were later vowel changes too. Baugh gives a table which shows the pronunciation of *name* in Shakespeare's time as /neːm/ (to rhyme with modern British English *hem*), where the diacritical mark [ː] indicates that the vowel is long rather than short.

Wrenn gives a slightly more complex table, suggesting a sound change pattern as follows:

Word	O.E. spelling	Chaucer's pronunciation	Shakespeare's pronunciation	Modern southern pronunciation
name	nama	/aː/	/e/	/eɪ/⁵

Simeon Potter gives it century by century, thus:

XIV	XV	XVI	XVII	XVIII	
/a/	/æ/	/ɛ/	/e/	/eɪ/	name⁶

It may be useful to look at a diagram which shows where in the mouth these vowel sounds were articulated, since that shows a clear progression from the open back vowel of Old English, /ɑ/ (British English *father*) in the International Phonetic Alphabet, to the slightly less open front vowel /æ/ (British English *hat*), to the half open front vowel /ɛ/, to the half closed front vowel /e/[7] and finally to the diphthong British English uses today, / eɪ/. However, although we can be sure of the progression, we cannot pinpoint exactly when and where the changes in pronunciation took place, or how fast they occurred and spread, but we can be reasonably confident that they began in the London area and spread out from there.

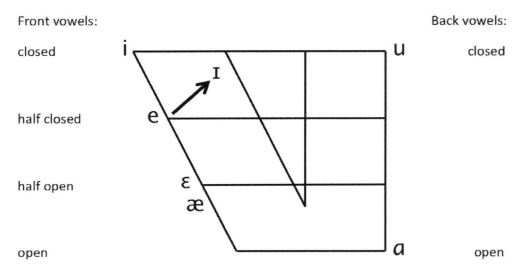

This diagram shows the places of articulation for the vowel changes from *sc(e)acan* to *shake*, including the three cardinal vowels /ɑ/, /u/ and /i/ as well. The right hand side represents the back of the mouth, and the sloping line on the left hand side represents the front of the mouth.

It is therefore reasonable to assume that whatever the pronunciation of 'Shak-' or 'shake' in Elizabeth I's day, the vowel sound would have changed in the London area earlier than in Warwickshire. 'Shak-' might reflect Warwickshire pronunciation and /æ/, a sound perhaps surviving a century longer in the regions than in London for 'shake.' However, the vowel diagrams above, from Baugh, Wrenn, and Potter, suggest the vowel sound would have been /ɛ/. We might note that one of the spellings of Shakspere is actually 'Shexpere' (Chambers 113), which suggests that the vowel sound was at that stage and that the writer was spelling the first vowel sound phonetically. The same writer spelled *Stratford* as *Stretford*, a pronunciation change not found today, but a spelling which is not unique: c.f. 'John Combe of Old Stretford' (Chambers 107).[8] However, the 'Shak-' spelling, where it existed, will have survived later than the pronunciation, because the pronunciation change for this sound will have occurred earlier than the change in spelling. This is generally true.[9] It was the change in pronunciation which drove the desire for spelling change.

There is another small complication, the dialectal word *shack*. This may be the sound associated with 'Shakspere,' since a variant of the name is also spelled 'Shackspere,' where the initial vowel is a monophthong rather than the diphthong in modern *shake*, and here assumed to rhyme with *back*. 'Shack' is reflected in some of the spellings of the surname 'Shakespeare' in the sixteenth century; Chambers gives a christening entry at Budbroke for a 'Henrie Shackespere' (Chambers 13), for instance. *The Shorter Oxford English* dictionary – the two-volume edition – opens its entry on *shack* thus:

Shack…Now dial[ectal]. 1536. [f. Shack, dial var[iation] of SHAKE.]

In other words, regional dialects (it is not clear which ones) in the sixteenth century might have used *shack* for *shake*. Of course, the writer Shakespeare did use *shake* in its modern form in e.g., *As You Like It*, when Orlando says 'thou shalt hear how he will shake me up,' and the Crystals' glossary in *Shakespeare's Words* does not offer any use of *shack* in the plays. But if *shake* was part of the standard and of London usage, then probably that would be the form the playwright and/or his printers would employ. The same dictionary tells us that Old English *spere* gives us today's *spear*. What this shows is that the spelling 'Shakspere' might have a hint of a dialect word and of an older spelling.

What about **orthography**? In 1490, William Caxton, who had brought printing to Britain, wrote a preface to his *Eneydos*, his translation (from French) of *The Aeneid*. In it he tells a story of a man called Sheffelde, who temporarily unable to make progress with his sea journey, went to a house and asked for *mete [food]*, 'and specially he axyd after eggys.' The lady of the house couldn't understand him, so eventually another of the men travelling with Sheffelde asked for 'eyren.' The point is that the first man had asked for the northern version of *eggs*, while the second asked for the southern version. The old southern plural inflection, <en>, is retained in five words today, e.g., *men* and *children*. And Caxton metaphorically throws his hands up in the air and asks as a printer, 'Loo, what sholde a man in thyse days now wryte, egges or eyren?' (Baugh 236). Of course Caxton's concern is to spell in such a way that most readers will understand him, in order to ensure as many readers (and purchasers) of his books as possible.

By the mid to late sixteenth century the desire to ascertain the correct spellings of words was even stronger. The spelling issue was complicated by the fact that by the mid-sixteenth century spellings were not always phonetic renderings of the words, because, as we have seen, pronunciation had changed in some circumstances while orthography had not. Nor was this the only reason. Contributions by the French scribes after the Norman Conquest – who contributed delights such as the <c> in *mice* – hadn't helped, and the variability of individual writers was also a matter of concern. The second half of the sixteenth century saw several would-be spelling reformers making proposals. Sir Thomas Smith was one of those who wished to improve English orthography, in his 1568 proposal for the *Correct and Emended Writing of the English Language*. He wanted to increase the alphabet to thirty-four letters, among other suggestions (Baugh 252). John Hart in 1570 wanted more phonetic spelling (Baugh 253), and in 1580 William Bullokar employed accents and apostrophes among his suggestions.

It was Richard Mulcaster[10] who made the most progress with encouraging 'right writing,' by adopting the customary spelling 'wherein the skilful and best learned do agre' (Baugh 254). One of his guidelines was to use word-final <e> consistently to indicate a preceding long vowel, in order to distinguish between *mad* (/mæd/) and *made* (/meːd/), for example. Today the word-final <e> tends to indicate that the preceding vowel is a diphthong (/meɪd/ in modern British English). Mulcaster's proposals came in his *Elementarie* in 1582. English spellings have followed his suggestions more than any of the other reformers of the time. Gradually, spellings became less varied and more fixed as printing spread and as writers tended to adopt the orthography they saw in printed books. Spelling is seen as largely standardised, or fixed, by 1650, though it is possible to find non-standard spellings in documents later than this – often explained by the writer's distance from London or by the writer's level of education.

This background to orthography is necessarily rather brief and summative, but it might permit us to make a generalised prediction. Since we know that changes occurred in the capital and spread out, we might speculate that older spellings would survive longer in areas more distant from London, while 'modern' spellings would be more likely to be used first in the London area and thereabouts. It may be too that the spelling 'Shak-' reflects a dialect word rather than Standard English *shake*. We have already commented that 'Shak-' may reflect a pronunciation that became less common in London at an earlier time than in Warwickshire. Both 'Shak-' and *spere* are more likely to be found later in parts of the country some distance from London than in the capital itself. Those in the capital who were involved in printing would be trying to produce spellings which would please the majority. It is therefore also likely that 'Shakespeare' would be found in London a little earlier than well outside the capital. With spelling reform actively promoted in London, and a considerable amount of printing done there, it is also more likely that consistent spellings would be found earlier in London. Writers who used 'Shakspere' are perhaps courteously using the spelling Shakspere preferred, as suggested by the six signatures, or have not yet adopted the word-final <e> to indicate a preceding long vowel.

We now turn to the spellings associated with the W. 'Shakspere' of Stratford and the spellings associated with the 'Shakespeare' on the title pages of the canon.

The records in Stratford show the record keepers there wrote 'Shakspere' more frequently than any other variant, from 1566 to 1600 (Chambers 2-4), for the family of W. Shakspere. Chambers does show one Stratford entry with the now standard spelling:

> 1583, May 26. C. Susanna daughter to William Shakespeare.

But this is an error, and 'Shakspere' is what is found in the facsimile in Schoenbaum's *William Shakespeare: A Documentary Life*. Shakspere's marriage license has the spelling 'Shaxpere', and the bond of sureties, also in 1582, has 'Shagspere' (Chambers 41).

In 1597 an extract in Latin – presumably by a reasonably well-educated writer – from an *Exemplification of Fine* concerning New Place mentions 'Shakespeare' three times, with consistency (Chambers 95-6). A 1602 document, again in Latin, and again an extract, from *Foot of Fine*, gives 'Shakespeare.' In contrast, also in documents relating to Stratford, the Chamber Account – written in English – records 'Shaxpere' for a load of stone and, on an endorsement for a lease of property, gives us 'Shaxpeare.' As a maltster his name is spelled 'Shackespere.' The old Stratford Freehold conveyance of 1602 refers to 'Shakespere' five times. This spelling is found again in 1610, in the *Finalis Concordia* in Common Pleas – another document in Latin. Not all these documents in Latin are consistent: one – in 1602, from *Copy* of an entry in the *Court Roll* – has both 'Shackespere' and 'Shakespere.' After his death in 1616, a note gives his name as 'Shakespere' (Chambers 96-112).

W. Shakspere of Stratford himself allegedly left six signatures, but does not spell his name as 'Shakespeare.' Jane Cox, writing in the HMSO book on *Shakespeare in the Public Records*, comments that the six signatures do not come from the same writer.[11] The earliest signature is 1612 'Shakp', and the 1613 ones are both 'Shakspe', with the line over the top of the word-final <e> to indicate a predictable next letter (or two). In 1616 he apparently signs his name as 'Shakspere' (twice) and 'Shakspeare' (once) on his will, a will made out on behalf of 'William Shackspeare' (Chambers 171, 173-4). The signatures are presumably all spellings of his choice, though the contrasting spellings of his name in the documents and in his signatures on those documents are disconcerting to a modern reader.

Some of his acquaintances and family mention him by name. It is noticeable that 'Shaksper' is the spelling in the letter from Abraham Sturley to Richard Quiney in Stratford. This might have suggested these two local people knew Shakspere's apparently preferred spelling, if it were not for Quiney's letter to Shakspere, which is addressed to 'Shackespere' (Chambers 101-02). The Welcombe Enclosure documents from 1614 include extracts from memoranda by Thomas Greene, who refers to 'my Cosen Shakspeare,' 'Mr Shakspeare,' 'my Cosen Shakespeare' (these last two in the same sentence), with several repeats of 'Shakspeare' (Chambers 142-3). Greene was presumably one who knew Shakspere reasonably well, but he still does not spell his cousin's name consistently. It is also rather curious that Greene appears to have attended Middle Temple, where his shield is displayed in the Middle Temple Hall. It records him as a 'lector' (reader) in 1621, a role he is likely to have taken up towards the end of his career, according to the stewards on duty on the 19th of September 2015. Do Greene's spellings represent a mixture of his cousin's preference and his own awareness that in London, 'Shakespeare' was the expected spelling? Interestingly, Chambers doesn't quote Greene as mentioning the performance of *Twelfth Night* on 2nd February 1602, which one might expect Greene to do somewhere, since his 'Cosen Shakespeare' is supposed to have written the play performed there. And somewhat earlier, Augustine Phillips's will (in London) has a legacy for 'Shakespeare' (Chambers 73). It is unlikely he did not know his legatee well, but he doesn't use W. Shakspere's apparently preferred spelling.

In London the records are a little different. In 1588, the bill of complaint in the Queen's bench regarding the Arden inheritance is in Latin. It has Johanne[s] or Willielmo 'Shackespere' quite consistently thirteen times, though the writer also produces two instances of 'Shackspere' and one of 'Shackspeare.' In 1596 the application for a grant of arms has the spelling 'Shakespere,' and John 'Shakespeare' (Chambers 18-9). These two – the bill of complaint and the grant of arms – undoubtedly refer to a Shakspere of Stratford, as does the Belott-Mountjoy lawsuit, though these are to father and son respectively. The Belott-Mountjoy suit is dated 1612 and states clearly that 'William Shakespeare of Stratford vpon Aven' is the man giving the deposition, spelled thus eleven times, with one 'Shakespe<are>,' and one 'Shakspeare' (Chambers 90-94).

A different set of records concerns London residences. These see him failing to pay taxes which have been levied, with spellings like (1597) 'Shackspere,' twice (1598) 'Shakespeare,' and twice (1599) 'Shakspeare' (Chambers 87-88).

As an actor, 'Shakespeare' leads the cast list in *Every Man In his Humour* in 1598. It is the same spelling in 1603 for the license for the King's Men, and for the red cloth for the procession of King James through London in 1604 (Chambers 71-73). It is also 'Shakespeare' at the top of the cast list in the First Folio.

On the narrative poems and on the plays, where a name is given, the spelling tends to be 'Shakespeare' or 'Shake-speare.' This isn't true for the 1608 *Lear* ('Shak-speare') (Schoenbaum 202) or *A Yorkshire Tragedy* where the author's name seems to have been 'borrowed' ('Shakspeare'), and the entry on the Stationers' Register in 1623 appears to have 'Shakspeer[']s' or perhaps 'Shakspere[']s' (Schoenbaum 203, 257). It is rather peculiar that it is the earliest spellings on play texts in London which have the now modern spelling of this name, on the whole.

Regarding the Globe theatre, a Latin document from 1615 mentions 'Shakespeare,' consistently spelled eight times. The 1619 document about the interest of 'Shakespeare' in the Globe and Blackfriars spells the name 'Shakespeare' six times without variations (Chambers 58-63, 52-54).

In 1607, the burial records of St Giles' show a burial of a child of 'Edward Shackspeere, Player,' while later that year the records of St Saviour's show the burial of 'Edmond Shakespeare, a player' (Chambers 18), assumed to be Shakspere's brother.

One much later example is that of Cuthbert Burbage, in 1635. The text is 'From the Answer of Cuthbert Burbadge . . .' It is not immediately clear in Chambers' entry whether this was actually written by C. Burbage. If it was, we would have to note and consider the significance of the (mis)spelling of his own name, as 'Cutbert'. He clearly knows 'Shakspere,' and in the same text spells the name both 'Shakspere' and 'Shakspeare' (Chambers 65-66). The text might merit closer examination, because it is the latest considered briefly here, and it demonstrates several non-standard spellings.

This paper doesn't list every single use of the name which is widely thought to refer to William Shakspere of Stratford. It isn't easy to decipher some of the English Secretary hand-writing in *William Shakespeare: A Documentary Life*. Nevertheless, there are some distinct patterns. It appears that however the name was pronounced, in the Stratford records it was usually spelled 'Shak-' at the turn of the sixteenth to seventeenth century. There is also a trend for those who have a higher level of education (and are able to write in Latin) to use 'Shakespeare,' and for that spelling to be more frequent in London, but still there are unsurprising spelling variations, even by the same writer. Those who know Shakespeare and are writing in Stratford appear to mix their spellings. His cousin, who spent some time at Middle Temple, in London, veers towards the spelling version more common in London.

There does appear to be a clear link between Shakspere of Stratford, 'Shakespeare ye player,' and Shakespeare the Globe share owner (Schoenbaum 171-2). The last two also link in their spellings with Shakespeare the playwright. Yet it seems that Shakspere to the end of his life preferred the spelling 'Shak- 'at the beginning of his name, despite the name 'Shakespeare' appearing on play lists, and narrative poems and plays. The six signatures showing this preferred spelling are dated 1612, 1613 and 1616.

The above outline of some of the changes affecting the language during the Renaissance shows it is sensible to be cautious about the pronunciation of 'Shakspere' and 'Shakespeare,' and also about the significance of the spelling of the name. The records of the fourteenth and fifteenth centuries show 'Shake-' was hardly unusual for the beginning of a name (Chambers 354ff). Online registers of births, marriages and deaths in England for plus or minus forty years around 1580 show clearly that names beginning 'Shake-' are by far the most common; then there is a much smaller number of 'Shaksp-', with a dozen 'Shackes-' and no 'Shex-'. Consequently it would not be surprising that a printer, especially a London one, would spell the surname the more common way. The online records also show that a certain 'S*, William' died in 1616; the spelling of his surname is not something the recorders appear certain about. It may be worth examining these records more closely, to understand the distribution of spellings. Is 'Shakspere' found more in Warwickshire? Perhaps too it is worth studying the whole of the texts where the name occurs, in case the context provides some indication of how particular or standard the writer is about other spellings.[12] But that might be for another paper. The intention here is to give a general overview of pronunciation and orthography regarding 'Shak-' and 'Shake-' in the Elizabethan and early Jacobean period, and to offer a context for discussion of the names 'Shakspere' and 'Shakespeare.'

It is not easy to establish whether the orthographical differences are significant. Different name spellings are found among Shakspere's contemporaries. For example 'Oxeford', 'Oxenford', 'Oxenforde' are found at the end of three of the seventeenth Earl's letters.[13] Yet we are left with a series of questions and anomalies regarding 'Shakspere' and 'Shakespeare.' *Venus and Adonis* was first published in 1593. F. T. Prince comments in his edition, which was printed from the first quarto of the poem:

> . . . the First Quartos, which have been generally accepted as well printed, [are] probably from the poet's fair copies. Some trouble would probably be taken, both by author and printer, in the production of pieces such as these.[14]

If the printing of *Venus and Adonis* in 1593 was so carefully overseen, shouldn't we assume the spelling of its author's name – 'Shakespeare' – was approved by the author – that the spelling has the author's authority? It is also disconcerting that Shakspere of Stratford apparently spent time in London, where printing was contributing to the regularization of spelling, yet he did not adjust the spelling of his own name in his six (alleged) signatures to the most widely found form, 'Shake-', particularly when that form was being used on most of the plays which presumably had some prominence among the printed books of the day. Then the lack of fluency in the penmanship of the signatures is odd. It is also curious that he does not have a clearly legible and stylish signature – as many who have left signatures in Henslowe's *Diary*[15] did – and that he is not mentioned in the *Diary*. Additionally if (as traditional scholars believe) Shakspere was the playwright, it seems peculiar that those printing his poems and plays did not use his preferred spelling. Of course, the playwright Shakespeare and/or his compositors are not entirely consistent with spellings in the plays, but as we have seen, this was not surprising or unusual at the time. Why would Ben Jonson, so particular about no <h> in his own name, use 'Shakespeare' rather than 'Shakspere' on cast lists and on the title page of the First Folio? And all of that is before we consider the will, three pages long, yet not mentioning one book by 'Shakespeare' or even a Shakespearean source. And – in only an interlineation at that – he bequeaths a 'peece to buy . . . Ringes' for 'John Hemynge Richard Burbage & Henry Cundell' without remembering any contemporary playwrights.

Works Cited

Baugh, A. C. *A History of the English Language*. London, Routledge & Kegan Paul Ltd, reprint 1968.

Bolton, W. F. *The English Language: Essays by English and American Men of Letters 1490-1839*. Cambridge University Press, 1966.

Chambers, E. K. *William Shakespeare. Vol 2*. Oxford, Clarendon Press, 1930.

Crystal, David & Ben. *Shakespeare's Words*. Somerset, UK: Penguin, 2004.

Davis, Frank. "Shakespeare's Six Accepted Signatures." *Shakespeare Beyond Doubt? Chapter 2*. Tamarac, Florida: Lumina Press, 2013.

Fowler, William Plumer. *Shakespeare Revealed in Oxford's Letters*. Portsmouth, New Hampshire: Peter E. Randall, 1986.

Jolly, M. *The First Two Quartos of Hamlet*. Jefferson, North Carolina: McFarland, 2014.

Potter, S. *Our Language*. Middlesex, England: Penguin, reprint 1969.

Schoenbaum, Samuel. *William Shakespeare: A Documentary Life*. Oxford, Clarendon Press, in association with The Scolar Press, 1975.

Shakespeare in the Public Records. London, Her Majesty's Stationery Office, 1985.

Shakespeare, William. *Venus and Adonis*, edited by F. T. Prince. London, Methuen, reprint 1982.

Wrenn, C.L. *The English Language*. London, Methuen and Co. Ltd, reprint 1970.

Notes

1. These divisions are used by A.C. Baugh, *A History of the English Language* (London, Routledge and Kegan Paul Ltd, reprint 1968).

2. Modernized spellings of Trevisa's comments; taken from Baugh, p 232.

3. The symbol in slashes or obliques [//] indicates it is drawn from the International Phonetic Alphabet, as are later symbols similarly marked.

4. The sound, or phoneme, /r/ is articulated in several different ways around the world. Each different version is known as an allophone. The French, for instance, pronounce the sound towards the back of the mouth. Rhotic <r> describes the allophone many Scots use to articulate <r> after a vowel. This is why it is also sometimes called post-vocalic <r>.

5. Wrenn actually uses /eɪ/, pronounced as in 'play'. C. L. Wrenn, *The English Language* (London, Methuen and Co. Ltd, reprint 1970), p 86.

6. S. Potter, *Our Language* (Middlesex, England: Penguin, reprint 1969), p 66.

7. Note that today British English speakers produce /e/ just above midway between the half open and the half closed front vowel positions, in words like 'yet' and 'bed'.

8. The vowel sound in 'Shakspere' and 'Stretford' could have been as close as /ɛ/ and /æ/.

9. There are a very small number of examples of spelling affecting pronunciation. One of these is in the word *perfect*. Middle English quite happily used the French spelling and pronunciation, 'parfait', 'parfit' (cf. Chaucer's *Knight*), but when it was decided to 'correct' the spelling and show its Latin root (Latin *perfectus*), the new spelling, *perfect*, affected how we pronounce the word today.

10. Headmaster at Merchant Taylor School, where Thomas Kyd attended.

11. 'It is obvious at a glance that these signatures, with the exception of the last two, are not the signatures of the same man.' *Shakespeare in the Public Records* (London, Her Majesty's Stationery Office, 1985). Comments by Jane Cox, p 33.

12. It is noticeable that the Revels Account in 1604-5 which records the

name 'Shaxberd' has a high proportion of now non-standard spellings, and inconsistent ones at that (Chambers 331).

13 These are all found in William Plumer Fowler's *Shakespeare Revealed in Oxford's Letters* (Portsmouth, New Hampshire: Peter E. Randall, 1986), pp 56, 164 and 803.

14 *Venus and Adonis*, edited by F. T. Prince (London, Methuen, reprint 1982), p xiii.

15 Explored by, inter alia, Frank Davis in chapter 2 in *Shakespeare Beyond Doubt?* (USA, Lumina Press, 2013).

Twelfth Night:
How Much Did De Vere Know of Dubrovnik?

by Richard Malim

We know that Oxford incurred an injury to his knee on a Venetian galley in 1575 during his stay in Italy (Anderson 87, 93).[1] On the 23rd of September 1575 an Italian banker wrote from Venice: "God be thanked, for now last [lately] coming from Genoa his lordship found himself somewhat altered by reason of the extreme heats: and before [earlier] his Lordship hurt his knee in one of the Venetian galleys, but all is past without further harm" (Nelson 128). A Venetian galley would only be used on a sea voyage as opposed to a canal or river journey. This might tie in with de Vere possibly making a trip to the free city state of Ragusa (its Italian name) or Dubrovnik (its Croatian name). If so, he could have seen for himself a culture and location that he would later use as background for *Twelfth Night*.

Here we will try to discover how much Oxford knew of Dubrovnik and its politics. Illyria is the classical name for the territories on the Eastern side of the Adriatic Sea, covering a large part of twentieth-century Yugoslavia, and is the name of the Duchy employed by Oxford for the play.

In the 16th century, the title of Duke of Illyria was used by the Hapsburgs in Vienna, and in 1575 it was one of the subsidiary titles of Archduke Charles (1540-90), the Emperor Ferdinand's third son. Oxford's reference in *Twelfth Night* is to a specific city and its home-grown ruler. For the reasons below, I think it can be identified only with Dubrovnik. In the first place, in 1575 it was a small city with a little hinterland and outlying islands with its own government, entirely surrounded by territories recently conquered by the Ottoman Turks but peopled by Christian Croatians.

Dubrovnik paid tribute to the Ottomans, an arrangement which was supposed to suit both parties – the Turks interfered as little as possible and benefited from Dubrovnik's position as a trading post, and the inhabitants could carry on with their trade and life-style unhindered. The city was very rich as a result, but its status was always precarious, as it had to placate the Hapsburgs, the Venetians, and the Ottomans, each with their separate interests.

After the Ottoman conquests in the 1520s and 1530s, the ancient kingdom of Croatia was reduced to a small strip of coastline and some inland territory, and as a result of the rulers' various matrimonial arrangements, it became virtually a part of Hungary and then of the Hapsburg Empire. The Hapsburgs thus became responsible for the defense of the frontier between the Muslim Ottomans and the Catholic Austrians with Dubrovnik now far to the south. The Hapsburgs did not take much interest in their responsibilities until new wars threatened. They failed repeatedly to finance the defenses and pay the defending troops, notwithstanding that they were the Christian power in the area. The result was that the garrisons each took on independent lives. By 1550 the Ottomans had reduced the number of garrisons to just one, namely that at Senj (*Segna* in Italian). Senj became the destination of persecuted Christians from the Christian interior of the new Muslim empire, as well as dispossessed and criminal types from Venice and the Austrian Hungarian Croatian Christian interior. While it could be and was attacked by sea, from land it was virtually impregnable because of the thick forest around it.

The other player in the game was Venice which was the sovereign power over a number of islands and parts of the coast of the North Adriatic. While they fought small wars with the Turks, their principal interest was trade and for the most part they had no desire to provoke the Turks into any action any more than their co-religionists in Dubrovnik had.

The problem with Senj was that its trade and hinterland, let alone the non-existent or haphazard Hapsburg financial support, gave its independent-minded inhabitants insufficient resources to live on, so they became in effect professional looters, rather than part of the frontier garrison. Always under cover of their elastic Christian consciences, these looters or *uskoks* survived on the raids they made on the Ottoman interior, sometimes with the support of the Christian peasants, except when they 'collected' from them as well. To get to the interior they had to cross the Venetian and Dubrovnik lands. The uskoks were also redoubtable seamen who conducted piracies against Venetian and Dubrovnik trade, stopping ships ostensibly only to remove Turkish goods and citizens, but in practice kidnapping, and purloining much else. Diplomats from Venice and Dubrovnik were fully exercised trying to convince the Ottomans that they were not supporting their fellow Christians or approving of their actions. Meanwhile the looters sold their loot where they could, which frequent-

---

Richard Malim *was an English provincial lawyer who became involved with the Oxfordian claim over 25 years ago. In 2003, when he retired, he became – and still is – the secretary of* The De Vere Society. *Malim was instrumental in the genesis of* Great Oxford, *an acclaimed collection of 31 articles put together to commemorate, in 2004, the quatercentenary of Oxford's death. Spotting a gap in the Oxfordian case and studies, Malim then wrote an all-round reference book,* The Earl of Oxford and the Making of Shakespeare - The Literary Life of Edward de Vere in Context *which places de Vere in the context of the development of literature in English.*

ly meant in markets controlled by the Venetians. (This is a broad-brush sketch of the political background in 1575.)

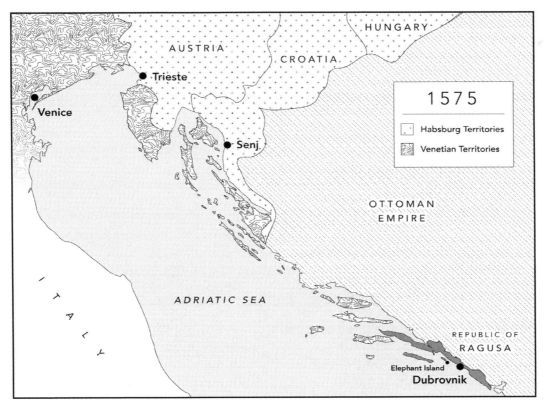

The principal historical event affecting Dubrovnik in the 1570s occurred when a band of uskoks led by one of their senior men tried to come back through Dubrovnik territory and their leader was murdered by the Dubrovnik defense force. This resulted in a classic vendetta which began in 1571 and was still flourishing in 1575 (Bracewell 135).

How Are These Events Reflected in *Twelfth Night*?

From the perspective of history, the really interesting character in *Twelfth Night* is Antonio, who is shown as an uskok leader. Antun seems a reasonably common uskok name. He appears with Sebastian, the romantic young hero he has rescued from a shipwreck in Act 2, Scene 1. Sebastian, as the lost brother, would immediately recall to mind the 'lost' king of Portugal who disappeared after the total defeat of his army in Morocco in 1578. At first, the depressed Sebastian wants to leave Antonio even though Antonio wants him to remain (2.1.1-6). He will not tell Antonio where he is going (2, l, 10) and then says "I perceive that you will not *extort* from me what I am willing to keep in" (2.1.11-13). Then there is this curious passage at 2.1.34-35, where Antonio is still anxious to stay and look after Sebastian, so he says, "If you will not murder me for my love, let me be your servant." Antonio, while recognizing Sebastian's superior social status, is a man expecting violence wherever there is disagreement.

Sebastian recognizes this and says, "If you will not undo what thou hast done, that is, kill him whom you have recovered, desire it not." Then he reveals: "I am bound to the Count Orsino's court." This shocks Antonio, who says, after Sebastian has left the stage:

> The gentleness of all the gods go with thee!
> I have many enemies in Orsino's Court.
> (2, 1, 43-44)

Nevertheless, he concludes:

> The danger shall seem sport, and I shall go. (47)

It is interesting that in *Twelfth Night*, Antonio is even more obviously a homosexual infatuated with Sebastian than is Antonio with Bassanio in *Merchant of Venice*. This connection is made more pointed with multiple references in *Merchant of Venice* to 'argosies,' whose original meaning covers the large cargo boats of Ragusa in which Venetians sought to get round the city's laws for the carriage of trade goods (Roe 116). Both Bassanio and Sebastian are young male characters beloved by a character named Antonio. In *Twelfth Night*'s next act, Antonio and Sebastian appear together in the streets of the city and Antonio confesses to Sebastian:

> I could not stay behind you. My desire,
> More sharp than filed steel, did spur me forth:
> And not all love to see you (though so much
> As might have drawn one to a longer voyage)
> But jealousy what might befall your travel,
> Being skill-less in these parts.
> (3, 3, 4-9)

Sebastian puts Antonio off from going to lodgings as he wants to see "the relics of this town" (19), but Antonio says:

> I do not without danger walk these streets.
> Once in a sea-fight 'gainst the Count his galleys
> I did some service, of such note indeed,
> That were I taken here, it would scarce be answer'd.
> …I shall pay dear.
> (3, 3, 25-28, 37)

Sebastian asks him if he slew "a great number of his [Orsino's] people," and he replies:

> Th' offence . . .
> . . . might have since been answered in repaying
> What we took from them, which for traffic's sake,
> Most of our city did.
> (3, 3, 30-35)

This reference to the city seems a precise allusion to the business of the citizens of Senj, especially as:

> Th' offence is not of such a bloody nature
> Albeit the quality of the time and quarrel
> Might well have given us bloody argument.
> (3, 3, 30-32)

This may well be linked as a reference to the 1571 vendetta referred to above. So they part, but not before Sebastian advises Antonio: "Do not walk then too open," to which Antonio replies:

> It doth not fit me. Hold, sir, my purse,
> In the South suburbs, at the Elephant,
> Is best to lodge.
> (3, 3, 38-40)

Suburbs means outside the city or underneath the walls, and yet there are only rocks and sea immediately south of the walls of Dubrovnik. If, as we think, the play could have been conceived before 1587, when the first theatre south of the Thames was opened – before the writer was concerned with, or had a play put on at any Thames south bank theatre – then *south* is a subsequent editor's post-1587 interpretation or a concession to the London groundlings. (No doubt some of them were customers of the Elephant Inn at Southwark.) If we look west, we come to the *Elephant* Islands, part of the Dubrovnik Republic but out of the immediate reach of the ruler, where Antonio would be much safer.

Then by mischance Antonio gets himself arrested while defending Viola, whom he mistakes for Sebastian, and is hauled off in Act 5 to appear before Orsino, who well remembers him. I have not found any references to the sort of ships used by the uskoks but they do appear in an engraving of 1617 (see following page) to be quite small, and thus suitable for inshore activities where the great galleons of Venice and Dubrovnik would be less maneuverable.

To this point, Orsino says:

> A baubling [contemptible] vessel was he captain of,

> For shallow draft and bulk unprizeable;
> With which, such scatheful grapple did he make
> With the most noble bottom of our fleet,
> That very envy and the tongue of loss
> Cried fame and honour on him.
>
> (5, 1, 52-57)

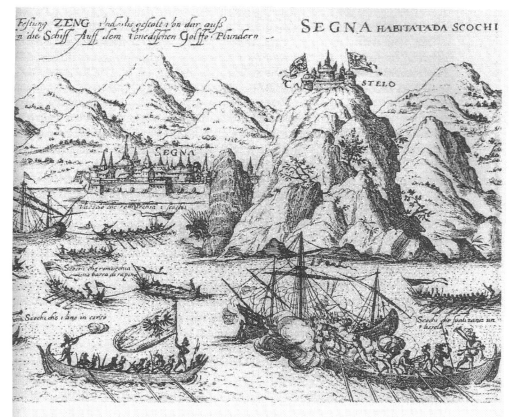

1. "Abriss der Festung Zeng" (Sketch of the Senj Fortress) (1617). A fanciful view of Senj and the Nehaj fortress by Georg Keller. In the foreground, uskoks plunder bales of merchandise from a trading vessel. (Reproduced from *Senj, Hrvatski kulturni spomenici*, vol. 1, ed. Artur Schneider [Zagreb: JAZU, 1940].)

The arresting officer recounts Antonio's triumphs/crimes, and Orsino says: "Notable pirate, thou salt-water thief (5, 1, 67).

But Antonio denies it:

> Orsino, noble sir,
> Be pleased that I shake off these names you give me.
> Antonio never yet was thief or pirate,

> Though I confess, on base and ground enough,
> Orsino's enemy.
>
> (5, 1, 70-74)

This a clear representation of the Venetian / Dubrovnik attitude to the uskok ("thieves and pirates") and equally the uskok attitude to their own activities as Christians. Antonio as a sea fighter has clearly played some leading role. Noticeably there is no pardon in the play for Antonio, so the play's political aspect is maintained. The pardoning or ransoming of a distinguished a leader, as Orsino clearly regards him, would immediately have brought down the wrath of the Ottomans on the citizens of Dubrovnik and the Venetians would have not been far behind. Oxford has deliberately left a very important point of the plot unresolved as a sign of his background knowledge (and as a covert signal of his authorship). He does a similar thing at the end of *Taming of the Shrew* where Sly the drunken peasant is left on stage asleep but in charge of all the lord's riches, which can be read as an allegory for Shakspere's title to Oxford's literary masterpieces. In *Twelfth Night* he is giving us a clear signal of his specialized knowledge of local politics.

So far we have a political and historical picture of Dubrovnik in 1575. If the play was post 1588 (i.e., after the Spanish Armada) one might have expected mention of the three Ragusan ships supplied to Spain for the Armada in 1588. There is no such mention. In addition there is one cast-iron English reference for dating the play.[2] The Oxford pioneer and scholar Admiral Holland pointed out the following:

> Feste: *Primo, secundo, tertio* is a good play; and the old saying is, 'The third pays for all'; the triplex, sir, is a good tripping measure; or the bells of St. Bennet sir, may put you in mind – one, two, three.
>
> (5, 1, 33-6)

The bells of the three churches of St. Bennet in London would ring out at the same time for Sunday afternoon prayers and sermon, precisely at the same time a trumpet would sound at the Theatre at Shoreditch, north of the Thames, to advertise the plays on a Sunday and with them, the dancing on stage. Sunday performances were banned beginning in 1581, so *Twelfth Night* must have been written earlier. By leaving Antonio's fate hanging, I think Oxford is signaling his political knowledge.

Other connections could be the identification of Malvolio with Sir Christopher Hatton and Count Orsini with the visit of a senior Orsini to Queen Elizabeth in 1601. Two hundred years earlier an Orsino had ruled in Dubrovnik and the Orsini family had recently been rulers of Epirus in northwest Greece, as well as being a very prominent family in northern Italy. I think the name was inserted as a compliment to the Italian visitor in 1601, and the character in earlier versions of the play probably had a different name.

The Constitution of Dubrovnik specified that one from the qualified noble families became sole ruler, rector of Dubrovnik for one month and that person was not personally allowed to act again for two years (quoted from Harris throughout). The qualified nobles were called Counts or Grofs (or Grafs). In English, they would called be Earls. The term Duke (or Doge) was not used but it would be clear to an English audience who was intended. Curiously, the title "Duke" is used in the earliest scenes of *Twelfth Night*, up to Act 1, Sc. 4, line 1. However, beginning with line 9, Orsino is referred to and addressed as "Count." During that one month the ruler was not allowed to leave the Rectory Palace without permission and was expected to attend to the State's business completely. In scene 1 he does not want to (be let out to) hunt the hart, presumably on the Elephant Islands (*elaphos* is Greek for deer). The change of title is a bit of a mystery as Oxford is so particular about titles in his other plays but it may reflect the situation under the Dubrovnik Constitution.

Much of Dubrovnik was destroyed in an earthquake in 1667. The area within the walls is small, barely five hundred square yards. It includes The Rectory, the Ruler's palace unaltered after major rebuilding after 1667. This building could be identified with Orsino's palace in the play to which the characters return in Act 5. Antonio is taken as a prisoner to Orsino (in his palace) and the situations of the characters in the plot are resolved. Much more difficult is the placing of Olivia's palace. There is only one building in Dubrovnik with a decent-sized garden and that is the Franciscan Monastery at the West end of the Placa – Stradun (these are Croatian terms for a main street). The solution may be that Oxford apparently remembered this very substantial building and adopted it into the play. Characters wait for admittance at its gateway, but it would be impossible to build a lover's bower at the gateway of this monastery as Viola/Cesario suggests to Olivia in Act I Scene 5. (So this is presumably a poetic fiction on the part of Viola/Cesario.) The garden at the rear is certainly big enough for the deception scene (2, 5). Olivia herself walks "like a cloistress" (1, 1, 29) as if she was in a religious house –this is possibly a hint. Malvolio, in his madness, could be readily kept in darkness in an interior room of a monastic building (4, 2), and there is evidence that the pre-earthquake buildings did remind Oxford of England with Feste jeering at Malvolio on his complaint of the dark: "Why it has bay windows as transparent as barricadoes, and the clerestories toward the south-north are as lustrous as ebony" (4, 2, 37-39). The Monastery is on the north side of the main street and runs "south-north." On the Sponza Palace on the eastern end of the road and almost opposite the Rectory, the clerestory has survived the earthquake on the south side.[3]

The Dubrovnik nobility were anxious to secure its continued dominance by making good marriages with the nobility from other towns. Presumably Sebastian's family from 'Messaline' would qualify. There is no doubt that Viola and Sebastian are good catches and Olivia is impressed when Viola / Cesario tells her that his parentage is "above my fortunes, yet my state is well. I am a gentleman." (1, 5, 279). The play notes the Dubrovnik custom of allowing the unmarried sons like Sir Toby, Olivia's uncle, to live in the family palace while unmarried girls as a general rule were not allowed out of the palace at all (Harris 257).

While I have tried to adduce all the evidence which points to a visit to Dubrovnik by the author of *Twelfth Night*, and I think certainly on the balance of probability that he did, I cannot prove beyond reasonable doubt that Oxford visited. There is nothing in theory that Oxford might not have learned from his visit in Venice, but by the 1570s the Croatian community in London was much reduced. In any case, I do not believe that the Croatians of London in 1570 should be relied on as a source of the Ragusa color in the play, let alone at the time of orthodox dating, approximately in 1600. The general volume of evidence, particularly the political flavour, gives the impression that Oxford's deep and specialized knowledge went beyond book learning and notes from conversations during his stay in Italy. Rather, it favours that he learned about Dubrovnik from an actual visit there, and took his inspiration from being there. He seems to capture the claustrophobic atmosphere of the tiny walled city hemmed in by formidable mountains and by hostile powers, which would seem to mirror recent history when it was besieged and shelled by Serbian and Montenegrin forces in 1991.

Author's Note

Before developing this article, I consulted Croatia's leading authorities on Shakespeare and was directed to Ogledi Naslovanica's paper (with Mladen Engelsfeld) "Shakespeare's Illyria: Facts and Speculations," *Zagreb University Kolo 3-4*, 2013. There, with the help of the Google's computerized translations, I read the gist of it. It was clear that the authors had conducted a survey of all of Shakespeare's plays that were relevant to them, including the unlikely possibility that any other Illyrian city might provide source material. Of course, since they were not challenging the 'orthodox' school of Shakespeare authorship and its c. 1600 dating for *Twelfth Night*, their conclusions were not particularly helpful. Their contentions and ideas did however produce slants on the problems this essay identifies, and my thanks is now recorded.

Additionally, my account of the history and constitutional arrangements owes a great deal to Catherine Wendy Bracewell, Robin Harris, and Noemi Magri.

Notes

1. See Richard Roe, *The Shakespeare Guide to Italy* for information about Oxford's visit to Italy in 1575/6. Noemi Magri also deals with the history of Illyria and the knee injury in her two essays "Shakespeare in Illyria and Bohemia" and "Shakespeare's Knowledge of Illyrian History in Twelfth Night" both of which are printed in *Such Fruits Out of Italy* (Laugwitz Verlag, Buchholz 2014).

2. Clark, Eva Turner. *Hidden Allusions in Shakespeare's Plays 3rd edition*. Page 383. From an essay by Loyd Miller based on Holland. *British Shakespeare Fellowship Newsletter*, Autumn 1958.

3. Personal visit by the author. September 2015.

Works Cited

Anderson, Mark, *"Shakespeare" By Another Name, The Life of Edward de Vere, Earl of Oxford, the Man Who Was Shakespeare*. New York, Gotham/Penguin, 2005.

Bracewell, Catherine Wendy, *The Uskoks of Senj*. Ithaca, NY, Cornell University Press, 1992.

Harris, Robin, *Dubrovnik – A History*. London, Saqi Books, 2006.

Magri, Naomi, *Such Fruits Out of Italy*. Laugwitz Verlag, Buchholz, 2014.

Nelson, Alan, *Monstrous Adversary*. University of Liverpool Press, 2003.

Roe, Richard, *The Shakespeare Guide to Italy*. New York, Harper 2011.

Evermore in Subjection
Edward de Vere and Wardship in Early Modern England

by Bonner Miller Cutting

When Henry Tudor ascended the throne of England as Henry VII in 1485, he found his royal coffers empty and set about to remedy this by asserting his right to feudal dues. Even as England was evolving past the feudalism of the Middle Ages, looking toward a more enlightened era, Henry was taking a hard look at the medieval customs from which revenues for his royal administration could be extracted. The newly-minted monarch wasted no time, and within the first year of his reign, his ministers were working to revive the moribund medieval system known as wardship (Hurstfield 7).[1]

One: Wardship

It is difficult for modern society to fathom what feudal dues and the wardship system it fostered were all about. Feudalism was a form of social order based on land tenure. *Tenure* is a term for how land is owned and feudal tenures were built on the relationship between a property owner and his overlord. From the time of the Norman Conquest, if not before, it was understood that every man who held land owed service to someone of higher social standing. The *tenant* was at a lower rung of the ladder; the individual at the higher level was a *lord*. The king stood at the top of this hierarchy as the supreme landlord of the entire country (Bell 1-5).

In medieval centuries, most of the land of England that was not in royal possession was held by barons. They had initially been given their lands and titles by the monarch, often as a reward for military service. A baron was to continue to provide military service – called *knight service* – to the king in return for the title and property that the king bestowed on him. The king expected his barons to be at the ready to render knight service when he had a war to fight or needed to defend his kingdom from an enemy. At this time, the barons put on their armor, got on their horses, gathered together the men who lived and worked on their properties, and led their men into the fray to support king and country.

This scenario may have worked well enough with an able-bodied father in the household, but if a baron died while his heir was still a minor, then his child was not physically able to give the required knight service. When this happened, the king felt entitled to compensation that came in the form of income from the lands that the child would inherit (Bell 1-2).[2] The revenue generated from wealthy estates could include rents from the cottages, sales of crops and livestock, wool from the sheep, wood from the forests, and control of any minerals on the land. But there was more. The king assumed the right to the custody of the child in order to supervise his upbringing and ensure that he would be a loyal tenant in adulthood. Furthermore, it was considered morally justifiable for the king to direct the child's eventual marriage so the property – which at an earlier time was regarded as crown property – would stay in friendly hands. Thus the king had, as a feudal right, the physical custody of the heir along with the income from the heir's property during his minority. Moreover, with the right to bestow the ward in marriage, the king controlled the ward's future – a future that could encompass the destiny of the ward's family. Indeed, the right of marriage came to be considered the greatest of all the evils that the ruling class visited upon the less fortunate of the monarch's subjects (Bell 125, Hurstfield 134).

Cold Blooded Profiteering

If a modern reader chances to pick up H. E. Bell's 1953 book on wardship or Joel Hurstfield's 1958 book *The Queen's Wards*, they would find it hard to believe that so outrageous a social system could have existed in a nation on the eve of a great humanistic renaissance. One might even be tempted to doubt the existence of the feudal wardship system, especially since most histories of early modern England treat the subject lightly if at all. But in spite of historical neglect, wardship was a reality in which the custody of children, the income from their lands and the right to direct their marriage were auctioned off to the highest bidder (Bell 119). Hurstfield has summarized wardship as "a squalid organ of profiteering from the misfortunes of the helpless" (Hurstfield 241). In 1549, the clergyman Hugh Latimer exclaimed against it. Sir Thomas Smith wrote that it was "unreasonable and unjust, and contrary to nature that a freeman and gentleman should be bought and sold like an horse [sic] or an ox."[3] Sir Nicholas Bacon wrote that wardship was "a thing hitherto preposterously proceeding," a peculiar statement coming from a man who was the

---

Bonner Miller Cutting *is a frequent presenter at Shakespeare authorship conferences and has researched many subjects including* Lady Anne Clifford's Triptych, *the Van Dyke portrait of Susan Vere at Wilton House, and censorship and punishment in early modern England. She has published articles on the will of William Shaksper of Stratford-upon-Avon and her transcript of the Stratford will was published in the Shakespeare Authorship Coalition book* Shakespeare Beyond Doubt? Exposing an Industry in Denial. *Cutting holds a BFA degree from Tulane University in New Orleans and a Masters of Music in piano performance from McNeese State University in Lake Charles, Louisiana.*

attorney for the Court of Wards, and who benefited from its very existence. Yet proceed it did, gaining strength as the 16th century marched on – a phenomenon that Bell credits to the administrative proficiency of the Tudors (Bell 10-15).[4]

Henry VIII showed his Tudor aptitude for administration by setting up a court in 1540 to handle the workload engendered by the business of wardship. Called the Court of Wards and Liveries, it brought a legal and judicial underpinning to what had previously been a societal custom, giving it the trappings of social justice (Bell 13, Hurstfield 12). Using a Court to oversee the buying and selling of wards facilitated the Tudor objective to centralize authority in the Crown, shifting the balance of power from the old aristocracy to the monarchy (Stone 97, 131-134). It also contributed to furthering a bureaucracy filled with new men who were loyal to the Tudors (Hurstfield 16-17). It was a brilliant innovation on the part of the Tudor monarch.

With the dissolution of the monasteries in the late 1530s, vast tracts of land were purchased by the members of the king's elite court circle who were in a position to buy property, bringing an estimated £90,000 a year to the royal coffers (Hurstfield 11). Even so, the wily king had something more in mind than just immediate profits. Unbeknownst to the purchasers, the seized church lands that would enrich them came with a twist: to the monastic lands, Henry VIII attached the feudal tenure of knight service.

It mattered not a whit to Henry that the lands of the church had not the slightest connection to the feudal duties of knight service. But it would eventually matter a great deal to the buyers, for it meant that the children of those who had participated, often zealously, in the seizure and acquisition of monastic property would be subjected to the charges of wardship in the event of the father's death before the heir reached his majority. At a time when this occurred in one of three well-to-do families, it was certain that subsequent generations of the king would continue to reap profits from subsequent generations of his courtiers' families. Hurstfield notes that "There is almost an Old Testament concept of retribution in the way the descendants of Henry VIII inflicted suffering upon the descendants of those who had bought up the confiscated lands of the church" (11).

I Bury a Second Husband

Many a Tudor widow could identify with the opening lines in *All's Well that Ends Well* when the widowed Countess says, "In delivering my son from me, I bury a second husband." Historians Bell and Hurstfield recount the crippling blow to a family if the father died leaving a minor to inherit his estates. But what exactly were the problems with wardship? Who profited from it? Was social injustice inherent in the system?

Wardship was remarkable because it exploited the upper strata of society. It was based on feudalism, and feudalism was based on ownership of property. Thus, wardship affected the propertied classes, not the poor. Upon the death of a father with a minor heir, the Tudor administration sent out agents to determine if the property was held by the tenure of knight service. If the government official suspected that the land, or even a small part of it, had once been part of a royal land grant, he would call for an *inquisition post mortem*. This was a legal examination by which the Court of Wards accessed the manner of tenure and the value of the property that the heir stood to inherit. Significantly, even at this initial stage, the deck was stacked against the heir's family. If only an acre of land could be proven to have originated in knight service tenure, then all the property of the estate, down to the last blade of grass, was pulled into the undertow of wardship (Bell 50). After the verdict of feudal tenure was rendered by the inquisition – and this was usually a foregone conclusion – the machinery of the Court of Wards was set in motion. The estate valuations from the *inquisition* were sent to the Court as one of the estimates of value used to determine the all-important price that someone would pay for the wardship (Hurstfield 83-85).[5] From this point forward, the fate of the child and his property would be in the hands of the Master of the Court of Wards.

The influence that the Master of the Court held over the landed families of England reached far and wide. Once it was known that a wardship was available, the Master would be besieged with pleas and petitions of suitors (as the prospective buyers were called) wanting to purchase the wardship. It was the Master's job to set the price that the suitor would pay and then select the fortunate individual with the winning offer. This sordid process was made all the more noxious by the fawning petitioners who swore their loyalty to the Master, often broadly hinting at gifts. In a less than ambiguously worded note, a suitor wrote to Robert Cecil that "If the ward prove well, I would be glad to buy him at the full value of your Honour for one of my daughters" (Hurstfield 264).

Mothers and relatives who likely had the welfare of the child at heart were rarely successful and could get in the queue, beseeching the Master with a bid for the custody of their own child. Curiously, a wardship could be resold at a price higher than the original one set by the Master, and at this juncture mothers or relatives often succeeded in buying back their own children, though at a much higher price than was initially paid (Hurstfield 124). Hurstfield notes that "In essence, a considerable body of the landed classes of England was each year held to ransom" (192).

It became common practice for families to attempt to hide potential wardships from the watchful eye of the government (Bell 52-52). Landowners countered with efforts to conceal how they owned their property, hiring battalions of lawyers to devise bogus transactions to mask possible feudal tenures left over from earlier centuries (Hurstfield 5-7).[6] The discovery of concealed wardships became "one of the great outdoor sports of Elizabethan England" (Hurstfield 34)[7] as the prospect of discovering one gave rise to a multitude of government employees, professional informants, and even neighbors who could look to a monetary reward for revealing a wardship illegally concealed from the Queen (Bell 50-53).

In the scramble for wards, participants came from all walks of life: from the grandest of the royal court down to the humblest servants in the Queen's stables. Officials of all stripes pursued wardships, including many that are well known to us: Attorney General Edward Coke, Lord Chief Justice John Popham, Sir Walter Raleigh, Sir Nicolas Bacon and his famous son Sir Francis, Lord Chancellor Thomas More, Sir John Fortesque of the Queen's Exchequer, and Dr. Bull of the Chapel Royal. The Earls of Leicester, Bedford, Rutland, Essex, and Cumberland were among the nobility who threw their hats into the fray (Hurstfield 66, 123-125, 274-275, 301, 347). According to Hurstfield, "No less a person than Lord Cobham, hearing of a man's death, wrote the same evening to Cecil for the wardship of the heir, adding that his haste was due to his fear of being forestalled" (62).[8] Aristocratic ladies had wards as well. Lady Leighton, Lady Paget, Lady Derby, and Lady Burgh are on lists of successful purchasers (Hurstfield 123-125). In explaining that the redoubtable Bess of Hardwick had wards, biographer Mary Lovell writes: "These were much sought after, being a perfectly legitimate manner of earning extra money" (484).[9] Unsurprisingly, the richest suitors scooped up the richest wardships, while the heirs with more modest estates went to junior court officials, clerks, under-clerks, messengers and ushers (Bell 35, Hurstfield 222). One historian remarks, "Wardship was a good thing for everyone except the wards." [10]

Wardship was a major source of finance for the Elizabethan administration. But with one caveat: for each pound that went into the Queen's royal coffers, an estimated twelve pounds went into private pockets (Hurstfield 344). The ever expanding bureaucracy mulcted official fees from hopeful suitors for an unimaginable litany of services. Sir Julius Caesar, an eminent lawyer and administrator of the time, kept records of the expenditures he incurred while purchasing for his wife the wardship of her two daughters from her prior marriage. He made payments to those he called "solicitors and friends," to auditors and attorneys, feodaries (a financial agent of the Court of Wards), the Pettibag Office of Chancery, and the Scheduler of Lands. He was charged for privy seals and the engrossing of leases, and hosted several dinners for the commissioners and the jury, paying the sheriff's bailiff's servant for making the arrangements. He concluded that his expenses came to £1,739 in addition to the £1,000 purchase price for the young ladies (Hurstfield 81-82). This would be well over a million dollars in modern currency.

Oblivious to conflicts of interest, the chief officials of the Court of Wards sought wardships for themselves and benefited from the lands of the wards as well as the fees that came with their offices (Bell 35). The big money was in the unofficial fees. The giving and taking of "gifts" was standard practice in Tudor government, and modern historians accept the rationale that the parsimonious Queen allowed this mischief because she did not adequately remunerate her court officials for the jobs they did. As Hurstfield explains, "their unofficial fees bridged the gap" (211, 238, 346, 348).[11] Bell states laconically that "the fees mentioned in the accounts are relatively small and in no way represent the real value of the positions" (34). This may clarify why the Queen remained blind to the flood of riches that went into private hands rather than her Royal Exchequer.

Burghley facilitated the practice by keeping initial valuations low enough to allow room for the pay-offs to Tudor officials throughout the administrative hierarchy (Hurstfield 276). Upon questioning what his office was worth, the last clerk of the Court of Wards replied "It might be worth some thousands of pounds to him who, after his death, would instantly go to heaven; twice as much to him who would go to purgatory; and nobody knows what to him who would adventure to go to hell."[12] It would not have been lost on Burghley that feudal wardship would continue to flourish – to the betterment of his own purse – as long as it was widely profitable.

The Extraction of Wealth

When William Cecil became Master of the Court of Wards in 1561, wardship was well entrenched in Tudor society. (Cecil would be elevated to Baron Burghley in 1571 by the Queen.) He held the Mastership for thirty-seven years until his death in 1598. After a nine-month vacancy, the Queen appointed his son Robert Cecil to the office and Robert retained it until his death thirteen years later (Barnett 51).[13] Thus father and son presided over one of the most powerful and lucrative offices in England for half a century. Although the records that have survived are not complete, it is estimated that over three thousand young people were processed through the Court of Wards during the Masterships of the Cecils (Bell 34).[14] The prospects for fees, both official and unofficial, were further augmented by the fact that the lease of the lands of the heir was allocated by the Master in another, separate transaction (Hurstfield 84). If calculated at two transactions per ward – one for the custody of the ward and right to bestow him in marriage and the other for the leases of his lands – this looks like six thousand opportunities for money to be made during the fifty years the Cecils controlled this office.

In the introduction to her book on the early Cecils, Pauline Croft recognizes "the sheer scale of the Cecils' extraction of wealth" (xviii). As we might expect, Burghley covered his tracks well. Only two scraps survive to shed some light on how much money might have come his way. A note preserved at Hatfield reveals a quarrel between two perspective guardians over the wardship of a Mr. Cholmeley. The unknown writer says he had paid "my Lord" £350. Though unnamed, this lord can be none other than Burghley (Hurstfield 82-82, 266).

Another remarkable fragment has survived in the Public Record Office. Appearing at the bottom of the page of this document are the words "This note to be burnt." It is fortunate for posterity that this was not done, for eleven suitor/guardians are named with the payments they made to an unidentified person. As the account ends on August 4, 1598, the date of Lord Burghley's death, it is hard to deny that this individual was Burghley (Hurstfield 266-288). These payments totaled £3103.[15] An examination of the records shows that the Queen received £906 for nine of these wards. For these particular wards, Burghley took in more than three times as much as the queen (Hurstfield 268). These two documents show that Burghley received over £3400 for thirteen wardships in the last three years of his life, nicely augmenting his official salary of £133 per annum (Stone, 192). Hurstfield extrapolates that the ninety wardships handled each year toward the end of Elizabeth's reign could have brought Burghley £27,000 annually, but does not venture to speculate how much three thousand wardships processed over half a century might have brought the Cecils.

In addition to the unofficial fees that Burghley received directly, the Cecil fortune was augmented by the profits to his family as a result of their proximity to him. Paper trails with direct evidence rarely survive, but there is one that tells of six people who claimed perquisites for transmitting a suitor's request to Lady Burghley, and she in turn received £250 for interceding with her husband. Amusingly, for this very wardship, the Queen received £233, £16 less than Burghley's wife (Hurstfield 265-266). Pauline Croft recognizes that a most likely source of Lady Burghley's wealth came from acting as an intermediary with suitors. Even her chamberlain accepted money to pass letters to her that, in turn, went on to her husband (291).[16] On another occasion, Burghley's son Thomas Cecil had the wardship of Edward, Lord Vaux, and he profited handsomely by selling it back to the boy's mother (Hurstfield 80, 249, 269). The resale market was hot, and wards could be sold more than once. Another wardship purchased by Burghley's elder son was that of Elizabeth Long, bought for £250 and immediately re-sold for £1,350, more than five times the price fixed by the Court of Wards. The young lady's wardship was sold again for £2,450 (Hurstfield 275).

It is not surprising that Lord Burghley allocated wardships, leases and opportunities for profits to his closest servants, but what is shocking is that he did this in lieu of paying them a salary. In his study of the Cecil servants, Richard Barnett posits that the ordinary household servants were paid wages, but the gentlemen were not salaried. They were paid in gratuities (15-16). Barnett traces fifty-five wardships granted to thirty-three servants and provides details in an appendix to his book (17, 159-169).

Described as an "astute and cynical trader in wards," Burghley's secretary Michael Hickes fielded requests from all over the social spectrum. The Earl of Huntingdon wrote to him, "I have been beholding to you for your travail and pains taken in soliciting my causes for me to my good Lord, for which I hold myself in your debt and will come out of it ere it be long" (Hurstfield 68). Yet for all this labor, there is no record that secretary Hickes ever received a penny in wages from either Cecil, father or son (Barnett 85-87). Moreover, Hickes died a rich man, leaving to his executors a wardship to increase his daughter's marriage portion. Henry Maynard, another of Burghley's secretaries, was among the gentlemen who received no salary but "whose service placed him in the way of considerable reward." Somehow Maynard accumulated vast landed wealth. Like Hickes, the executors of his will had the profits of a wardship to allocate for the marriage portions of his daughters (Barnett 100-103). Hickes and Maynard, among others, learned well from their years of service in the Cecil household.

The accumulation of family fortunes and political clout were not the only matters to which wardship could be directed. Inherent in the system was the power to transform England from a Catholic country into a Protestant one. When wardship was visited upon landed Catholic families, the sons were sold to Protestant guardians and given Protestant upbringings. This process can be seen in the Wriothesley family. Henry Wriothesley, the second Earl of Southampton married the daughter of Anthony Browne, Viscount Montagu, uniting two staunchly Catholic families (Stone 342-343).[17] The second Earl had his own Catholic chaplain to conduct mass in his private chapel, and even suffered imprisonment for his Catholic faith in 1571 and again in 1581 after anti-recusancy laws were passed.[18] When the second Earl died, his minor son Henry became Burghley's ward and was removed to Cecil's London house where he was subjected to daily Protestant services. Burghley later sent him to St. John's College, Cambridge, his alma mater and a center of the Protestant Reformation. The third Earl of Southampton converted to the Church of England during the reign of King James (Akrigg 177-181). In short, wardship served many purposes. In addition to its more salient economic functions to provide funds for the Tudor monarchy and rewards to its loyal servants, wardship was a useful tool to convert prominent Catholic families to Anglicanism. As such, it had the capacity to influence the religious direction of the English nation (de Lisle / Stanford 41).[19]

Two: The Cecils and Edward de Vere

In her article "The Fall of the House of Oxford," Nina Green examines the financial crisis of John de Vere, the sixteenth earl that resulted from the extortion of his lands by Edward Seymour, the First Duke of Somerset during the reign of Edward VI. She follows the money through the restoration of the sixteenth Earl's properties and, most importantly, through the nine years of his son, Edward de Vere's wardship in the London home of his guardian, Sir William Cecil, later Lord Burghley (Green 41-95). It is well known that de Vere married Cecil's daughter Anne upon reaching his majority and that this marriage was deeply troubled (Cecil 84-85). Less well known is the information revealed in Green's remarkable research. In carefully sifting through the documentary evidence, Green shows how Elizabeth mismanaged de Vere's properties in order to benefit her favorite courtier, Sir Robert Dudley. After the death of de Vere's father, the Queen allowed Dudley to take de facto control of the core lands of the Oxford estates, a move which gave Dudley the underpinning in landed property that was necessary to make him Earl of Leicester (Green 68-69). The Queen also allowed Cecil to abrogate the contract that the sixteenth Earl of Oxford had made for his son's marriage with the daughter of the Earl of Huntingdon, thus paving the way for de Vere's marriage into the Cecil family. Hurstfield observes that the ascendancy of the Cecils from the yeoman to the aristocratic class – a feat accomplished in a mere two generations – was largely derived from the marriage of Anne Cecil to the ancient de Vere family (252). In addition, the Queen sued the young seventeenth Earl for revenue from his mother's jointure, and later ignored clauses in the sixteenth Earl's will that provided for the payment of his son's livery when he came of age (Green 67-77).

While a ward in Cecil's London house, Edward de Vere accrued large debts in the Court of Wards. It could be supposed that these wardship debts might have been forgiven as part of de Vere's marriage settlement with the Master's daughter; but, in fact, he was charged with a rigid payback schedule during his marriage to Anne. This he could not maintain, and large fines were levied at each forfeiture. Documentation in the Lansdowne collection at the British Library shows that in 1591, three years after Anne Cecil's death, Lord Burghley claimed that his son-in-law and former ward owed the Court of Wards the staggering sum of £14,553, of which £11,446 were fines (Green 77).[20] Although Hurstfield joins the historical consensus in laying the blame for these debts on de Vere himself, it seems that de Vere's financial downfall was predestined from the moment his father breathed his last.

One might feel for the plight of the youth who entered Cecil's magnificent London house in 1562. Even the brightest of twelve-year-olds would be no match for the wily, experienced Cecil, a man who commanded the Privy Council, the Court of Wards, and the Treasury. Because of wardship, de Vere accrued backbreaking debts and entered into a disastrous marriage. In the end, he lost everything: his property, his children, and his reputation – all the tangible and intangible things that make the patrimony so highly valued by the aristocracy. Burghley himself wrote "The greatest possession that any man can have is honor, good name, and good will of many and of the best sort" – sentiments that Shakespeare ascribes to Iago (Anderson 118). Furthermore, it's hard to see how the bitter frustrations expressed in the *Sonnets* fit the blissful, upwardly mobile life of the Stratford man. Sonnet 66 is a litany of griefs, and Sonnet 29 opens with a grim assessment that the writer is "in disgrace with fortune and men's eyes" (Anderson 329-330).[21]

The loss of his patrimony stoked a fury in de Vere that drove him to transform the magisterial education of his youth into a weapon of vengeance. What resulted was a contest of wills between the Queen's brilliant, calculating minister and his brilliant literary son-in-law, a family feud made all the worse as it played out on the public stage. Polonius in *Hamlet* is modeled on William Cecil himself, an identification recognized by leading twentieth century historians (Stone 265). Hurstfield calls Burghley's *Precepts* "the authentic voice of Polonius" (257). Richard III may well be modeled on Robert Cecil (Akrigg, *Jacobean Pageant* 109-112).[22] In *Shakespeare by Another Name*, Mark Anderson finds plenty of surrogates for de Vere's innocent wife Anne Cecil. She is the falsely accused heroine Ophelia in *Hamlet*, Desdemona in *Othello*, Imogen in *Cymbeline*, Hermione in *The Winter's Tale*, and Hero in *Much Ado*. Set in the backdrop of wardship, the parallels between de Vere and Anne Cecil and the action of *All's Well* can hardly be denied (47-48, 51, 125, 144, 146-147, 219-221, 342). In *Merry Wives of Windsor*, Anne Cecil is thinly veiled as Anne Page and her father is William Page. But why is the name *Page* substituted for *Cecil*? Could it be that the dramatist took the opportunity to point out that the Cecil family began their rise to power when Burghley's grandfather *became a page* in the court of Henry VIII? (Collins ix-x).[23] How infuriating this must have been to the hyper-sensitive Burghley who took pride in a genealogy that he proposed went back to Charlemagne (Hurstfield 251).[24] The dignity of the Cecil family was at stake. The situation called for some kind of cover story.

The Dénouement

It is often asked how the Stratford narrative developed and why it has held sway for so long. Though a comprehensive discussion of the evolution of the Stratford mythology is beyond the scope of this paper, suffice it to say that it took several centuries to put the narrative in place. But the middle of the eighteenth century was a crucial juncture and is worth a moment of consideration. By this time, a Shakespearean tourist industry was getting underway in Stratford-upon-Avon and the normal accoutrements of a writer's life were missing. There was nothing for an eager public to see by way of manuscripts, books, or letters belonging to the Bard. The Birthplace had not yet been purchased or even identified and Ann Hathaway's cottage was far in the future. If bardolatry was to continue its forward march, the world needed something to venerate and admire.

With the fledgling Shakespeare industry gaining traction, people wanted to know what Shakespeare looked like, and the only two images held out to be the author were the Droeshout engraving in the First Folio and the wall monument in the Holy Trinity Church in Stratford-upon-Avon. Both have serious flaws. The Droeshout engraving is a preposterous floating head with two right eyes peering out of the mask-like face and left sleeves on both arms of the disproportionate torso. Before its "beautification," the figure on the church monument was a dour fellow with a drooping mustache and arms resting on a sack, perhaps a sack of grain or wool (Whalen 145-161). Neither the harlequinesque Droeshout engraving nor the Woolsack Man was particularly appealing. The developing Shakespeare narrative was in great need of more satisfying imagery. It also needed to be in the right place. A place like Westminster Abbey.

Visitors today to Poets' Corner will see a life-sized statue of Shakespeare. He is a pleasant looking, well-attired gentleman leaning on a pedestal, his elbow resting, appropriately, on a stack of books. The heads of Queen Elizabeth, Henry V and Richard III are carved around the base of the pedestal, and the Bard points to a scroll floating down the side. Notwithstanding the strangely inaccurate passage from *The Tempest* inscribed on the scroll, it makes a definitely acceptable impression.

Some helpful information about this monument is on the Westminster Abbey website. It was erected in 1741 by Richard Boyle, the third Earl of Burlington, along with Alexander Pope, Dr. Richard Mead and Tom Martin. The monument was designed by William Kent and sculpted by Peter Scheemakers. Two theatrical companies assisted with fund-raising events.[25] This is fine as far as it goes. But questions remain. With no portraits of the Bard from his lifetime, what inspired this iconography? Were the men involved in this project connected in some way? What motivated them to put up this cenotaph?

The Monument Men

The patron of the Westminster Abbey Shakespeare monument, the third Earl of Burlington, is credited with almost single-handedly making Italian Palladianism the national style of Georgian England. One of the wealthiest peers in England, the "architect Earl" was influential in areas beyond architecture, including the fields of politics, literature and the arts. His resolve to see the Shakespeare monument through is evident in his financial underpinning of the project when there was a shortfall in fundraising (Prendergast 100).

Of the other participants, Alexander Pope often gets a billing that outshines Lord Burlington. Alexander Pope's literary legacy is well known, and his biography in the *ODNB* details the important people who held him to be the best poet of the age. His celebrated literary friend Jonathan Swift sought to have one of Pope's *Epistles* addressed to him (*ODNB* xliv, 867). Pope successfully cultivated friendships with the highest strata of English society, and his correspondence with the Earls of Oxford, Orrery, and Bathurst, as well as other notables of the time, has been published. Pope's association with Lord Burlington began sometime before 1716 when the Pope family moved into a home at Chiswick Lane – just a few steps from Burlington's Chiswick House (Berry 205). It is said that the Popes lived "under the wing of my Lord Burlington" (Erskine-Hill 218). Controversial throughout his life, Pope was known for "the wretched series of complex quarrels, maneuvers and falsifications in which he was plunged from his youth." One acquaintance reportedly said that he "could hardly drink tea without a stratagem" (*DNB* xvi, 122-123). But in spite of his character flaws and physical deformities from a childhood illness, Pope dominated both the literati and the high society of London.

William Kent, the artist who designed the statue, was a "bold associate" of Pope and another of Burlington's protégés (*DNB* xi, 25). Burlington met Kent when the artist was working as a painter at a villa in Italy. The Earl brought Kent back to England where he lived in Burlington's apartments for the rest of his life. Upon his death, Kent was interred in the Burlington family vault at Chiswick. In spite of many prestigious appointments secured for him over the years by Burlington, Kent turned out to be a man of limited artistic talent (Barnard / Clark xxiv). His portraits of his aristocratic clientele suffered from "feeble composition and bad draughtsmanship." Perhaps his best qualification for the job of creating the image of Shakespeare was his expertise in garden statuary, an important element in architecture and landscape design that he learned in Italy (*DNB* xi, 24).

Dr. Richard Mead was a physician, writer, and collector of considerable influence. He was elected to the Royal Society in 1703, and in 1720 was named governor of the hospitals of Bridewell, Bethlehem and St. Bartholomew. He is credited with persuading his friend and patient, Thomas Guy, to found the hospital that to this day bears Guy's name (Jones 87-92). Dr. Mead gave the Harveian lecture at the Royal College of Physicians in 1723, and was later appointed physician to George the Second. Mead was as well known for his collection of books, art, antique medals and coins as he was as a physician, and was consulted by Lewis Theobald in his preparation of Shakespeare's works. His library at his London home, one of the largest of the time, contained among other treasures the coveted 1632 second folio of Shakespeare – the very book that had been owned by Charles the First (*ODNB* xxxvii, 639-640). Dr. Mead was Alexander Pope's physician, for which he received several mentions in Pope's *Epistles*. Judging from the many occasions in which Pope tells of his illnesses in his correspondence, he must have required frequent medical advice (Berry 141). Although probable, it is not clear if Mead was Lord Burlington's physician, but it is noted that Mead sold to Burlington a valuable consignment of Palladio's drawings. (Lees-Milne 125).

The least documented of the four, Tom Martin is likely to be Thomas Martin of Palgrave, a man who held a stellar place among the collectors of the time. He was an attorney by trade, practicing law with his brother, but "his thirst after antiquities was as great as his thirst after liquor." His longstanding membership in the Society of Antiquaries began in 1720 under the mentorship of Peter Le Neve, the Norroy King of Arms, who was the President of the Society at that time. He is likely to have come in contact with Lord Burlington after the Earl became a fellow Antiquary in

1724. Admired as a "skillful and indefatigable antiquary," Martin was appointed executor of Le Neve's estate and charged, by terms of the will, to organize Le Neve's massive collection of books and manuscripts for a public repository. (*ODNB* xxxvi, 984). This he did not do, but instead married Le Neve's widow and moved the collection to his home in Palgrave. (*DNB*, xii, 1182).

There is no mention of participation in the Westminster Shakespeare monument in the *DNB* biographies of Mead, Martin, or the third Earl of Burlington, an absence that is particularly puzzling in the life of the architect-Earl. In a recent book about Burlington, *Lord Burlington: Architecture, Art and Life,* editors Toby Barnard and Jane Clark detail his illustrious career along with his many accomplishments. The family genealogy takes up two pages, and an entire chapter is devoted to the third Earl's famous ancestor, the second Earl of Cork who became the first Earl of Burlington (Barnard & Clark 167-199).

However, the Burlington family tree has an even more notable ancestor: the grandfather of the first Lord Burlington's wife was Robert Cecil, Earl of Salisbury. It appears that this Cecil was dropped from the publication, as one finds the following in the index: *Salisbury, earl of, see Cecil, Robert.* But there is no entry for Robert Cecil. Nor is any mention of his name to be found anywhere in the book (Barnard & Clark 325). This is odd as the writer underscores the importance of the marriage of the second Earl of Cork to Elizabeth Clifford – a marriage that ultimately brought the Burlington earldom to the Boyle family. The third Earl of Burlington is a direct descendant of Robert Cecil through the marriage of Robert Cecil's daughter Frances to Henry Clifford, the Earl of Cumberland. Elizabeth Clifford, the only surviving child of this marriage, is the third Earl's great-grandmother. Also, the Burlington and Salisbury families were entwined; the Burlingtons had the guardianship of the Salisbury minor children in the seventeenth century (Cecil 178).[26]

That the Burlington family lineage from the Cecil family is absent from a treatment of Lord Burlington is puzzling. Perhaps equally strange is the omission of any mention of the third Earl of Burlington's patronage of the Shakespeare monument in Westminster Abbey, surprising given the substantial cultural impact that the sculpture of Shakespeare had when it was unveiled in London in 1741. According to Ingrid Roscoe, it "inspired a Shakespeare revival."[27] Connecting the dots: the Shakespeare monument in Poet's Corner in Westminster Abbey was designed and erected under the direction of a descendant of William Cecil, Lord Burghley.

The All-Pervading Presence

Elizabethan and Jacobean historians have, for the most part, eliminated Edward de Vere, the seventeenth Earl of Oxford, from the chronicles of the times. If for some reason he must be mentioned at all, the writers hasten to attach to his memory as many harsh adjectives as possible. The explanation for this is invariably that de Vere mistreated his wife, Anne Cecil. One might think that de Vere is the only person in a millennium of English history who maligned his wife and didn't get along well with her family. Clearly, Edward de Vere lives in the doghouse of history.[28]

It might be asked how baggage such as this can be carried from century to century? An answer may lie in the longevity of the Cecil family dynasty. In his *History of the House of Lords*, Frank, Lord Longford, a twentieth-century leader of the House of Lords, provides insight into the House of Cecil:

> When I became a member of the House of Lords in 1945, it was impossible not to feel the *all-pervading presence of the Cecils*. The fifth Marquis, 'Bobbity,' was still active and much admired in the House. He had been Leader of the House or of the Opposition in the Lords from 1942 to 1957, and had been throughout that time the leading personality there. His father's bust was in the corridor just opposite the entry to the dining room; his grandfather's portrait was in the same corridor, shown destroying the Home Rule Bill of 1893. His great-grandfather's photograph was in the room I later occupied as Leader. *Four generations of Salisburys, successive Leaders of the House of Lords. An awe-inspiring record.*
>
> (Longford 52) [emphasis added]

Lord Longford continues with a discussion of the early Cecils, father and son, and closes with the comment that "From that day to this, the Cecils have enjoyed a reputation for a certain ruthlessness when their minds are thoroughly made up" (Longford 53). About the seventeenth Earl of Oxford, the minds of the Salisbury Cecils have been made up for centuries.

Conclusion

Bertram's words in the opening scene of *All's Well That Ends Well* describe Edward de Vere's predicament as well as that of many other wards: "And I in going, madam, weep o'er my father's death anew; but I must attend his Majesty's command, to whom I am now in ward, evermore in subjection." The word *evermore* is prophetic. Who would have thought that a story initially constructed to ameliorate the feelings and safeguard the privacy of a grandee family would last through the centuries? Yet the name of Edward de Vere has all but disappeared from history while ostensible admirers of Shakespeare pour through the turnstiles at the supposed birthplace of their Bard in Stratford-upon-Avon.

Works Cited

Akrigg, G. P. V. *Jacobean Pageant*. Boston: Harvard University Press, 1963.

------- *Shakespeare & the Earl of Southampton*. Hamish Hamilton, 1968.

Anderson, Mark. *Shakespeare By Another Name*. New York: Gotham Books, 2005.

Barnard, Toby and Jane Clark, eds. *Lord Burlington: Architecture, Art and Life*. Hambledon Press, 1995.

Barnett, Richard C. Place, *Profit and Power: A Study of the Servants of William Cecil, Elizabethan Statesman*. University of North Carolina Press, 1969.

Bell, H.E. *An Introduction to the History and Records of the Court of Wards & Liveries*. Cambridge University Press, 1953.

Berry, Reginald. *A Pope Chronology*. Boston, G. K. Hall & Co., 1988.

Cecil, David. *The Cecils of Hatfield House: An English Ruling Family*. Houghton Mifflin Company, 1973.

Collins, Arthur. *The Life of That Great Statesman William Cecil, Lord Burghley*. London: Robert Gosling and Thomas Wotten, 1732. Reprint,` Kessinger Publishing.

Croft, Pauline, ed. *Patronage, Culture and Power: The Early Cecils*. Yale University Press, 2002.

De Lisle, Leanda and Peter Stanford. *The Catholics and Their Houses*. HarperCollins, 1995.

Dictionary of National Biography, Sir Leslie Stephen and Sir Sidney Lee, eds. Oxford University Press, 1968.

Erskine-Hill, Howard. "Avowed Friend and Patron: The Third Earl of Burlington and Alexander Pope" in *Lord Burlington: Architecture, Art and Life*, Toby Barnard and Jane Clark, eds. London, Hambledon Press, 1995.

Green, Nina. "The Fall of the House of Oxford" in *Brief Chronicles*. The Shakespeare Fellowship, Vol. 1, 2009.

Hurstfield, Joel. *The Queen's Wards: Wardship and Marriage Under Elizabeth*. London, Green and Co., 1958.

Jones, Roger. "Richard Mead, Thomas Guy, the South Sea Bubble, and the Founding of Guy's Hospital" in *The Journal of the Royal Society of Medicine*, 2010. 103 (3)

Lees-Milne, James. *Earls of Creation: Five Great Patrons of Eighteenth-Century Art*. New York: London House & Maxwell, 1963.

Lord Longford. *A History of the House of Lords*. Sutton Publishing Limited, 1999.

Lovell, Mary S. *Bess of Hardwick: Empire Builder*. New York: W.W. Norton, 2006.

Matthew, H. C. G. and Brian Harrison, eds. *Oxford Dictionary of National Biography*, Oxford University Press, 2004.

Prendergast, Thomas A. *Poetical Dust: Poet's Corner and the Making of Britain*. University of Philadelphia Press, 2015

Roscoe, Ingrid. "The Monument to the Memory of Shakespeare" *The Journal of Church Monuments Society*. IX, 1994.

Russell, John W. Review of *The Queen's Wards* in *Shakespeare Authorship Society Review #3*.

Smith, Sir Thomas. *De Republica Anglorum*, 1583; Menston, Scolar Press Limited. Reprinted 1970.

Stone, Lawrence. *Crisis of the Aristocracy*, abbreviated edition. Oxford University Press, 1967.

Stopes, Charlotte Carmichael. *The Life of Henry, Third Earl of Southampton, Shakespeare's Patron*. New York: AMS Press, 1922.

Whalen, Richard. "The Stratford Bust: A Monumental Fraud" in *Report Me and My Cause Aright: The Shakespeare Oxford Society Fiftieth Anniversary Anthology*. 2007.

Notes

1. Hurstfield traces the revival of wardship initiated by Henry VII and continued in the reign of Henry VIII. He also discusses the use of royal power to exploit the landed classes. pp. 3-17.

2. Stone notes that one in three peers was a minor when he inherited the title.

3. Sir Thomas Smith, *De Republica Anglorum*, as quoted by Hurstfield in The Queen's Wards, p. 110.

4. In his chapter "Agitation against the Court," Bell details the political battles to end the wardship system in the reign of King James. But wardship was so deeply ingrained that it lumbered along for several more decades before its final elimination by Parliamentary decree in 1646. A condition of the Restoration was that wardship would never again be reinstated. See also Hurstfield 329.

5. Lord Burghley used three estimates of value, and the Inquisition was often the lowest. A survey was made by the agent of the Court of Wards, and a "particular" was prepared by the suitor. Of the three, the Master placed the greatest reliance on the agent's land valuations, though many additional intangibles – such as the age, health, social status, and younger brothers as back-up heirs – were taken into consideration.

6. Bell documents payments to private informers "whose aid was enlisted by a species of bribery," and grants of wardships to informers on "easy terms." pp. 50-51.

7. For a thorough examination of the practices of concealment and discovery, see Hurstfield's chapter 3, pp. 33 – 57.

8. The amusing use of the word *forestalled* indicates that Lord Cobham knew that there would be much competition and time was of the essence.

9. Lovell embellishes the official story, explaining that "the law on wardship was greatly improved under Queen Elizabeth when in 1561 the Court of Wards came under the benign and efficient influence of William Cecil, who was to be its Master for thirty-seven years."

10. John W. Russell, Review of *The Queen's Wards* in *Shakespeare Authorship Society Review #3*.

11 Hurstfield adds "The salaries of the Elizabethan administrators were small and notoriously out of line with their responsibilities, their importance, and their standard of living."

12 Bell 35. Hurstfield 344. Quoted from page 14 of *The Way to be Rich, According to the Practice of the Great Audley*, 1662.

13 Upon the death of the Robert Cecil (Earl of Salisbury), the office stayed in the hands of the Cecil court faction, first going to Cecil's close friend and confident Sir George Carew and then to Sir Walter Cope, the Cecil stalwart who served both father and son.

14 Bell estimates that sixty to eighty wardships were processed each year. Hurstfield concurs, noting that by the end of Elizabeth's reign, "Burghley and his officials had broken through the barriers of silence, concealment and fraud … to uncover more than ninety wardships in a year." p. 262.

15 See also Bell, pp. 31-35. Bell identifies the letter as the work of Edward Latimer, the clerk to Receiver-General Sir William Fleetwood, and posits that Fleetwood was responding to a request from the Earl of Essex for this information. Hurstfield concurs that the Earl was interested in gauging what his profits might be if he was successful in his bid to become the next Master after Burghley's death.

16 How Lady Burghley financed her benefactions is unknown, but Croft suggests that gifts from suitors "for intervening in Burghley's favour" are a likely source. This is supported by a letter from a suitor that is archived in the Lansdowne. This letter, passed on by Lady Burghley, is endorsed by Lord Burghley himself. p. 300.

17 Stone continues: "The ancient power of wardship, first revived by the early Tudors for purposes of finance, now took on a new function as an instrument in making the country safe for Anglicanism. Lord Burghley was far more successful in his self-appointed task of giving aristocratic heirs a taste for Protestantism than he was in inducing them to buckle down to their books. In family after Catholic family the process can be seen at work."

18 The family chaplain was Alban Langdale, a Catholic priest known for his disputations with Protestant clergy.

19 In their study of sixteenth century Catholic families, de Lisle and Stanford relate a story of a Catholic heir taken away from his family to be raised in the new religion, noting that it "was the fate of other Catholic heirs in this period of persecution." See also: Bell 124-125.

20 Hurstfield notes that "some of his lands were seized and held for payment" to satisfy the debts that "had long hung over him in the Court of Wards." 253.

21 For an introduction to historical people mocked in Shakespeare's works, see Anderson, pages xxxii, xxxiii.

22 Akrigg observes that "Cecil was hardly cold in his grave when there burst a storm of revulsion and spite against him. Men who had been afraid of him and his spies while he lived now spoke freely." Soon after Cecil's death, an anonymous broadside connected him to the last Plantagenet king: "Here lies little Crookbacke Who justly was reckon'd Richard the 3rd and Judas the 2nd." (Folger M.S. 452.1).

23 In this early biography of Lord Burghley, Collins traces the family genealogy, noting his father's employment in the Court of Henry VIII. Richard Cecil, the Lord Treasurer's father, was one of the Pages of the Crown in the eighth year of the reign of Henry VIII and rose to a Groom of the Robes fourteen years later. After further promotions to Yeoman of the Robes and steward of several of the king's manors, his career culminated in the grant of 299 acres of arable land in Stamford.

24 Hurstfield expounds on this quirk: "He [Burghley] failed, it is true, to erect an authentic aristocratic past for himself, but there can be no doubt about the nobility of his descendants."

25 The Abbey's website notes that both Kent and Scheemakers signed the monument and dated it 1740, still using the Old Style in which the new year began at the end of March. The appearance of the monument in the Abbey was announced in *Gentleman's Magazine* in February, 1741.

26 In his account of his family history, Lord David Cecil refers to the Countess of Burlington as a Salisbury "cousin."

27 Ingrid Roscoe, "The Monument to the Memory of Shakespeare" in *Journal of the Church Monuments Society*, IX, 1994. pp. 72-82. An indication of the favorable public reception of the Westminster monument can be seen in the increased popularity of the sculptor Peter Scheemakers. Thereafter, he was often preferred to the better established Michael Rysbrack.

28 Edward de Vere would be glad to know that the negative historical view of him actually puts him in good company. William Cecil, the family patriarch, had two surviving sons. Robert, Lord Salisbury was his younger son from his second marriage, and the Salisbury line has dominated

the political and social structure of England to the present day. Thomas Cecil, his elder son from his first marriage, became the Earl of Exeter and left a large family whose descendants had successful careers, many in the church and the military. However, the Exeter line does not receive the admiring commentary that writers of history regularly bestow on their Salisbury cousins. Barnett disparages Cecil's first marriage to Thomas's mother, "It was probably the only major personal strategic mistake Cecil ever made. Mary's early death corrected his error, but a very ordinary son was the reminder of an imprudent love. There were times when the son even appeared to the distraught father as a punishment" (3). This deplorable reportage may stem in part from the Exeter Cecils' connections to the de Vere family. Edward de Vere's son Henry, the 18th Earl of Oxford, married Diana Cecil, Thomas Cecil's granddaughter. Also, Henry de Vere is buried with the family of Thomas Cecil in his chapel in Westminster Abbey.

The Sycamore Grove, Revisited

by Catherine Hatinguais

> ... underneath the grove of sycamore
> that westward rooteth from the city's side,
> so early walking did I see your son.
> *(Romeo and Juliet* 1.1.119-121)

Now the trees are in separated stands, the ancient grove cut and hacked away by boulevards and crossings, by building blocks and all the ruthless quirks of urbanization. But the descendants of Romeo's woodland are still growing where they grew in Romeo's day. Rejoined in the mind's eye, erasing the modern incursions, those stands form again the grove that once, four and far more centuries ago was the great green refuge of a young man sick with love.
(Roe, 10)

A group of Oxfordians and assorted Shakespeare enthusiasts went to Italy in June 2016 to see the cities, palaces and artworks that, judging from his Italian plays, we can be fairly sure the playwright had to have seen with his own eyes. For this pilgrimage of sorts, we followed in the footsteps of Richard Paul Roe, taking his book as a guide. It was a wonderful trip, which left us both dazzled and hungry for more, but all our visits didn't quite turn out as expected.

During our visit to Verona, our bus stopped briefly near Porta Palio to allow us to see Romeo's sycamore grove. I asked our Italian guide – just to be sure – if those trees that we glimpsed through the bus windows were indeed the famous sycamore trees. She answered bluntly and without hesitation: "No, those are plane trees. Sycamores are a different species." Once I recovered from my surprise, I started thinking this question was worth investigating further. Are there really two different tree species, each with its own unique name? Or is there only one species of tree, but with two different names depending, say, on the region or the era? Such cases of terminological confusion are very frequent in botany when one deals with vernacular – as opposed to scientific – names. To get to the root of this problem, we first had to get to the leaves. So, after a somewhat shortened lunch, Julia Cleave, Susana Maggi, and I went back to Porta Palio to gather some evidence. Little did I know how far this modest inquiry would lead.

Verona's Fortifications

From Verona's Castel Vecchio, in the old city center, if you walk almost due west – a five-minute stroll on Stradone Porta Palio in the cool shade of the horse-chestnut trees which line the avenue – you will reach the famous Renaissance gate Porta Palio, built between 1550 and 1561 by the Venetian military architect Sanmicheli.

Porta Palio is part of a string of gates, angled bastions, and low ramparts built by Verona's Venetian rulers between 1531 and 1561, that follow the trace of the previous medieval wall, the old 'Scaligera wall' dating from the 14th century which ran from Porta Catena to Bastione San Francesco and guarded the western and southern side of the old city (Gray 7-13). Such high but thin medieval walls had been shown to be ill-suited to withstand the new siege cannons of Charles VIII of France when he invaded Italy in 1494. In response, Renaissance architects, inspired by Roman, Byzantine, and Ottoman practices (Vigus 4, 13), redesigned their fortifications and adapted their military works to the new reality of gunpowder artillery.

Verona's Renaissance fortifications were destroyed by Napoleon in 1802. Starting in 1833, the Austrians, Verona's rulers at the time, reused the materials left in the rubble to repair the walls and enlarge the bastions, adapting them to 19th century artillery, while still following the same trace as the Renaissance walls (Gray 14). In other words, the Verona fortifications you see today go back only two centuries, but they run along the same line as the medieval Scaligera wall and its Renaissance successor.

Verona's Trees, Then and Now

There is a map of Verona published (1581-1588) as part of the popular atlas of European and world cities, Civitates Orbis Terrarum, showing the 16th century walls. It is hard to know how accurate or up-to-date the maps included in this atlas were (Krogt 12). In particular, the map of Verona shows the Porta Nuova (built in 1531) in its distinctive Renaissance style, topped with the winged lion of Venice, but shows

---

Catherine Hatinguais *worked for the United Nations in New York for thirty years, first as a translator and later as a terminologist. During this time, she conducted research and created multilingual glossaries for use by translators and interpreters on technical subjects reflecting UN activities, such as military affairs (peacekeeping, demining, arms control, nuclear fuel cycle, chemical weapons), law of the sea (geology, cartography, continental shelf, fisheries), climate change, and the environment. She holds a BA in political science and an MA in English literature from the University of Bordeaux in France. She also studied biology and ecology at Hunter College in NYC and trained as a botanical illustrator at the New York Botanical Garden. Now retired, she devotes her time to studying Shakespeare and the authorship question.*

stretches of the medieval 'enceinte,' or curtain wall, crenellated and unchanged and the other 'portas' facing west – Porta Palio and Porta San Zeno – as high and square medieval towers with arched gates. These are not the lower Renaissance structures that Sanmicheli designed and that are still seen today. It is therefore possible that the source drawings on which the map was based were actually made at least three decades earlier, i.e. sometime between 1531 and 1550, and those source drawings reflect the fortifications in a transitional or hybrid state, before Sanmicheli's innovations were fully implemented and the work completed.

Whatever the case may be, the map is interesting as it also shows the countryside to the west and south of the walls. Open fields and roads are clearly seen but hardly any trees, let alone woods. It would have made little sense from a military standpoint to allow trees to grow right outside defensive ramparts, as they would obstruct the view and protect attacking forces from detection by the city's defenders and from projectiles. The immediate surroundings of a fortified city, especially the moats and glacis, were cleared of anything that could give cover to the attackers against the defenders' musket fire. Farther out, it was important that there be nothing within the range of cannon shot that enemies could use to conceal themselves (no hills, valleys or buildings), in order to ensure that a stronghold could 'command the country' (Vigus, 17).

Today, Porta Palio stands at the center of a traffic roundabout and is one of the main access points to the old city. On either side of the Renaissance gate, the sloping ground still rises to the top of the old ring of fortifications, which are remnants of the earthen banks that abutted and reinforced the defensive walls. Outside this narrow green belt of urban park, called Parco delle Mura e dei Forti, with its footpaths, benches and ornamental trees, lies a series of wide boulevards and beyond, modern Verona. (See map on following page.) In particular, the modern Viale Colonnello Galiano, along which Roe imagined the surviving stands of trees were growing, runs precisely where the Renaissance fortifications' moat and glacis were located.

The mounds themselves are planted with a variety of bushes and trees, among them, linden trees, cypresses, cedars and pines, while both the inner ring road ('circonvallazione') and the outer boulevards ('viale') running roughly parallel on either side of the old fortifications, are lined almost exclusively with plane trees. Most of these planes are young – a few still have their planting supports – while some are clearly older, perhaps as much as two centuries old.

These are not the gnarled and besieged survivors of an ancient grove which was reduced by urbanization but who are, centuries later, still defiantly holding out, huddled together near Porta Palio in discernible "separated stands" (Roe 10). No, these trees that line the neighborhood streets and protect passers-by from the beating sun were planted at different times over the last century or two, as Verona expanded and municipal authorities beautified its streets. And there is no substantial ancestor grove visible on that old 1580s map. Something is therefore amiss in Roe's picture.

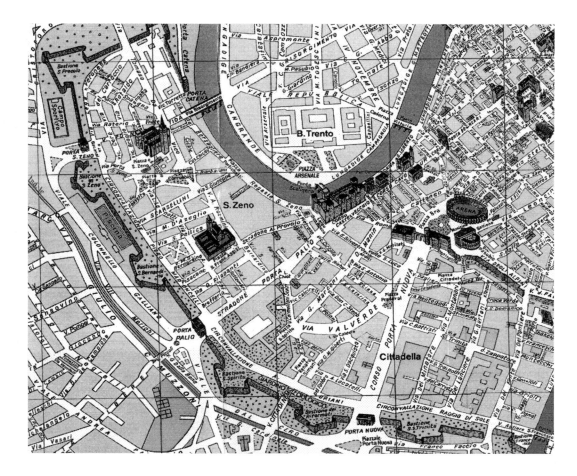

There is also uncertainty about the actual identity of the trees mentioned by Shakespeare in the 16th century and Roe in the 21st.

A Botanical Exploration

Let us assume for now that there was indeed in the late 16th century a small grove of trees growing in the general direction of Porta Palio or Porta San Zeno, the other gate on the western side of the city, not right against the fortifications but perhaps farther out into the countryside, and that Shakespeare did refer to it in *Romeo and Juliet*. Couldn't the trees that we see today be at least individual descendants of that now-disappeared grove, as Roe also suggests in the opening quote?

Investigating that question will have us diving into a terminological thicket, unfortunately common in botanical vernacular nomenclature (Pavord 31, 42). Let's start with our cast of botanical characters. (See illustration 1, third page following.)

Platanus orientalis (Linnaeus, 1753). Variant: *P. vulgaris. Platanus* (Gerard, Johnson)

English: Oriental plane tree, chenar

Other languages: Platanus (Lat.); platano orientale (It.); plátano oriental (Sp.); platane d'Orient, plane (Fr.); chinar, chenar (Pers.).

Native Range: Balkans & Anatolia to Northern Iran and as far as India.

Introductions and cultural history: Frequently used in Persian gardens; planted as a shade tree in ancient Greek cities and venerated for its size, shade (Pavord 67) and a longevity measured in centuries. Introduced by the Romans to Sicily around the 4th century BCE, then to Italy and Gaul. Prized in private gardens, country estates and avenues and praised by Pliny, Martial and Vitruvius (Bowe 46).

Introduced in England as an ornamental tree by the mid 16th century (Pokorný 112; Knight 97) at the latest, and possibly earlier in medieval times (Thomas and Faircloth 266) but it did not naturalize there and remained rare (Pavord 254). In wider cultivation since the 17th century.

Gerard praises it for its shade in his *Herball*; he notes that the tree is 'strange' in Italy (i.e., non-native), is nowhere seen in Germany and the Low Countries, but is plentiful in Asia and Crete (1304). He mentions a "fine plane tree in my Lord Treasurer's garden at the Strand" (Pavord 340).

In 1633, Johnson writes in his revision of Gerard's *Herball* (Johnson 1489) that "there are one or two young ones at this time growing with Mr Tradescant" (the botanist and gardener).

Its tenderness to frost makes it ill-adapted to northern climates, but it is cultivated in temperate regions and is still common in Mediterranean countries.

Habitat: Riverbanks, beside willows, alders and poplars; tolerates dry soils once established.

Botanical description: Tender. Three to six spherical fruit heads, rarely two. Palmate leaves, alternate, deeply lobed, coarsely toothed; 5-7 lobes, lobe longer than wide. The species is highly variable in leaf shape, branching pattern and bark formation.

Platanus occidentalis (Linnaeus, 1753)

English: American sycamore (US), American plane tree, occidental plane, buttonwood

Other languages: platano occidentale, platano americano (It.); plátano occidental, plátano de Virginia, sicómoro americano (Sp.); platane d'Occident (Fr.).

Native Range: Eastern US (Ontario & Maine to Florida & Texas).

Introductions and cultural history: Introduced to England in 1636 by botanist J. Tradescant (David H.). It does not grow well in Britain and failed to naturalize in Europe (More & White, 453); today it has almost disappeared from the Old World.

In North America, used in park landscaping and for furniture. English settlers in America followed a long tradition (Pavord 39) when they chose for this newly encountered tree the vernacular name *sycamore* to signal that its leaves resembled those of the European sycamore maple they remembered from the old country.

Habitat: Riverbanks, wetlands, wastelands.

Botanical description: Tender. One fruit head, rarely two. Alternate leaves, with 3-5 shallow lobes; lobes wider than long.

Platanus x acerifolia (Wildenow, 1805). Variants: *P. hybrida, P. hispanica, P. intermedia*

English: common or London plane

Other languages: platano comune (It.); plátano de sombra (Sp.); platane commun, platane à feuilles d'érable (Fr.).

Native Range: Fertile and hardy hybrid of *P. orientalis* and *P. occidentalis*. Long disputed, this hybridization has recently been confirmed by DNA analysis (Gibson). The two parents didn't come together in England until 1636 at the earliest. The hybridization event, alternatively located in Spain, Southern France or England depending on the author, was probably spontaneous, and had occurred by 1663 when the new hybrid was first recorded in England (More & White, 451). Propagated at the Oxford Botanic Garden about 1670 (Campanella; Mabey, 57).

Introductions and cultural history: Since the 19th century, it is the dominant tree in the streets of London, Paris, Rome, and in many European cities (Campanella), as well as in towns and along roads and canals in Southern France; now planted worldwide.

In Europe it interbreeds freely with *P. orientalis* so that there is a continuous gradation of traits from the hybrid plane to the true Oriental plane.

Similarly, in the US, it can back-cross with its parent species, *P. occidentalis*, which gives rise to a range of mixed characteristics (David H.).

Habitat: Cities and towns. It is highly tolerant of air pollution, drought and compacted soil. Rarely escapes to the wild.

Botanical description: Hardy. Palmate leaves, broader than long, with five shallow lobes (rarely 3 or 7), scalloped with broad teeth. Two fruit heads, rarely three.

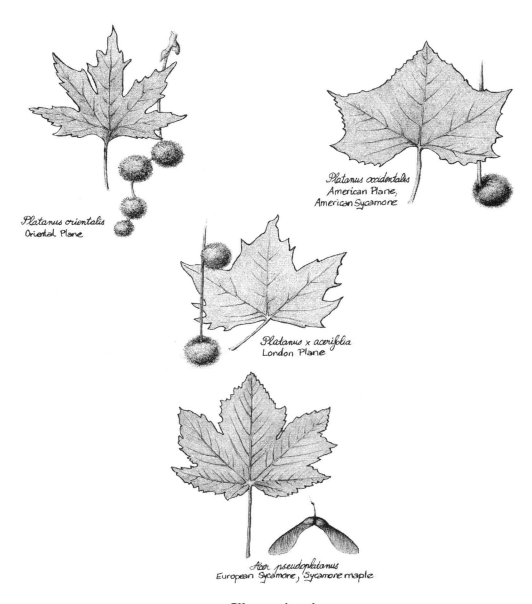

Illustration 1

Acer pseudoplatanus. Linnaeus (1753); Variants: *Acer maior* (Gerard), *Acer maius* (Johnson)

English: sycamore (UK); sycamore maple (US); European sycamore maple

Variants: false plane tree, great maple, Scottish maple, mount maple, mock-plane, plane-tree maple, Celtic maple.

Other languages: arce blanco, falso plátano, arce sicómoro (Sp.); acero di monte, acero montano, sicomoro (It.); grand érable, érable sycomore, faux platane, érable plane (Fr.).

Native Range: mountain ranges in Central and Southern Europe (Pyrenees, Alps, Carpathians).

Introductions and cultural history: possibly introduced initially to Great Britain by the Celts. Its presence was recorded in England as early as 1280 (More & White, 633; Mabey, 265).

In his *Herball*, Gerard praises *Acer maior* for its shade. He notes that it is "a stranger in England and only it groweth in the walkes and places of pleasure of noblemen where it especially is planted for the shadowe sake and under the name sycomore tree."

Nowadays in widespread cultivation, it is tolerant of air pollution, wind and salt spray and is used for shade and for wind breaks on the sea coast (More & White, 633). Its wood has been used for musical instruments and spears.

Habitat: Alpine and maritime, cool and temperate climates (Pokorný, 136).

Botanical description: Hardy. Double samaras (two winged seeds), bunched. Palmate leaves, opposite, with five lobes.

Analysis

Which of those four trees would Shakespeare have known in England? Which could he have seen in Verona in the mid-16th century? Let us proceed by elimination.

He could not have known the American plane tree (aka American sycamore, *P. occidentalis*), which arrived in Europe (more specifically, in England) in 1636; nor *a fortiori* the London plane hybrid (*Platanus x acerifolia*) which arose only in the late 17th century in England.

He may seen have seen some of the rare specimens of *Platanus orientalis* on the estates of a wealthy botany and garden enthusiast (such as Lord Burghley's on the Strand) (Pavord 340). It is known that noblemen had imported the tree from south-east Europe by the mid 16th century and planted it as an ornamental. He could also have read about it in Pliny and Vitruvius, and in Gerard's *Herball*.

It is highly probable that he was familiar with the European sycamore maple (aka simply "sycamore" in British English, *Acer pseudoplatanus*), which was a common feature "in the walkes and places of pleasure of noblemen" (Gerard, 1300), notably at Theobalds and Wimbledon where it was planted by the Cecils (Thomas and Faircloth, 331). But it is unlikely that this tree of mountains or cool climates was present in Verona, as it is notably rare in the lower altitudes of the Po valley with its torrid summers. The one tree that was common in Italy at that time – thanks to the Romans, and whose leaves could easily be unwittingly confused with, or deliberately compared to those of a sycamore maple – is the Oriental plane tree (*P. orientalis*). It seems only natural that, based on this resemblance, he would name the Italian plane trees for the trees he knew back home. This, after all, is what travelers, explorers, conquerors, and settlers have done since ancient times when encountering strange new plants (Pavord 39). Now, let's go back to the 21st century.

Which Trees Would Roe Have Seen Near Porta Palio?

Judging from the admittedly very limited but totally random sample that we took of two different and neighboring trees near Porta Palio **[see Illustration 2, next page]**, we can be reasonably certain that:

> Sample (1), with its two fruit heads and shallow-lobed leaves, is from a London plane tree (*P. x acerifolia*) – a recent (19th century) but extremely successful introduction in Italy – and

> Sample (2), with its three fruit heads and deeply lobed leaves, is from an Oriental plane (*P. orientalis*), or possibly a hybrid of an Oriental with a London plane (since such back crosses are not uncommon). Only DNA analysis could establish the true identity of this second plane.

Short of a complete census of trees found in the park and along the avenues around Verona's western gates, it is impossible to know the present distribution of the various tree species or cultivars in that neighborhood. Our sample is unlikely to be representative in that regard. But at least it attests to the presence in today's Verona of both London planes, the newcomers, and Oriental planes, present in Italy since antiquity. The continuity presumed by Roe lies here and only here: not in surviving or self-propagating 'stands' living in the exact same location as their 16th century ancestors, but in the often hybridized genomes of relatively young trees, grown in Verona's nurseries and planted by the city. They are the modern descendants of Oriental planes now long dead and of the cosmopolitan and ubiquitous London planes.

Illustration 2

But then, why did Roe call them sycamores? Was he so eager to agree with Shakespeare that he ignored the obvious diagnostic feature of the spherical fruiting heads of *Platanaceae* and thus misidentified the trees as *Aceraceae* – sycamore maples, when any field guide would make it easy to distinguish between the two? In fact there is a simple explanation to this puzzle. Roe (9) did identify them correctly as *Platanaceae* – he did note their "broad-lobed leaves and mottled pastel trunks" after all – but being an American he gave them the name commonly given in the United States to the Occidental plane (*P. occidentalis*): i.e. 'sycamore' which is short for 'American sycamore.' And not being a botanist, he did not realize that broad lobes are a specific trait of the modern London plane and that the only tree that Shakespeare could have seen in Verona, *P. orientalis*, had – and still has – narrow lobes.

It would seem therefore that Shakespeare and Roe both gave the name *sycamore* to Verona's plane trees, but for different reasons: Shakespeare, by analogy with a tree he knew in England whose leaves looked similar, *Acer pseudoplatanus*, or sycamore maple. Roe gave the name by analogy with the American plane tree he knew, *Platanus occidentalis*, a.k.a. American sycamore.

A question nevertheless remains: was there, in the 16th century, a grove of 'sycamores' – or, as we now know, Oriental planes – somewhere out in the countryside west of Verona's walls, that Shakespeare could have recalled in *Romeo and Juliet*? It is doubtful. Roe certainly did not settle it and neither did we. Only further research might.

Only two things seem sure. If there was a grove, it would not have been growing right outside the city walls where Roe pictured it, along Viale Colonnello Galiano. And today, there is no identifiable stand or remnant of an ancient grove of *P. orientalis* near Porta Palio, but only – at most – individual descendants, heavily hybridized with the modern London plane and deliberately planted by Verona's authorities.

In conclusion, we are left with another question. As we have seen, it was usual for early travelers to name the plants they observed on their journeys by analogy with similar plants they remembered from their home country. We have also seen that Shakespeare would likely have been familiar with the Sycamore maple, common in gardens of noblemen, and also with the Oriental plane, which was much rarer in England, but was a prized ornamental and was famously extolled in classical literature. In other words, he may have been aware of both trees and quite capable of differentiating between the two. If so, why didn't he, at least in his plays?

The reason might be that, as a poet, Shakespeare would have delighted in the wonderful resonance of the word *sycamore* as compared to the duller sound of *plane*. Several authors have also plausibly argued that he devised a clever bilingual pun with the meaning of *sick amore* (or 'lovesick'), since the context in all three occurrences of the word in the canon is indeed love sickness. The combination of a beguiling sonority and an added layer of meaning might have proved irresistible to the poet, especially one as addicted to verbal wit as Shakespeare. *Sycamore* it had to be. In this particular case at least, we should not exclude the possibility that the poet's playfulness may have spoken louder than the traveler's memory.

Works Cited

Gerard, John. *The Herball or Generall Historie of Plantes.* John Norton, 1597.

Gray, James A. *The Walls of Verona.* A brief of a study written in 1954. International Fund for Monuments. Venezia, New York. //www.wmf.org/sites/default/files/article/pdfs/IFM%20Walls%20of%20Verona.pdf (Accessed 15 July 2016).

Johnson, Thomas and John Gerard. *The Herball or General History of Plants: the Complete 1633 Edition as Revised and Enlarged.* Calla Editions, 2015.

Krogt, Peter van der. "Mapping the towns of Europe: The European towns in Braun & Hogenberg's Town Atlas, 1572-1617." Belgeo, *Belgian Journal of Geography/Revue belge de géographie.* [En ligne] 3-4 2008. *Formatting Europe – Mapping a Continent.* National Committee of Geography of Belgium / Société Royale Belge de Géographie. https://belgeo.revues.org/11877 (Accessed 6 August 2016).

Mabey, Richard. *Flora Britannica: The definitive new guide to wild flowers, plants and trees.* Sinclair Stevenson, 1996.

Ministère des affaires culturelles. Chapitre XVII "Architecture militaire." *Principes d'analyse scientifique: Architecture, Méthode et Vocabulaire.* Imprimerie nationale, Paris, 1972.

More, David and White, John. *The Illustrated Encyclopedia Of Trees.* Second Edition. Timber Press, 2005.

Pavord, Anna. *The Naming of Names: The Search for Order in the World of Plants.* Bloomsbury, 2005.

Pokorný, Jaromir. *Arbres. Illustrations de Vlasta Matousouvá et Milena Konecná.* Gründ, 1987.

Roe, Richard Paul. *The Shakespeare Guide to Italy: Retracing the Bard's Unknown Travels.* Harper Perennial, 2011.

Thomas, Vivian and Faircloth, Nicki. *Shakespeare's Plants and Gardens: A Dictionary.* Bloomsbury, 2016.

Vigus, Robert T. *Fortification Renaissance: The Roman Origins of the Trace Italienne.* Thesis, 2013. http://digital.library.unt.edu/ark:/67531/metadc271911/m2/1/high_res_d/thesis.pdf (Accessed 7 August 2016).

Online sources

Articles

Bowe, Patrick. *Gardens of the Roman World*. Getty Publications, 2004. Google Books. (Accessed 11 July 2016).

Campanella, Thomas J. "The Roman Roots of Gotham's London Plane." *Wall Street Journal*, July 20, 2011. http://www.wsj.com/articles/SB10001424052702304314404576414091335186456 (Accessed 11 July 2016).

"David H." Article, *London Planes and American Sycamores*. Posted on March 13, 2012. https://growinghistory.wordpress.com/2012/03/13/london-planes-and-american-sycamores/ (Accessed 11 July 2016).

Figuier, Louis. *Les Merveilles de la science ou description populaire des inventions modernes: L'Artillerie ancienne et moderne*. Furne, Jouvet et Cie, 1867 (3, pp. 309-462). French Wikisource.org (Accessed 9 August 2016).

Gibson, Arthur C. "Speaking the Plane Truth." *Mildred E. Mathias Botanical Garden Newsletter*. Volume 5, Number 2, Spring 1999. www.botgard.ucla.edu (Accessed 11 July 2016).

Knight, Charles. "The Plane Tree." *The Penny Magazine of the Society for the Diffusion of Useful Knowledge*, Volume 11. 1842. Google Books. (Accessed 8 August 2016).

Websites on Botany

(last consulted, 8 August 2016)

Kew Gardens. http://www.kew.org/science-conservation/plants-fungi/platanus-orientalis-oriental-plane

Jardin! L'encyclopédie. http://nature.jardin.free.fr/arbre/nmauric_platanus_orientalis.html

http://nature.jardin.free.fr/arbre/nmauric_platanus_occidentalis.html

http://nature.jardin.free.fr/arbre/nmauric_platanus_acerifolia.html

http://nature.jardin.free.fr/arbre/ft_acer_pseudo.html

Hortus Camdenensis. http://hortuscamden.com/plants/view/platanus_orientalis_1

http://hortuscamden.com/plants/view/platanus_occidentalis_1

Wikipedia.

https://en.wikipedia.org/wiki/Platanus_orientalis

https://en.wikipedia.org/wiki/Platanus_occidentalis

https://en.wikipedia.org/wiki/Acer_pseudoplatanus

https://en.wikipedia.org/wiki/Ficus_sycomorus

https://it.wikipedia.org/wiki/Platanus_orientalis

https://it.wikipedia.org/wiki/Platanus_occidentalis

https://it.wikipedia.org/wiki/Acer_pseudoplatanus

Miscellaneous.

http://www.feow.org/ecoregions/details/gulf_of_venice_drainages

https://naturando.wordpress.com/le-platane/

Websites on History

(last consulted, 11 August 2016)

Verona

www.parcomuraverona.it

https://it.wikipedia.org/wiki/Porta_Palio

https://it.wikipedia.org/wiki/Porta_Nuova_(Verona)

https://it.wikipedia.org/wiki/Porta_San_Zeno_(Verona)

Fortifications and Weapons

https://en.wikipedia.org/wiki/Star_fort

http://www.castlesandmanorhouses.com/types_10_star.htm

http://www.castlesandmanorhouses.com/architecture.htm

https://en.wikipedia.org/wiki/Glacis

https://weaponsandwarfare.com/2015/08/13/renaissance-fortifications/

https://fr.wikipedia.org/wiki/Discussion:Fortifications_et_constructions_de_Vauban

https://fr.wikipedia.org/wiki/Trac%C3%A9_%C3%A0_l%27italienne

Maps

Google Maps: https://www.google.com/maps/

British Library: http://www.bl.uk/collection-items/view-of-verona-in-civitates-orbis-terrarum

Sanderus Antiquariaat: https://www.sanderusmaps.com/en/our-catalogue/detail/166476/old-antique-map-bird's-eye-view-and-plan-of-verona-by-braun-and-hogenberg

The Great Reckoning
Who Killed Christopher Marlowe and Why?

by Stephanie Hopkins Hughes

> "His life he contemned in comparison of the liberty of speech."
> Thomas Nashe, *Jack Wilton The Unfortunate Traveller*

The Oxfordian thesis has forced us into areas of psychology, biography and history – English, continental, and literary – that we would not have had to deal with if it were not that the issue of Shakespeare's identity has forced us to. Seeking the truth about the author of the western world's most important and influential literary canon has required that we examine the facts surrounding the production of other literary works at the time, facts that demonstrate that the Stratford biography is not the only one rife with anomalies. Although Christopher Marlowe's biography holds together far better than most, his death remains as much a mystery as Shakespeare's identity. Could these two mysteries be related?

Birth of the Media, the Fourth Estate

It was during the period when Marlowe was writing, in the decade from 1583 to 1593, that the first modern commercial theater was built in England. By this we mean a permanent structure meant solely for theatrical performance, one that opened its doors to the public on an almost daily basis, and that did not rely (solely) on aristocratic patrons or the Crown for financing, one that paid its taxes and supported its owners, managers and the companies that performed in it on the proceeds of ticket sales to the public.

For centuries, theater had been produced either at court or in noble households for the entertainment of courtiers and nobles, enacted by choirboys, musicians or other members of the household, many of whom had other duties the rest of the year. At the other end of the social scale, rural and small town communities were entertained in churches, the courtyards of inns, on village commons or in the halls of trade guilds, by actors who were often little better than beggars in costume. Burbage's Theatre, built in 1576, was a start, but it wasn't until Marlowe's *Tamburlaine* exploded on the London scene in 1587 that actors, playwrights and theatre owners could see the public stage as having the potential to provide them with a dependable living.

This same period also saw the first glimmers in publishing of what would eventually evolve into modern journalism. Penny ballads – single sheets that put topical lyrics to well-known tunes – had been in production for years, but these functioned intellectually at the level of comic strips and commercially at the level of peanut vending. True journalism, or one form of it – an inexpensive format produced at regular intervals consisting of entertaining or informative material that generated enough sales that printers found them profitable to publish – did not take off until the uproar created by Martin Mar-prelate in the late 1580s created a reading audience that, having found itself, was eager to support storytellers and satirists like Robert Greene and Thomas Nashe. Greene and Nashe can be seen as the first modern English journalists and their pamphlets as the first magazines. Thus were the commercial stage and the commercial press born at roughly the same time, the final quarter of the 16th century.

The people of London, starved for entertainment by the grim strictures of the Swiss Reformation thrust upon them earlier in the century,[1] were the ground out of which the commercial stage and press first thrust forth tender and uncertain shoots. This burst of popular enthusiasm for the stage, and to a lesser extent, for the press,[2] created a situation whereby their producers could live, or at least could hope to live, on the proceeds of a large number of small transactions, a significant first in English history. For the first time, writing for the public would be driven more by popular demand than by wealthy patrons, religious polemics, or court propaganda.

The importance of this new development, the tremendous power that it represented (the vox populi, the voice of the people, the Fourth Estate of government), may have taken awhile to sink in, but soon enough both court and city officials realized the threat it posed to their hegemony. Their concern is evidenced by the Crown's efforts to control the press through censorship and licensing, and the city's many efforts to "pluck down" the theaters (Chambers 2.236 et seq.).

Scanning history for clues to the human forces behind these developments, the decade when they began, roughly the 1580s, presents a smooth facade, lacking in specifics. Despite a scattering of facts, names, and dates, nothing provides the kind

---

Stephanie Hopkins Hughes *is an independent scholar who since 1987 has been researching issues of 16th-century authorship in libraries and archives in the US and UK. Appointed in 1995 by Charles Beauclerk, then President of the Shakespeare Oxford Society, to design and establish* The Oxfordian *as the first scholarly journal dedicated to publishing research articles on the Authorship Question, Hughes was its editor from 1998 to 2007. She has published articles in the SOS and DVS Newsletters as well, and has spoken at numerous authorship conferences in the US, the UK, and Canada. In 2008 she launched* www.politicworm.com, *a popular online journal of essays on authorship issues, from which this article is reprinted. She is currently at work on a book that examines the authorship question from the point of view of the author's education as proven by his works.*

of connections necessary to get a reliable picture of who or what was propelling events. Not until March of 1595 comes the first occurrence in a theatrical record of the name Shakespeare,[3] the name that, in time, will come to represent the peak of this new force. Strangely it will not appear again in any similar connection until 1598 when it's published on the title pages of two popular plays, *Richard II* and *Richard III*. Its appearance in these two places, so widely separated in time, so late in the development of the stage, is puzzling.

As for the Earl of Oxford, so difficult to locate later, he does appear during this early period, obviously and publicly in connection with the stage, less obviously in the press. In 1580 his name surfaces as patron of at least two companies that perform at court and in the provinces throughout the decade, one of boy actors and another of adults (Chambers 2.100-01). If, as we believe, he was also doing most of the writing for the Queen's Men,[4] then he and his plays dominate the revels at court throughout the 1580s. We see him stepping in to lease the first Blackfriars Theater in 1583 when it was in danger of being shut down (Smith 151). In the early 1590s his persona (if not his name) is dragged by Thomas Nashe into his pamphlet duel with Gabriel Harvey.[5]

The University Wits

Nashe, along with Robert Greene, George Peele, Thomas Watson, Thomas Lodge, and Thomas Kyd is included as a member of the mysterious coterie of early writers termed by 19th-century scholars the University Wits. Marlowe and Lyly are often included though, unlike the others, their connections with other members of the group are less significant than their individual biographies. Having surfaced in London in the early 1580s with the advent of the amorphous Robert Greene, all but Nashe had disappeared from "the paper stage" by the middle of the 1590s and he appears only once after 1596. That within such a narrow time-frame this group should appear and then vanish like a batch of out-of-season mushrooms has not only not been explained by orthodox scholars – not one so far as I know has even noticed that it needs explaining.

Investigations into their individual biographies reveal an assortment of anomalies much like those that bedevil the Stratford biography. The one thing that most have that William of Stratford does not is time spent at a university; for the rest their histories are equally problematic. Since there also exists at that time a group of erudite courtiers, who, like Oxford, were known for their writing skills, but who left little or nothing signed with their names (Puttenham's *Arte of English Poetry* (1589) as quoted by Ogburn 687), today's authorship scholars must consider the possibility that William of Stratford was not the only proxy for courtiers who wished to see their works in print. That being the case, where does Marlowe fit in this early modern publishing scenario?

Of one thing we can be sure, at least where his plays are concerned, Marlowe was nobody's proxy. His passion, his point of view, are all his own.

Marlowe's Success

It may be that Marlowe had more to do with the commercial success of the London stage than any other single individual (apart from Oxford). Of course without the acting talent of Edward Alleyn his scripts would not have been brought to exciting life, and without the entrepreneurial skills of Alleyn's father-in-law and partner, Philip Henslowe, owner and manager of Southwark's public stage, the Rose, their combined talents might have blazed and died away like so many holiday fireworks.

But strong acting and the entrepreneurial instinct were probably present all along. It took someone of Marlowe's genius to create the vehicles for Alleyn to bring in the crowds night after night, crowds who would be willing to pay once more to see Tamburlaine thunder down his adversaries, and in the process, show potential investors that, given the right elements, theater had the potential to become a profitable venture.

Nor could he have done it without Oxford, who created the first public stage in 1576,[6] provided the most popular plays, as revealed by Henslowe's Diary,[7] and showed him the way. But it may be that Oxford hadn't yet acquired the common touch that gave the shoemaker's son the edge with the 16th-century public. It may be that, although Oxford (as we believe) taught him the craft of writing plays, it was Marlowe who showed Oxford how to reach, if not his most important audience, certainly his largest.

Was Marlowe Shakespeare?

Because the name Shakespeare begins to appear so late in the record, Marlowe is often given credit for shared tropes, scene construction, even particular phrases. According to the poet Swinburne, "He and he alone guided Shakespeare in the right way of work." Malone, the first real Shakespeare scholar, attributed *Titus Andronicus* to Marlowe, while dozens of others have claimed for him Shakespeare's early quartos and particular scenes from his earlier plays. Others have gone so far as to claim that Marlowe continued to write behind the name Shakespeare, that he survived his assassination and, protected by patrons, went on to write *Hamlet, Julius Caesar*, etc.

While the reason for these mis-attributions lies with the out-of-sync dating scheme bequeathed us by the Stratford biography, the best argument comes from Caroline Spurgeon's close examination of their differences in her great book, *Shakespeare's Imagery* (1935). Having sifted their works for their favorite comparisons, metaphors and similes, in classifying and comparing them she finds too great a difference for them to have come from the same mind.[8] Oxfordians might ask, could Oxford have used Marlowe as a proxy before he began using Shakespeare? No, and for the same reason. And there are other differences.

Shakespeare was a deeply humorous person. We sometimes get the feeling that it was his sense of humor that saved him from madness. Marlowe on the other hand is always in earnest and what humor he shows rarely reaches beyond a sort of savage irony. His wit is meant to wound, not amuse. If the clown roles in *Dr. Faustus* are his, then he wasn't half trying when he wrote them; many scholars can't hear his voice in them at all, believing that they were added after his death by a second writer (Ribner xxiv). Himself a product of the working class, it's understandable that creating the kind of working-class clown that Shakespeare's audience delighted in might go against the grain.[9] Had Shakespeare written the clown parts in *Dr. Faustus* they would probably have been funny.

Marlowe has a different rhythm than Shakespeare: heavier, more insistent, less flexible. Shakespeare moves us in many ways, but frequently by stinging us into awareness. Marlowe moves us in an almost opposite way, by hypnotizing us into a state of excitement. Shakespeare can sound like Marlowe, but he will shift away from it. Marlowe can sound like Shakespeare in the quality and timing of his one-liners, but he hasn't the Bard's flexibility. Shakespeare's genius shifts with ease from one mode of expression to another, from singsong to imperative, poetry to rapid-fire dialogue; Marlowe's is a rhythmic and hypnotic rising, rising, rising, like an opera chorus, to a climax. Clearly these are two separate voices. If there are crossovers of style and construction, of phrasing and tempo, the explanation must lie elsewhere.

Seemingly fairly equal in skill at the time that we first catch sight of them, they were different in just about every other way. Unlike the Stratford Shakespeare, there is ample evidence that Marlowe had the necessary education to write the works attributed to him. Unlike the Stratford Shakespeare, Marlowe's works reflect his nature as portrayed by his origins and the incidents of his life. His protagonists were not noblemen, but were, like himself, men of obscure background who raised themselves to positions of power through their talent, charisma, and strength of will. Tamburlaine, who wants to conquer everything, and Faustus, who wants to know everything, spoke for that ambitious new middle class into which Marlowe was thrusting himself through his writing – while Barabas, the money-lender who wants to own everything, was its villain.

This burgeoning class, surging into prominence with the development of the modern market economy, needed role models. Neither the timeless folk myths that sustained the yeomanry – like Robin Hood or *George á Greene* – nor the chivalric romances like Arthur and Lancelot or *Orlando Furioso* that fueled the psyches of aristocrats, could have much meaning for this new entrepreneurial class. The author himself, as a writer forced to live by his wits, the son of a man who lived by his hands, was clearly one of these.

It was Marlowe who had the kind of reckless Icarian genius that the orthodox are forced by their short timetable to claim for William of Stratford, and it shows in the style and themes of his most popular works and the kinds of heroes he created, as it most manifestly does not in Shakespeare. Unlike Shakespeare, whose early themes tend to call on classic ideals of chivalric loyalty, there is no trace of these, either pro (thematic) or con (satiric), in any of Marlowe's works – though he may cast an ironic eye their way in passing. Marlowe's world-view is, in almost all points, the diametric opposite of Shakespeare's.

Shakespeare's ideology hearkens back to a feudal world where peace and harmony depend on the hero keeping – or, returning, after a pleasant sojourn in a sylvan fantasy – to his proper place in the scheme of things – or, as in the tragedies, going mad or dying because for some reason he can't return. In contrast, there is no possibility of peace or harmony in Marlowe's world. His heroes are admired for their very refusal to remain at their predestined level, and for the passion and perseverance with which they create a new world, however cruel and unstable, with themselves at the center.

The accusations of atheism directed at Marlowe shortly after his death were written to order for those who wished to portray his killing as a boon to society – but taken for what they're worth, they too strengthen our impression of this writer as a man not contented with the orthodox explanations of things, one hungry for the kinds of truths that the Church regarded as off-limits, one in fact much like his own Dr. Faustus.

Marlowe vs. Shakespeare

With the little we know for certain at this time, we can only guess at the kind of relationship that might have existed between these two brilliant artists whose works place them together in time. While history strangely ignores it, one thing we can be sure of, there was – there had to have been – some sort of relationship. The world of the London stage was simply too small then for these two powerful voices to be unaware of each other. That being the case, their influence on each other must have been at least as vital as any of the other factors in their individual developments.
At their best they were in close competition with each other, and although others occasionally approached them in their lesser moments, no one else ever came close to approaching either of them at their lyrical best. It simply has to be that, during the brief period when they vied for the public's favor on the stage of The Rose theater – when they brought a new and more polished speech to the stage, and when, together, they helped give birth to a commercially successful theater industry, a brief period of some five or six years – each measured himself against the other.

Like knives, did Marlowe and Shakespeare sharpen their skills on each other? If not directly, one-on-one, over a bowl of sack at the Steelyard or the Mermaid Tavern, surrounded by a group of fellow wits, or in some even more direct relationship, but at the very least in the constant awareness that the other was watching and listening, perhaps slipping into the theater unseen to measure the intensity of the crowd's response to the other's latest play.[10] It simply must be that it was in large part competition with Marlowe that gave Shakespeare the thrust to become the greatest writer of his time – if not of all time. We'll never know, of course, what Marlowe might have become, since he never got the chance.

So, although there remain many unanswered questions, in comparison with the kinds and numbers of questions that swarm around Shakespeare and the University Wits, we feel secure in accepting Christopher Marlowe as what he appears to be: a young poet of stunning ability who rose in a few short years on a tide of circumstance to a height of popularity and influence. Marlowe's success was a quantum leap from his origins: a shoemaker's son who, when he got into hot water with authority, could use the cream of the peerage as character references.[11] Unfortunately, at the height of that success – much like one of his own heroes – he was dashed to destruction in a sudden turn of Fortune's wheel.

Did that wheel turn purely through the immutable workings of Fate, or was there a hidden hand at work in Marlowe's sudden fall? And if so, whose and why? Researchers Charles Nicholl, Leslie Hotson, A.D. Wraight, Calvin Hoffman, and Curtis Breight have left no doubt in many minds that the scenario of Marlowe's death was not at all the unfortunate result of accidental violence that it was made out to be in the coroner's report. Yet of all the scholars who have dealt with Marlowe, few agree on why he was killed or who was responsible.

Marlowe's Background

A shoemaker's son from the cathedral town of Canterbury, educated first through a scholarship meant to provide the Canterbury Cathedral choir with young singers, and then at Cambridge University through a scholarship for poor but promising students from Canterbury, orthodox opinion holds that Marlowe arrived in London shortly after receiving his Masters degree at the age of twenty-three, sometime after March of 1587, and that he began writing for the theater right away, perhaps even with a play or two ready for production on his arrival. One of these was the super-hit *Tamburlaine*, performed for the first time in the summer of 1587. In the five years after *Tamburlaine* he and Alleyn produced one hit after another; roughly one a year from 1587 to 1592.

When the Cambridge dons, nervous over religious dissension on campus, were set to deny him his Masters degree in 1587 because they saw his extended absences from Cambridge as trips to Rheims, a Catholic stronghold on the continent, the

Privy Council overrode their decision with a letter stating that Marlowe deserved his degree because he had been engaged in important service for her Majesty. This interference by the Crown in the affairs of a poor scholarship student, together with Marlowe's absences during the final three years of his studies, has led scholars to the conclusion that the only possible explanation is that he was spying on Catholics for Francis Walsingham.

Since nothing remotely connected with spying can be found in his record until the year before his assassination, it seems far more likely that these absences were periods during which the gifted young playwright was testing his wings on the London stage. Facing the gathering storm that would result in the attack by the Spanish Armada in 1588, by 1584, when his absences began, Walsingham and the Privy Council would have been just as concerned with the need for artful propaganda as they were for spies.[12] When examined closely, it becomes apparent that the periods of Marlowe's absences from Cambridge correspond to periods when plays would be prepared for rehearsal for court performance, which means they would also have been performed at the public theaters for the groundlings. In any case, it should seem unlikely that the government would set someone as gifted as Marlowe to spy on his fellows when his native talents could be put to so much better use doing what nobody else could, and where but with the playwright whose theaters and plays had created the London Stage.[13]

What, Where, and When?

A close look at events, locations and dates puts Marlowe and Oxford physically close in the mid-to-late 1580s. From 1580 to late 1588, Oxford was living in Shoreditch, just outside the London Wall, at the manor known as Fisher's Folly, a fifteen-minute walk north to the Theatre built by James Burbage in the Liberty of Norton Folgate, where Burbage's family and a number of other actors and musicians were living by then. Next door but one to Fisher's Folly and Bishopsgate was the inn known as the Pye, the home of young Edward Alleyn (*ODNB*), with whom Marlowe would form the partnership that brought them both such success.

On June 1, 1583, Oxford was officially reinstated at court after his two-year banishment for impregnating a Queen's "maid of honor." Immediately upon his return he combined the Children of Her Majesty's Chapel with the Children of Paul's into a single company known variously in the records as Oxford's Boys, Paul's Boys, or the Earl of Oxford's Company (Chambers 4.101), rehearsing them at the little school in Blackfriars where evidence shows him holding the lease in 1583 (Smith 151).

The Revels account for that winter shows three plays by the Queen's Men, their first at court. For two of them, the payee is Oxford's man John Dutton.[14] Two of the plays were performed by the Children of the Chapel (recorded as "Oxford's boys") and one was performed by the Earl of Oxford's "servants" (where the payee was John Lyly). The following winter, 1584-5, there were four plays by the Queen's Men, one by "the children of the Earl of Oxford," one by "servants to the Earl of Oxford for feats of activity and vaulting," and one by "the Earl of Oxenford his boys" (Chambers 4.160-61). Doubtless Oxford was overwhelmed.[15] That he, Hunsdon and Walsingham would have been on the lookout for someone who could assist with providing these companies with new plays makes sense, and in fact it was in the fall of 1584 that Marlowe's first long absence from Cambridge occurs.

By the summer of 1585, fears of Spain and Jesuit infiltrators had driven the Crown to fund Walsingham's growing intelligence operation to the tune of £2000 per annum (Read 2.370-1). While Oxford was dealing with military matters that summer – first in petitioning the Queen and Burghley to give him a command in the Netherlands – then in going, and then almost immediately returning (his promised cavalry post transferred to the 19-year-old Earl of Essex), Walsingham and Hunsdon must have felt pressured to find someone who could replace him for the coming winter holiday at court. This was not necessary as it turned out, since Oxford was back in England by late October.

The following summer Oxford was allotted a grant of £1000 per annum in the Privy Seal Warrant, the Queen's personal funding source, the source also of Walsingham's secret service grants. It's been assumed that this was to finance an appropriate lifestyle for one of England's premiere earls, but since no purpose was stated, it could just as easily have been meant to fund a behind-the-scenes operation to provide anti-Spanish propaganda in the theaters and bookstalls.[16] Just as the unsavory agents who were being gathered by Walsingham began to appear with his increased funding, so did the University Wits begin to appear with Oxford's annuity.

In his detailed account of the circumstances surrounding Marlowe's assassination, Charles Nicholl provides data that supports our assumption. Drawn from two sources, the Cambridge buttery books record what the students spent on food and drink, and Marlowe's scholarship account; it records the shilling per week he collected as a scholarship student, but only when he was present. When both of these disappear during a particular time period, it is evidence he was away from campus (98).

According to Nicholl, during the four years Marlowe was studying for his BA, he rarely left the campus, even during the summers (99). The absences that so concerned the Cambridge dons began with the first year of his Master's program. For eight weeks from the middle of April until mid-June 1585, then another nine weeks from July through September, Marlowe was missing from Cambridge. Are there hints in the Revels record for the following winter holiday at court that this was the true reason for his absence?

That winter there were plays by "the Queens Men, Howard's [the Lord Admiral's]

Men, Hunsdon's [the Lord Chamberlain's] Men, John Simon's, and Mr. Stanley's [Lord Strange's] boys" (Chambers 4.101-02). Since this is the first mention in the Revels record of the Lord Admiral as a patron, this may be the hint we're looking for, because Lord Admiral Charles Howard was the patron at the Rose during most of the time that Marlowe dominated its stage. This is also the year that Marlowe's "actual spending at the buttery leapt from a customary few pennies to lavish weekly sums of 18 shillings and 21 shillings" (Nicholl 100). 1585 is also the year inscribed on the portrait found at Marlowe's college,[17] in which he's dressed like a young lord with 30 gold buttons prominently displayed on his over-sized jacket.[18]

Marlowe's final absence of seven or eight weeks out of the normal twelve (99) occurred the following spring. There is nothing to show that he was in Cambridge after March 1587. *Tamburlaine* was first produced at the Rose early that summer. Since *Tamburlaine* is both too innovative and too polished not to have been preceded by juvenilia, it's fair to suggest that Marlowe's rapid grasp of the techniques of successful playwriting was fostered by someone more experienced than himself. With his future partner Edward Alleyn located next door to Fisher's Folly and Alleyn's brother John working for James Burbage just up the road at Norton Folgate (Edward Alleyn ODNB) – with records that by 1589 place Marlowe with fellow poet Thomas Watson, recorded as living in or near Fisher's Folly during or shortly after Oxford's time as owner (Anderson 232) – there's more than enough evidence to place Marlowe with or near Oxford in the mid-to-late 1580s.[19] Certain plays produced for the Queen's Men at that time suggest Marlowe's developing style.[20] While there's no hard evidence, locating Marlowe so close to Fisher's Folly at this time helps to account for the links of style and construction that connect him to Shakespeare (i.e., Oxford), and for his unusually rapid leap to glory.

Was Marlowe Ever a Spy?

What then of Marlowe's purported involvement in government spy operations? Despite an exhaustive 400-year exploration of the records, there is still no solid evidence that Marlowe ever acted for the Crown in that capacity.[21] The entire structure that condemns him as a spy rests on the later conjecture by academics that the Privy Council's claim in 1587 that he was acting in the Queen's interest could only mean one thing: that he was spying for Walsingham.

Apart from the event that resulted in his elimination from the London stage, the only other incident in which Marlowe appears to have been involved with members of the Elizabethan spying community took place in January 1592 in the Netherlands, where it seems he was sharing a room in Flushing with two known government operatives, one Richard Baines and a "Gifford Gilbert." We know this because Baines denounced him to Sir Robert Sidney, then governor of Flushing, as having urged "Gilbert" to counterfeit a Dutch shilling and to have declared that he was about to "go over" to the enemy, i.e. the expatriate English Catholics in Brussels (Nicholl 234-249).[22] When interviewed by Sidney, Marlowe claimed that it was Baines who set up the coining episode while Baines claimed that Marlowe was intending to defect. The last we hear of the matter, Marlowe and the purported coiner[23] were on their way back to England under guard, for questioning by Burghley (Nicholl 238).

With Marlowe's emphatic denials of any involvement in the supposed counterfeiting scheme and no other evidence of any connection with the spy community, the idea that this identifies him as a double agent, either a counterfeiter working for the Jesuits or posing as one to attract catholic dissidents into the spymaster's web, is patently absurd.[24] Motivations may be difficult to parse from our place in time, but the maybe-this-maybe-that motivations attributed to Marlowe by Nicholl and others make no sense. Why they would choose to give credence to anything said by men like Baines and Gifford, why supposedly intelligent researchers would continue to lump Marlowe, "the muses darling," in with these blackguards, is an even greater mystery. With the end of the story in mind, it should be obvious that this coining adventure was a trap set by the government that Marlowe managed to escape. Next year he would not be so lucky.

"The Reckoning"

On May 12, 1593, in a sweep ostensibly to discover the author of a political libel pasted on the wall of the Dutch Church the day before, government agents found what they claimed was an atheist tract in the rooms of an impoverished scrivener named Thomas Kyd, a paper Kyd said must be Marlowe's because it wasn't his.[25] While Kyd languished in prison, Marlowe was brought before the Star Chamber for questioning about his "blasphemy," then released with orders to remain available for further questioning. Ten days later, supposedly having been invited to a feast in Deptford, a port town on the Thames a few miles from Greenwich Palace, he spent from ten in the morning until sometime after supper with three men, two government agents and a confidence racketeer, in a room and garden of the home of one Eleanor Bull, a widow who let rooms and provided meals to travelers.

At some point during this prolonged get-together, Marlowe was stabbed to death just above the right eye. A coroner's jury was hastily assembled; a plea of self-defense was offered by one of those present at the killing, attested to by the other two, and accepted by the coroner's jury; the body was buried immediately somewhere nearby and the killer freed on a verdict of self-defense.

These three angels of doom cooperated with the authorities like true professionals. Ingram Frizer, the self-confessed killer, "neither fled nor withdrew himself." All agreed that Marlowe, angered over "the reckoning" – the bill for the day's expenses – had grabbed Frizer's knife from him and was trying to stab him when Frizer accidentally stabbed Marlowe in the eye. Frizer was officially pardoned exactly a month later, apparently spending no time at all behind bars. This is the official story. It's a story that begs a number of questions. Without pretending to know all the answers, we'll consider some of them.

Questioning the Official Story

What kept these four men together for ten hours? Ten hours is a long time to spend at anything. People spend time like that when they're waiting for something; waiting for someone to show up, for a ship to sail, for a message to arrive, for it to turn dark. If the three government operatives had been ordered to convince Marlowe that he must do – or not do – something or take the consequences, ten hours without a resolution seems unlikely. Of course there is no way of knowing at what point during those ten hours he was actually killed.

Why was he stabbed in the eye? A stab in the eye is one of the few knife blows that can be certain to kill instantly since it cannot miss the brain.

Why were there three of them? Marlowe was young and strong, and knowing that he had acquitted himself in at least two street fights, there probably had to be enough men present to insure the success of their mission, two to hold him and one to do the deed. Since the last man to arrive was Robert Poley, whose reputation as a government agent suggests that he was the leader, the other two required to make sure that he stayed put until Poley arrived. Altogether they provided the requisite two witnesses to justify the killer's plea of self defense.

Why did they meet in Deptford? Was it because Deptford was in Kent, not far from Scadbury, where Marlowe was staying with Thomas Walsingham and his servant Frizer? Was it because Deptford was a port town filled with sailors and strangers, a rough town, used to having to deal with violent death, and thus not inclined to linger over details? Was it because it was a town where Marlowe would be unknown to any that might be on the jury, and where the body of someone other than Marlowe could be identified as his without anyone knowing the difference? Although Marlowe's *works* were well known, it's unlikely that many beyond the theater community or his audience knew his name or could recognize his face.

Or was it perhaps because the Queen was then in residence at Greenwich which put Deptford within the twelve mile verge of the court, so that it would not be the local coroner in charge of the inquest but William Danby, Coroner to the Royal Household, whose standing with high level Court officials would have meant a good deal more to him than the death of some atheistic playwright.

Why did they meet at Eleanor Bull's? Mrs. Bull, in whose house the killing occurred, was not just any old innkeeper. She was closely related to Blanche Parry, a long-time headmistress of the Queen's Privy Chamber and Elizabeth's personal confidante since childhood, who, when she died some time before, had left her cousin Eleanor Bull a sizable bequest (Nicholl 36-7). She was a person with Court connections and one who belonged to a prestigious network of individuals with the right to ask for – and the duty to grant – special favors to those in power.

Finally, did the fact that this was the worst year for the plague in many years contribute to the timing of the murder? Certainly the fact that the theaters were all closed, the players were on the road, and the powerful patrons of the theater who might have interfered, had all relocated themselves as far as they could get from the zone of contagion, make what appears to have been a government sting operation much more easily accomplished than if the plague not cleared the City.

During the period from a few days before the killing to several weeks afterwards, three notices were created that portray Marlowe as a scurrilous atheist and brawler. As Nicholl clearly shows, all three of these were written by what we would now regard as "disinformation" experts, meaning they originated from the same community of undercover agents to which, as Nicholl so clearly proves, two of the three parties to the execution belonged. One was written by the same Richard Baines who had attempted to get Marlowe arrested in Flushing the year before. These libels have so befouled Marlowe's posthumous reputation that for centuries he's been denied his place in literature.

Ingram Frizer and the Walsinghams

The man who confessed to the killing, Ingram Frizer, was a servant of Thomas Walsingham, who was second cousin to the Queen's former Secretary of State, Sir Francis Walsingham. Marlowe was staying with Thomas Walsingham when he was taken by Walsingham's servant Ingram Frizer to the "feast" that ended his life. Walsingham's role is sometimes described by the pundits who wrote about the assassination as that of Marlowe's homosexual lover. Less often is it noted that he was a member of the same undercover community to which all three of the men present at Marlowe's undoing belonged.

Thanks to Nicholl we have evidence that, as young men, both Thomas and his older brother had followed their father's first cousin Francis Walsingham into "the service," Thomas having worked for Sir Francis in Paris, then later as his secretary in London. Ingram Frizer began as a servant of their father, but when he died, rather than stay with the heir, Thomas's older brother Edmund, Frizer chose to stay with Thomas. Four years before Marlowe's visit, Edmund's death left Scadbury, the family estate, in the possession of the 26-year-old Thomas. Thus it was to Scadbury that the messenger was sent to fetch Marlowe to his Star Chamber hearing on the 10th of May and so it was also from Scadbury that Marlowe rode with Frizer to Deptford on the morning of May 30th.

Skeres and Poley

Nicholas Skeres, the servant of Thomas Walsingham who escorted Marlowe to his final feast, was, as records dug up by Nicholl reveal, a tout for the kind of London moneylender who paid scurvy types like Skeres to ensnare unwary young heirs, desperate for cash, into signing away their estates (Nicholl 25-31). During the Babington sting in 1586, Skeres functioned as a government provocateur, helping to steer the poor fool and his friends towards prison and the scaffold.

The third man, Robert Poley, was a government agent of long standing. Having orchestrated the Babington Plot that "beguiled" Anthony Babington into committing himself to treason and the gallows, the following year he was instrumental in getting the Queen of Scots to incriminate herself, thus enabling Burghley and Walsingham to put an end once and for all to the plots focused on getting her crowned Queen of England.

On May 30, 1593, the day Marlowe was led to the slaughter, Poley had just returned from passing important communiques between the English government and the Hague. Nicholl shows that payments later disbursed to Poley include the period from his arrival back from the Continent to several days after the inquest, proving that he was on the government payroll at the time of Marlowe's death. That he was involved in Marlowe's "reckoning" suggests that his government employers saw the popular playwright's elimination as something that required his particular experience as a seasoned professional.[26]

Which brings us to the question of *why* Marlowe was killed. Disinformation created by government agents after his death suggest a number of reasons, but these can be eliminated since they have served only to distract his audience, and generations of scholars, from the truth.

Was it Spying that Caused his Death?

Obviously Marlowe was silenced by members of the government spy community, but so far there isn't a shred of solid evidence that spying activities of his own had anything to do with his killing, either directly or by implication.[27] Suggestions by Kyd and Baines that Marlowe was on the verge of defecting to Scotland or to the Catholics overseas, ring hollow. Why should a brilliant young poet at the peak of an exciting career in the brave new world of commercial theater wish to leave the arena of his success – that is, unless he was forced to for some reason? Nothing in anything he wrote suggests an adherence to Catholicism, or any religion – quite the opposite.

Was Sex Involved?

Among the various reasons put forth to explain the murder, one of the more enduring held that he died in a brawl caused by jealousy over his love affair with Thomas Walsingham. In this, Walsingham is seen as Marlowe's beloved with Walsingham's servant Ingram Frizer as his violently jealous lover. In this scenario Marlowe is pictured in the midst of penning *Hero and Leander* as a gift for Walsingham when he's interrupted for the fatal jaunt to Deptford – total fiction, though there may be some truth to the relationship. That Marlowe was more attracted to men than women seems likely from his writing; in the three plays that we can be certain are his own, the female characters are little more than cardboard stereotypes; what's meant to be romantic dialogue comes off as little more than stilted rhetoric.

Records at Corpus Christi show that Marlowe had a lot more money to spend at school by 1585 than he had ever spent before. Writing for the theater didn't pay much (nor, presumably, would working for Oxford, whose £1000 would have had to cover a stable of writers and secretaries, some in need of bed and board, in addition to printers, theaters and acting troupes, and their costumes and props). Gifts from a gentleman lover would have put the kind of spending money in Marlowe's purse that enabled him to splurge at the buttery at school, as he evidently did, and to dress like a gentleman, as revealed in his portrait.

As for Thomas Walsingham, based on the little we know, it's impossible to conjecture with any assurance about his sexual bias. His youth, his rank, his time spent in Paris, would easily make him a likely member of one of the circles of young men-about-town who frequented the theater and patronized artists, one who could have been particularly interested in the author of the most popular plays in London. Thomas had returned to London at about the time Sir Francis organized the Queen's Men and that Marlowe's long absences from Cambridge began to occur.

It's difficult to look at the scenario as we now have it (thanks to Charles Nicholl and Leslie Hotson) and not see Marlowe as having been set up by Thomas Walsingham as a favor to someone in power.[28] In what would be the least malignant version, Walsingham may have had no choice.

Was it Because of his Atheistic Beliefs?

In the years immediately following his death, the claim that Marlowe was an atheist, though not portrayed as a direct cause, was certainly played up as a factor. The three documents that most immediately accused him of atheism originated either from members of the government disinformation crew (an especially impressive bit of delving by Nicholl), or from Thomas Kyd, whose condemnations of Marlowe's atheism can be discounted as a desperate attempt to end his own sessions on the rack. Thus all contemporary references to Marlowe's atheism can be seen as "written to order." That is, all but one.

All scholars are agreed that it was Marlowe that Robert Greene harangued in *Greene's Groatsworth of Witte*, as "thou famous gracer of tragedians" in an effort to stop him and two other playwrights – probably Nashe and Peele – from continuing to write for certain ungrateful actors. If it weren't for *Greene's Groatsworth* we might be satisfied with the conclusion that Marlowe's reputed atheism was no more than a slander created by his murderers to justify his brutal death. But Greene's warning has a genuine ring to it and since *Groatsworth* was published nine months before Marlowe's death, it seems unlikely that it was connected with the later official campaign to tarnish his memory. Did Greene actually know something nine months before Marlowe's arrest, or was his warning just a lucky shot?

The term *atheism* and what it meant in Marlowe's day can be defined perhaps as any belief system or philosophy that wasn't Christian – meaning Catholic, Anglican, evangelical or dissident – and since Catholics were condemned as pagan idolaters and dissidents as heretics, there was little room for an independent thinker. More to the point perhaps, charges of atheism were to the 16th-century English what charges of communism were to 20th-century Americans, a hot button used by politicians to rid themselves of rivals and enemies.

Marlowe's atheism, if we must call it that, was certainly publicized by his killers to excuse his killing, but it could not have been the reason *why* he was killed. Had it been, his story would have ended with an execution similar to that of the Catholic activist Edmund Campion and other enemies of the State, bloody dramas performed to as large a public audience as possible as a warning. Had religion been the real issue there would have been no gathering of government agents, no faked argument over the bill, no need to drag him all the way to Deptford so that it would be the royal coroner who led the inquest. We can probably state with a fair amount of assurance that although Marlowe's sexual bias and indifference to religion gave his killers sticks with which to beat his corpse, neither was the *reason* for his death.

Did His Killing Have Something to Do with Martin Mar-prelate?

Martin Mar-prelate was the pen name of a wickedly gifted satirist who began publishing anti-Church pamphlets in 1588. The authorities did what they could to stop him, not only because his calls to revolution threatened to reach all the way to the top levels of government, but also because he revealed embarrassing things about the Anglican bishops and seemed ready to publish more.

The hunt for Martin began right away, but it wasn't until 1593 that a suspect, John Penry, was run to ground. Penry was known to be the chief printer of the Marprelate tracts, but most doubt that he had either the wit or the inside information to write the pamphlets himself – something he continued to deny to the end, claiming that he never knew who actually wrote them. Returning secretly from Scotland the previous autumn in an effort to rejoin his religious community, Penry had managed to elude discovery until March 22nd of 1593, when he was finally nabbed by the authorities shortly before the anti-Marlowe libels were pasted on the wall of the Dutch Church. The rapidly-evolving chain of events that followed are of interest to anyone studying Marlowe.

Chronology of Penry/Marlowe events

- **April 10:** Penry is questioned by Richard Young and the Archbishop of Canterbury, John Whitgift, at Newgate Prison. The following day . . .

- **April 11:** Libelous tracts appear on the wall of the Dutch Church, so rousing that they push the Privy Council into taking action to discover the author or authors. These imitate Marlowe's style and refer to Tamburlaine. The following day . . .

- **April 12:** A paper is "discovered" during a supposedly random search of Thomas Kyd's lodgings. The authorities label it atheistical. Kyd, now in prison, identifies it as Marlowe's.

- **May 20:** Marlowe is brought before the Star Chamber for questioning by Burghley and Archbishop Whitgift, Penry's prosecutor. The following day . . .

- **May 21:** During his trial before the King's Bench, Penry continues to deny his authorship of the Martin tracts and begs Burghley for clemency, but (so we are told) Whitgift is set on vengeance. A week later . . .

- **May 29:** Penry is hurried to a remote location, and hanged in the courtyard of an inn on the Canterbury Road halfway to Deptford. The following day . . .

- **May 30:** Marlowe is "feasted" in Deptford, a feast – to take a phrase from his great contemporary – "not where he eats, but where he is eaten."

Was Marlowe the Author of the Mar-prelate Tracts?

How many writers could there have been in London capable of writing these brilliant and angry satires, that henceforth would set a standard for satirical writing? This was a question that the authorities must have asked themselves frequently over the four-year period while Martin had them under his ink-stained thumb. But Marlowe's style was nothing like Mar-prelate's, nor was he privy to Mar-prelate's inside information.

Was Marlowe Really Murdered?

It's also possible that Marlowe wasn't actually killed that day in Deptford, that his death was a covert action designed to put a stop to his writing and explain his disappearance without resorting to murder. This is the opinion of Calvin Hoffman, whose thesis, published in 1955, offers an answer to certain otherwise difficult questions.

One of the oddities of the Marlowe story is the long wait – some ten hours – that the men spent in each other's company before the killing took place. No scenario, whether of random violence or government sting can account satisfactorily for this ten hour wait before an action that could have been over in an hour. The only explanation is that they were waiting for something, a ship perhaps? Deptford was a port town that offered an easy passage out of the country. The arrival of a corpse to represent Marlowe? Penry's perhaps? Both ship and corpse?

In any case, whether dead or transported, Marlowe's voice, his sensibility, his rousing style, his almost operatic verse, were heard no more. Several works were published later under his name, but differences in style suggest that these may have not have been his.[29] Whatever the true scenario, one thing is certain, after May 30, 1593, there would be no new Tamburlaines to feed the public appetite for underclass heroes. Whether murdered or transported, Christopher Marlowe was silenced.

But why? And by whose orders?

Was It Raleigh?

It has been suggested by Dr. Samuel Tannenbaum (1926) and others that it was Sir Walter Raleigh who had Marlowe killed to prevent him from having to testify in Star Chamber regarding the "School of Night" that supposedly met at Durham House to discuss forbidden matters. Since Raleigh had no known connection with any of the killers, and since he was just as open about his occult studies as he was about most of what he did and never seemed to be paying much attention to possible repercussions, this seems unlikely. Raleigh was no Mr. Milquetoast, but murder was not his style.

In addition, all the documents of disinformation created to cast Marlowe's removal in the light of national security, starting from the beginning with the Dutch Church libel, mentioned Raleigh and his circle in their implications of the dangerous spread of atheism, something that the intelligent Raleigh would certainly not have done to himself. Now that we have clear evidence that the Dutch Church libel was part of a covert government operation, we can guess that the finger of blame that points to Raleigh does so because it was fixed in his direction from the start.[30]

Was It The Earl of Essex?

Based on a guess that Marlowe was questioned about Raleigh's atheism in his Star Chamber hearing and had refused to testify against him, Nicholl goes to some length to accuse Essex, chiefly because it was known that he detested Raleigh and so was seeking his destruction, a theory based, as Breight puts it, on "extremely thin evidence" (129). Not only has Nicholl no evidence that Raleigh's name was brought up at Marlowe's hearing, his thesis paints Essex as conspiring to destroy one of the Court's leading lights purely out of spite. What Nicholl does show is that Marlowe's murder was the work of professionals, which to my mind eliminates Essex. His one proven sting, the destruction of the Portuguese Jew, Dr. Lopez, was clumsy in the extreme. Had Essex been good at this sort of thing he would never have fallen into one trap after another himself as he would later.

Scholar Hugh Ross Williamson thinks Marlowe was killed because he refused to continue working for Poley, but it is simply not feasible that Poley would have dared to assassinate a government agent unless he had orders to do so. To assassinate someone who was undergoing investigation by the Star Chamber would certainly require orders from the highest level, and again, while Nicholl shows that all three of Marlowe's assassins had previous connections with each other, there's never been anything to show that Marlowe was one of them.

Whatever the full truth behind the Flushing sting and the Deptford "feast," one thing can be stated with assurance: it would be very hard to finish Charles Nicholl's book without becoming convinced that Marlowe was eliminated on someone's orders; someone who was central to government intelligence networks, someone with enough authority to order it done, someone with the skill to manage it, and with the kind of influence to control the outcome so that no embarrassing questions ever surfaced, either at the time or for centuries afterwards.

Was It Robert Cecil?

All of Nicholl's evidence points directly to Robert Cecil. Only he was in a position to bring it off and only he had the motivation for such an elaborate operation. Curtis Breight, in his *Surveillance, Militarism and Drama in the Elizabethan Era* (1996), provides voluminous citations proving that all of those involved in the assassination, killers and demonizers, were in the employ of either Lord Burghley or his son Robert Cecil, both before and after Marlowe's death (127-171). Although Breight accepts the Marlowe as spy thesis, he's one of the few who grasps that the reasons for the assassination were entirely political (134).

With Secretary Walsingham's death in April of 1590, his network of undercover operatives and spies was left without a director. Burghley, who had created the office of Elizabethan Secretary of State, spies and all, and who had seen to it that Walsingham got the job in 1573 when he himself moved over to the Treasury, urged that the office be given to his son Robert, then in his thirties. But so great was the weight of dissent from leading officials and courtiers, Essex in particular – so nervous were they about what a power bloc led by Robert Cecil could mean to themselves and England's future once the aging Queen was gone – that Elizabeth, at a loss, simply stalled.[31] While the office of Secretary continued to remain vacant, Burghley simply added the paperwork to his workload as Lord Treasurer and other offices, passing the legwork on to his son. For this reason, by July 1596, when he was finally officially appointed, Robert Cecil had been Principal Secretary in everything but name for six years.

Following Walsingham's death, we're told that his spy network was dispersed, Poley remaining with Cecil, while his other top agent, Thomas Phelippes, transferred to Essex. Nicholl, and those whose research could not be done without access to the archives at Hatfield House, would like to make much of this, but common sense would urge that in fact Phellippes never left the team, pretending to work for Essex while reporting what he could about Essex back to Cecil. Breight cites evidence that Burghley employed Phelippes to do some deciphering work long after Phelippes had supposedly joined Essex's intelligence team. Indeed, Burghley asked Phelippes to do some intelligence work for him . . . within days of Marlowe's death (281 n1).

Why Was He Murdered?

Since it's Marlowe's writing, or its popularity, that is the single most important thing we know about him, one would think that his plays would be front and center in any effort to answer questions about his life. Sidetracked and befuddled by the spy allegation, hardly anyone has considered it, even in passing. Anyone but Curtis Breight that is, who sees Marlowe's *Edward II* as the obvious and immediate cause of the Cecils' wrath. Breight guesses that one of the two unnamed plays performed at Court by Pembroke's Men in the winter of 1592-93 was *Edward II*, but had that been the case it would have said so in 1594 on the play's title page, rather than just that it was "acted by Pembroke's Men in the Honorable City of London."

It's even more likely because the onstage torture of the King in Act 5, Scene 2 and his grisly murder in Scene 5 so grossly violates the unwritten rule against portraying the deposition or assassination of an anointed king.[32] This was not the sort of thing that the Queen would ever have found entertaining; the Lord Admiral's Men may have been reckless, but they were not insane. The Queen would not have seen it, but the Cecils would certainly have known of it and would have been aware that anyone who could afford a penny in the "Honorable City of London" could have seen it. But Marlowe was either unaware of this rule, or more likely purposely ignored it.

As Breight quotes from another scholar, "Tamburlaine's assertion that, 'Nature . . . doth teach us all to have aspiring minds' "(150), might well be taken as encouraging the poor workers in his audience to rebel against their masters, a dangerous suggestion at a time when riots were breaking out all over London over high prices and the bullying of citizens by government officials.[33] Tamburlaine was a godless infidel, but that does not alter the effect on his audience when he drives a cart across the stage pulled by two kings on their knees, as he shouts, "Holla, ye pampered jades of Asia! What? Can ye draw but twenty miles a day?" And although it's supposed to be the Quran that he burns in Part II, that Marlowe's usurper and murderer of kings ultimately dies peacefully of old age would suggest to his audience, who paid little attention to details like differences in Time and Place, that when it came to Tamburlaine's sins, the Lord must have been looking the other way.

While the record has apparently been cleansed of anything that might lead future historians to this conclusion, common sense alone should suggest how the Cecils would have seen these plays.[34] Marlowe may have been warned by Robert Greene and others, but if so, it's clear he paid no attention, for his final play, *The Massacre at Paris*, portrays the brutal onstage stabbing of the French Duc de Guise just five years earlier, and ends with the murder of Henri III.

When the Cecils and the more conservative members of the Privy Council saw how *Edward II* and *The Massacre at Paris* were pulling audiences off the streets day after day at the Rose they could hardly have been ignorant of the message he was sending to that dangerous social animal, the apprentices of London, nor to the power he was beginning to acquire, not only with the public, but also with certain members of the ancient nobility, who saw reflected in his plots their outrage against the cruelties perpetrated by the Crown against their fellow catholics.

If Marlowe wasn't stopped now, later might be too late.

Did His Fellow Writers Leave Any Clues?

Unlike Shakespeare who appears to have said nothing at the time, three of the University Wits were quick to mention Marlowe's passing. In a poem dedicated to his patron, Henry Percy, 9th Earl of Northumberland, apparently for the Garter Ceremony of June 26, 1593, George Peele speaks of the "unhappy end" of "Marley, the Muses darling." In his book *Jack Wilton, the Unfortunate Traveller*, finished on June 27, 1593, a month after the assassination, it's assumed by those accustomed to Nashe's style, that when Nashe praises Pietro Aretino as "one of the wittiest knaves that ever God made," and adds "his life he contemned in comparison of the liberty of free speech," he was referring to the recently assassinated Marlowe.

While *Jack Wilton* wasn't published until the spring of 1594, it seems that immediately following Marlowe's murder, Nashe published instead the morose pseudo-religious *Christ's Teares Over Jerusalem*, in which he refers to Marlowe as an atheist whose death was simply good riddance to bad rubbish. *Christ's Teares* has caused some head-scratching by Nashe scholars, chiefly because it differs so markedly from anything else he ever wrote. Drenched in Calvinistic gloom and doom and with none of the nonchalance of his other works, what caused Nashe to rush this miserable book into print ahead of the far more entertaining and better written *Unfortunate Traveller*? What caused him to so abruptly change his attitude, his public attitude at least, towards Marlowe in the weeks immediately following his murder?

Marlowe's Variable Reputation

For a good four years after the publication of *Jack Wilton* there is nothing (extant) in print about Marlowe. Then, in 1597 comes the first of what would be many references to him and to his death in works by puritans using what Nicholl calls "demeaning and dismissive" terms. These have set the tone for most of the printed references to Marlowe from then until the late 20th century. In 1598, the author of *Wits Treasury* (aka *Paladis Tamia*) – famous as the first mention of Shakespeare as the author of ten currently popular plays – repeats the official view of Marlowe while performing the same disservice for the recently deceased George Peele, claiming he died of the pox, a total fabrication according to Peele's biographer David Horne. The usual imitators, repeating like parrots the official view of Marlowe's character and his death, caused his reputation to sink ever lower as the years went by.

In 1598 however, perhaps as a reaction, a very different picture of Marlowe begins to appear: Marlowe the literary genius. That year, Blount's publication of *Hero and Leander* refers to him in idealistic terms, while in *Lenten Stuff* Nashe returns to praising him. Two years later, Blount attributes Thomas Thorpe's dedication of the translation of *Lucan* to Marlowe, and he also praises him, despite its oddly jesting tone. Over the years, these perceptions have continued to survive alongside each other until the present: Marlowe the celestial poet, Marlowe the atheistic sexual deviate, Marlowe the double-agent and spy. Modern biographers have been hard-put to weave these into a believable whole.

Shakespeare's Comment

Shakespeare's references to contemporary personalities are generally so diffuse as to be hopeless of absolute identification, but he's more obvious than usual in *As You Like It* when the shepherdess Phoebe declares her feelings for Ganymede by quoting Marlowe: "Dead shepherd, now I find thy saw of might; whoever loved that loved not at first sight?" Few dispute that this refers to a line from *Hero and Leander*, though consensus is lacking, as usual, on his reasons for the quote. It seems likely that it was one of a number of additions Shakespeare made to this play during his final years – additions that contribute nothing to the story but appear to be messages of a personal nature embedded in the text, intended for a coterie of insiders, even, perhaps, for future readers.

In another late addition to *As You Like It,* again as an aside that has nothing to do with the plot, the banished Court jester Touchstone says: "When a man's verses cannot be understood, nor a man's good wit seconded by the forward child understanding, it strikes a man more dead than *a great reckoning in a little room*" (3.3.9-12, italics added). This comment has been chewed over by scholars for many years, again with no consensus. The fact that it is followed soon after by Touchstone's comparison of himself to the Roman poet Ovid, exiled to the land of the barbaric Goths by the Emperor Augustus, suggests that Touchstone (*aka* Shakespeare *aka* Oxford) is drawing parallels between his own fate and that of Marlowe and Ovid, both "tongue-tied by authority" (Sonnet 66).

Whatever the purpose of such asides, and whoever the individual or group to whom they were addressed, there seems no doubt that Shakespeare is using *As You Like It* to make a point of some kind about Marlowe. The phrase "great reckoning" is a direct reference to "the reckoning," the bill for the day's refreshments, named in the coroner's report as the cause of the quarrel that led to his death. The phrase "a little room" conflates the room in which Marlowe died with another famous Marlovian phrase, "infinite riches in a little room," (from *The Jew of Malta*). Shakespeare appears to be saying that for a poet to be misunderstood – by his audience? by the authorities? – is another kind of death. It is the death of his work, the death of its value.

But why does he amplify "the reckoning" into a "*great* reckoning?" Is the reckoning *great* – in the sense of mighty or powerful rather than good – because of its deadly nature, because it was the *final* reckoning for a great poet? Or was the reckoning *great*, not because it was with a great poet, but in the sense that it was payback directed at an entire community of writers, the community to which Marlowe belonged? Was this perhaps why Nashe withdrew his ebullient *Jack Wilton* shortly after Marlowe's death, rushing into print instead the morbid *Christ's Teares*, with its effulgent condemnation of almost everything, including himself and the poet he couldn't praise highly enough in just about every other reference he made to him? Was Shakespeare saying that "the reckoning" was meant to silence, not Marlowe alone, but the entire writing community? Was this why the University Wits began disappearing so soon after Marlowe's death?

Hardly a commentator on Marlowe fails to note the strangely prophetic tone of the final sentence in Robert Greene's *Groatsworth*, his warning to Marlowe to give up his atheistic ways, "for little knowest thou how in the end thou shalt be visited." Was this no more than an oddly coincidental prophesy? Or did Greene have some special insight into the forces that were gathering against them all? Did he write as he did in a genuine effort to get the message through to his hard-headed protégé, perhaps in the only way he could?

"His life he contemned in comparison of the liberty of free speech," wrote Nashe shortly after his demise. Of the circle of writers who knew Marlowe, and as one who more often than any other dared to speak the truth as he saw it, this forthright pronouncement by Nashe should be taken at face value, no less because of his strange about-face in *Christ's Teares*, but perhaps even more because of it, if it reveals his fear that by skirting so near the surface of truth in his pamphlets he had, like Marlowe, been taking a deadly risk.

Greene may be telling us that Marlowe was silenced because of his free-thinking. Shakespeare (in *As You Like It*) may be telling us that he was silenced as a warning to other writers. Nashe may be telling us that he was silenced because he couldn't be controlled any other way. In any case, it achieved one result that most certainly has had a lasting effect on the development of English literature – to the eternal confusion of its critics and historians – which is that certain 16th-century playwrights and poets, unable to resist the compulsion to tell the truth about life as they saw it, were driven ever deeper into strategies for hiding their real identities. Marlowe's mistake, or perhaps simply his fate, was that unlike Shakespeare, he had no place to hide.

Conclusion

I would venture that the Dutch Church libel, which Nicholl asserts "can be seen as the opening move in the smear campaign against Marlowe," was also the opening move in Robert Cecil's first big operation as the head of domestic intelligence. With the plague making an early and fierce appearance, the theaters were closed in February and everyone who could afford to leave town did so. With the nobility away in the country, the actors on the road, and the Court holed up at Greenwich, he could count on having a relatively free hand with a maneuver that at another time would have run into resistance from more liberal Court members (like Essex and Raleigh). The slanders were created by the crew he inherited. Robert Cecil's sting was calculated to demonstrate his muscle to those who were not ready to take him seriously. It was time to show the anti-establishment satirists and playwrights, and their noble patrons, who was now in charge.

As Nicholl shows, all three of Marlowe's killers, Frizer, Skeres, and Poley, had ties to either Burghley or his son Robert Cecil during this period. Once Walsingham was gone, Burghley could step back into the role of Court policeman, perhaps taking care of some matters that, in his view, Walsingham had let slide, perhaps even made possible, and he would train his son in the harsh realities of maintaining order at a Renaissance court, perhaps in a hands-on exercise of this sort. This seems not only possible, but it is the only possible explanation for Marlowe's murder and also that of his patron, Lord Strange, a year later (Wilson 172). England may have Burghley to thank in large part for her rise to power among the nations of the world, though it is unfortunate that among his many gifts was not included a greater appreciation of literature. As Hamlet said of Polonius, "He's for a jig or a tale of bawdry, or he sleeps" (*Hamlet*, 2.2.496).

Despite Nicholl's incessant flummery regarding how poets are inclined by nature to become spies he also wrote:

> Amid all these ructions that attended the last years of Elizabeth and the first years of James, there is one figure who continued to rise, and to ride the troubled waters of his succession, who was indeed the principal prosecutor of Essex, Raleigh, and Northumberland in his role as Mr. Secretary. That is, of course, Sir Robert Cecil . . . he is the one that emerges from these years as the chief manipulator and broker of political power. . . . Also beneficiaries of James' favors were the Walsinghams, Sir Thomas and Lady Audrey . . . .
> (333-34)

Perhaps faced with what he regards as a conclusion he dares not publish in England, Nicholl simply leaves it to the reader to arrive at the inescapable conclusion that it was Robert Cecil who was responsible for the violent end to the literary phenomenon that was Christopher Marlowe.

Works Cited

Anderson, Mark. *Shakespeare by Another Name*. New York, Gotham/Penguin, 2005.

Chambers, E.K. ed. *A History of the Elizabethan Stage. 4 vols*. Oxford UP, 1923.

Eccles, Mark. *Christopher Marlowe in London*. New York: Harvard UP, 1934.

Gurr, Andrew. *The Shakespeare Company: 1594-1642*. Cambridge UP, 2004.

Hart, Alfred. *Shakespeare and the Homilies*. (1934). New York, Octagon, 1977.

Harvey, Gabriel. *Foure Letters and Certaine Sonnets*. (1593). books.google.com.

Hoffman, Calvin. *The Murder of The Man Who Was Shakespeare*. New York, Messner, 1955.

Horne, David. *The Life and Minor Works of George Peele*. New Haven, Yale UP, 1952.

McMillin, Scott and Sally-Beth MacLean. *The Queen's Men and Their Plays*. Cambridge UP, 1998.

Nelson, Alan. *Monstrous Adversary*. Liverpool UP, 2003.

Nicholl, Charles. *The Reckoning, The Murder of Christopher Marlowe*. New York: Harcourt, 1992.

Read, Conyers. *Mr. Secretary Walsingham and the policy of Queen Elizabeth*. 3 vols. (1925). Hamden CT: Archon, 1967.

Ogburn, Charlton. *The Mysterious William Shakespeare*. New York, Dodd- Mead, 1984.

Ribner, Irving. "Greene's Attack on Marlowe: Some Light on Alphonsus and Selimus." *Studies in Philology 52*. (1955).

Riggs, David. *The World of Christopher Marlowe*. New York, Henry Holt, 2004.

Riggs, David. *Ben Jonson: A Life*. Cambridge, Harvard UP, 1989.

Smith, Irwin. *Shakespeare's Blackfriars Playhouse*. New York UP, 1964.

Spurgeon, Caroline. *Shakespeare's Imagery and what it tells us*. (1935). Cambridge UP, 1993.

Tannenbaum, Samuel. *The Assassination of Christopher Marlowe*. Hartford, 1926.

Williamson, Hugh Ross. *Kind Kit*. New York: St. Martin's Press, 1972.

Wraight, A.D. and Virginia Stern. *In Search of Christopher Marlowe*. New York, Vanguard, 1965.

Notes

1. The English Reformation that transformed the nation from Catholic to Protestant halfway through the 16th century, was a grim version of the Swiss or Calvinist form of Protestantism that eliminated all but a handful of the traditional holidays from the Church calendar leaving the public without the pleasures of their regular Saints Day feasts.

2. In the 1580s, the audience for plays was far greater than that for pamphlets since at that time it is estimated that only two to three percent of the population were literate.

3. The name William Shakespeare appears for the first time in a theatrical connection as one of the payees for the Lord Chamberlain's Men following their first season at Court, 1594-95. It had appeared in public for the first time two years earlier, in 1593, as a dedication on an inside page of *Venus and Adonis*, but only the tiny percentage of people who could read would have taken any notice.

4. The Dutton brothers who appear in leading positions in the developing theater scene of the early 1580s show connections to Oxford that are traceable at various points in the record. Lawrence Dutton was a payee for Oxford's company in 1580 (Chambers 2.100), John was a payee for the Queen's Men at their inception in 1583 (2.101), Lawrence joining later (2.107). Early versions of four of Shakespeare's early plays were produced by the Queen's Men plus a number of other early plays that would immediately be accepted as early Shakespeare were it not for the limitations imposed by Stratford-based dates.

5. In *Strange News of the Intercepting of Certain Letters* (1593) Nashe attempts to shame Harvey for his treatment of Robert Greene with the statement that Greene "would have drunk with thee for more angels than *the Lord thou libelst on gave thee in Christ's College*." This seeming non-sequitr was in response to Harvey's caricature of Oxford in his poem "Speculum Tuscanismo," published in 1580 in *Three Proper and witty . . . letters*. Harvey would defend himself later, claiming in *Foure Letters and Certaine Sonnets* (1593) that Oxford had taken the ribbing with Jovian aplomb, and that he had the right to address him since they'd been introduced by the son of Sir Thomas Smith, Harvey's patron and Oxford's old tutor (17). There are at least two similarly oblique references to Oxford in other Nashe pamphlets.

6. Oxford was clearly involved in the creation of the first two commercially successful public theaters in London, both having appeared shortly after his return from Italy in 1576: Burbage's big public stage in Shoreditch survived for 20 years, and the little rehearsal stage in the school for the Queen's Children of the Chapel known as the First Blackfriars Theater survived for 14 (Gurr Company 4).

7   That is, if, as we believe, he was the true author of plays like *Thomas of Woodstock*, *Edmund Ironside*, *King Leir and his Daughters*, or plays later attributed to Robert Greene such as *Friar Bacon*, *James IV*, *Friar Bacon and Friar Bungay*, or of *The Spanish Tragedy*, attributed to Kyd; or of the early quartos of Shakespeare's plays like *The Famous Victories*, the *True Tragedies*, the *True Contentions*, and many others.

8   As Spurgeon claims in her introduction, she embarked upon this painstaking and encyclopedic study on purpose to prove that neither of the claimants challenging William of Stratford at that time, Marlowe or Francis Bacon, could have been Shakespeare.

9   In his first words to the audience in *Tamburlaine*, Marlowe shows his disdain for the Queen's Men and the kind of humor that they were known for: "From jigging veins of rhyming mother-wits and such conceits *as clownage keeps in pay*, we'll lead you to the stately tent of war . . . ."

10 Their paths must have crossed on the stage of the Rose Theater in 1590-92, since plays by both writers were produced there within the same time period: Shakespeare's *Henry the Sixth* and *Titus Andronicus*, Marlowe's *Jew of Malta* and *Massacre at Paris*.

11 Lord Strange, heir to the Derby earldom, and Henry Percy, 9th Earl of Northumberland.

12 Largely due to the loss of his private papers, the orthodox view of Walsingham still sees him as little more than Elizabeth's "tough-fisted" spymaster, when in fact it was he who almost singly-handedly prepared England to defeat the Armada (Conyers Read). Walsingham was considered by the younger writers of the time as their Maecenas, their great patron, a facet of his biography almost totally ignored by historians.

13 One of our problems in connecting the plays in question with corresponding events is that the Academy treats history and literature as separate studies to the extent that almost no correspondence is ever drawn between the two, leaving history as little more than a dull recounting of dates, and literature as little more than myths and fables whose only external interest lies in which came first. This is unfortunate since literature could bring history to life and history could reveal the important role literature plays in human events.

14 The Dutton brothers, John and Lawrence, appear throughout this period in the role of payee and lead actor for companies either known to be Oxford's or as suggested by the available facts. Court scribes during this period rarely recorded the titles of plays, however there is one from the entry for that winter that records a play peformed "by the Earl of Oxenford his boys on St. John's day" (Chambers 4.160. F 365) titled *The History of Agamemnon and Ulysses*, which sug-

gests an early version of *Troilus and Cressida*.

15 That Oxford was writing for the Queen's Men at this time I believe will be borne out when the Stratford biography no longer blocks a clear view. Evidence that points in that direction include the fact that titles performed by the Queen's Men in the 1580s include several early versions of Shakespeare plays, among them: *The Famous Victories of Henry V*, *The Troublesome Reign of King John*, *The True Tragedy of Richard III*, and *King Leir* (McMillin 88-89).

16 Early versions of Shakespeare's history plays performed by the Queen's Men, created by Walsingham on purpose to tour the provinces, plays such as *The Famous Victories of Henry the Fifth* and *The Troublesome Raigne of King John* suggest propaganda meant to arouse patriotism in audiences along the southern coast where the Spanish would be most likely to land.

17 We cannot be certain that it's Marlowe, but the circumstantial evidence is impressive. It was discovered in a pile of rubble outside the Master's Lodge at Corpus Christi, Marlowe's college, in 1952. Now hanging in the Master's Lodge, it does provide a date: 1585, and the age of the sitter: twenty-one – Marlowe's age in 1585. More information on the portrait can be found in Nicholl's book and also in A.D. Wraight.

18 Gold buttons were a means of displaying the wealth of a gentleman. They were usually made with a metal loop on the back so a set like Marlowe's could be moved from little round button holes on one garment to those on another. Nicholl draws conclusions about Marlowe's personality from his pose and the size of his jacket, but this must be discounted since standard studio practice was to have the clothing painted by an apprentice. Marlowe having left the jacket with the artist, it would have been modelled by a clerk or another apprentice (the need to fill the space left on the canvas with just the arms and jacket would explain their out of scale size). That his hands are hidden has nothing to do with some aspect of his personality as Nicholl wants to believe; hands, being difficult to paint, would have added to the cost of the portrait. For the studio's leading artist to paint the entire portrait would have been very expensive.

19 In September 1589 records show that Marlowe was briefly jailed for having gotten into a sword fight in which another resident of Fisher's Folly, the poet Thomas Watson, also got involved (Watson *ODNB*). The fight occured on Hog Lane, a long winding road that ran past both the Curtain Theater and the rear entrance to Fisher's Folly.

20 *Alphonsus, King of Aragon, Selimus, Orlando Furioso,* and *A Looking Glass for London*, all somewhat Marlovian in style, were all produced by the Queen's Men sometime in the '80s (McMillin 91). Generally attributed either to George Peele or

Robert Greene, *Alphonsus* in particular has been labelled an attempt by Greene to beat Marlowe at his own game (Ribner).

21 Even Charles Nicholl, who so enthusiastically subscribes to the Marlowe-as-spy theory, admits: "The only record of [Marlowe's] early activities as an intelligencer is the certificate supplied by the Privy Council . . . in response to the particular problem of his MA" (110). But this says nothing about spying.

22 Coining and defecting were often linked because the catholics were supposedly desperate for money.

23 Since no one so far has ever come up with a background for "Gifford Gilbert," the purported coiner, the strong likelihood is that this was the same Gilbert Gifford who in the mid-'80s was central to the entrapment of Mary Queen of Scots and Anthony Babington. While evidence is cited for Gifford's death in a French prison in 1590, the name is simply too suggestive. If not Gifford himself, then it was someone who, for whatever reason, found it useful to call himself by this inversion of Gifford's name.

24 Breight agrees: "It makes little sense that Baines would inform on Marlowe if they were working together on some government operation" (152).

25 Nicholl makes it clear that the atheistic tract found (or planted) in Kyd's lodging was nothing more than a digest of Unitarian tenets copied from a book published many years earlier, and that the most inflamatory item in it was perhaps the notion that Jesus was a man of flesh and blood and not a supernatural being.

26 Having been incarcerated in 1597 for his involvement in *The Isle of Dogs*, Jonson mentions Poley later, as biographer Riggs suggests, as one of the "two damn'd villains" who entrapped him. Says Riggs, "the very mention of their names [by Jonson] reminds the reader that Jonson's liberty is imperilled by state-supported surveillance and repression" (Riggs, *Jonson: A Life*, 231).

27 Nicholl's persistent sleuthing reveals how all three men involved in Marlowe's death were connected with each other through previous government stings and confidence rackets. Missing is any evidence for a previous connection with Marlowe.

28 With the death of Secretary of State Walsingham, Robert Cecil inherits Thomas Walsingham along with the rest of his agents. As soon as Cecil receives his appointment, Thomas turns up at Court, is appointed Justice of the Peace, is knighted, is granted a visit by the Queen, and is made Member of Parliament for Rochester and granted the reversion of the keepership of the Great Park at Eltham. With the accession of James and the rise of Cecil to total power, further perks come Walsingham's way, largely it would seem through Cecil's relationship

with his wife (*ODNB*). A court record states that when she died she left the world "only her ill name" (Wraight 261).

29 Following Marlowe's death, various individuals saw to the publication under his name of translations of Ovid's *Amores*, of Lucan's *Pharsalia*, and the narrative poem *Hero and Leander*. The questionable histories of these works, the fact that none conform to the nature and style of Marlowe's plays, and that all are flagrantly in violation of either the sexual or political mores of the period, suggest that somebody simply made use of his name and his posthumous reputation to get them published. It would be immensely helpful to have this issue properly examined, as these attributions may well have distorted our perception of who Marlowe was.

30 Nicholl traces this animus against Raleigh and Northumberland through the various documents created to blacken Marlowe's reputation (291-93).

31 The Queen had run out of options; Sir Ralph Sadler had died in 1587, Leicester in '88, Walsingham in 1590, and Hatton in 1591. In her aging eyes, none of the younger men, none but Cecil that is, had the necessary experience.

32 As Alfred Hart shows in his *Shakespeare and the Homilies* (1934), there was an unwritten but nevertheless potent prohibition against portraying the downfall of an anointed monarch on the stage, evidence of which can be seen by the fact that during Elizabeth's reign *Richard II* was published in quarto three times without the deposition scene (Bullough 3.353); this because according to the Homily in question, required by law to be read aloud to the captive audience at Church once a year, to depose or kill an anointed monarch was a mortal sin that would inevitably bring down the wrath of God on the sinner and his entire community. Hart shows how faithfully Shakespeare conformed to this requirement throughout his career.

33 As reported by English Professor Chris Fitter and historians Barbara Freedman and Roger B. Manning, the 1590s were a violent period of political unrest.

34 Among the interesting gaps in the minutes of the Privy Council as noted by E.K. Chambers in *The Elizabethan Stage* (4.259), the period from August 1593 through October 1595, if intact, might have revealed something about Marlowe's assassination and certainly would have had something to say about what it was that caused two members of the Council to create the Lord Chamberlain's Men and the Lord Admiral's Men.

Essex, The Rival Poet
of Shakespeare's Sonnets

by Peter Moore

Shake-speares Sonnets appeared in 1609, apparently published without the author's consent, and probably suppressed by the authorities as they were not republished until 1640. There are 154 sonnets; the first 126 address a young aristocrat, commonly called the Fair Youth, with whom Shakespeare was infatuated – though whether the motivation was sexual is quite unclear. I join the majority who believe it was not. The next 26 describe Shakespeare's relations with his unfaithful mistress, the Dark Lady. These sonnets were apparently written during rather than after the fair youth series, and so Sonnet 126 may be taken as the closing poem. Sonnets 78 to 86 concern a rival poet who competed with Shakespeare for the affections of the fair youth. Sonnets 153 and 154 are an unrelated finial.

The principal questions about the *Sonnets* are the identities of the fair youth, the dark lady, and the rival poet, the dates of their composition, the problem of whether their 1609 order is correct, and what, if any, topical allusions are found in them. This article supports the consensus that the fair youth was Henry Wriothesley, third Earl of Southampton, a vain and reckless young man who, following a treason conviction and two years of imprisonment, matured into a model husband, a courageous champion of Parliamentary rights, and a hard working patron and director of the Virginia colony. He was born in 1573 and died on campaign in the Netherlands in 1624. Shakespeare's only dedications (of *Venus and Adonis* in 1593 and *The Rape of Lucrece* in 1594) were written to Southampton. No substantial candidate has emerged for the role of the dark lady. The most often proposed rival poets are George Chapman and Christopher Marlowe, but the arguments for them are thin. Even weaker cases have been offered for virtually every other contemporary professional poet. The conventional wisdom is that the *Sonnets* were begun in the early or mid-1590s and continue past the death of Queen Elizabeth and the advent of King James in 1603 (which events are referred to in Sonnet 107). This series of articles will argue that the conventional wisdom is correct. As has been indicated, I also feel that within the two subseries (Sonnets 1 to 126 and 127 to 154), the *Sonnets* are in the right order.

And now to the rival poet.

Robert Devereux, the second Earl of Essex, was the brilliant but flawed star of the late Elizabethan firmament. He was the Queen's most illustrious (though not her best) military and naval commander during the 1590s. He was her last great favorite and he attempted to take over her government from the astute and cautious dynasty of William Cecil, Lord Burghley and his son Robert. Desperation and mental instability led him into a botched coup that cost him his head in February 1601. He was intelligent, handsome, athletic, improvident, charming, a generous patron of writers, a commander of real talent, a confirmed womanizer, a devout Protestant who leaned toward Puritanism, a ditherer on several critical occasions, and a dangerously unstable egotist who finally lost touch with reality. He was also the best friend and hero of the youthful third Earl of Southampton. He was also a poet whose talent was admired by his contemporaries.

Essex exerted a major gravitational force on his age and he influenced William Shakespeare, who praised Essex in *Henry V*. Contemporaries also saw a resemblance, intended or not, between Essex and Bolingbroke in *Richard II*. It has plausibly been suggested that *Love's Labour's Lost* had something to do with Essex's circle, that the description of Cawdor's execution in *Macbeth* evokes the death of Essex, and that

---

Author Note: My research on the *Sonnets* resulted in a series of four articles. This one, the first of them, demonstrates why Robert Devereux, 2nd Earl of Essex, was the rival poet of Sonnets 78 to 86. The second shows that Sonnets 78 to 100 can be dated quite firmly to events in the life of the Earl of Southampton between his return from the Azores voyage in late 1597 and his departure for Ireland in early 1599. The third article discusses the implications of the first two articles with regard to the authorship controversy and will bring the 17th Earl of Oxford into the picture (particularly with regard to some of the later Sonnets). The fourth and concluding article argues that the *Sonnets* as published in 1609 are in the right order. It is partly motivated by original material, but also by the fact that most learned commentators believe the question of the order of the *Sonnets* is one of subjective literary judgment. In fact, there exist a number of completely objective, non-judgmental reasons for believing that the *Sonnets* are properly ordered.

Peter Moore *established himself as a scholar of the Renaissance in England by contributing articles to six peer-reviewed journals in Europe and the United States between 1993 and 2006. He was a professional military officer, graduating from the University of Maryland with a degree in engineering and achieving the rank of lieutenant colonel in the US Army. This article is reprinted from from his collected essays, edited by Gary Goldstein and published posthumously under the title* The Lame Storyteller, Poor and Despised *by Verlag Uwe Laugwitz in 2009. It is available in paperback and as an e-book via Amazon.com.*

"The Phoenix and the Turtle" glorifies Essex's love for Elizabeth. Above all, Essex appears in books about Shakespeare as the hero of Southampton, Shakespeare's sole dedicatee. There are more than ten good reasons for proposing Essex as the rival of the *Sonnets*, and, in Ben Jonson's words, "I therefore will begin."

First, Sonnets 78 to 86 describe a man who was Shakespeare's rival for the affections of Southampton during the 1590s. The man who is known to have had Southampton's affection during that period was the heroic and charismatic Earl of Essex. Southampton attempted to serve under Essex in the Cadiz expedition of 1596, but was forbidden by the Queen; he did serve under and was knighted by Essex on the Azores expedition of 1597. Southampton sought Essex's counsel when in financial difficulties, agreed to marry Essex's penniless cousin (whom he had gotten with child) in 1598, and named his daughter after Essex's sister. During the failed Irish campaign of 1599, Essex made Southampton his General of the Horse and was furious when Queen Elizabeth vetoed his decision.

In December 1599 Essex was near death with fever and wrote Southampton a moving letter of counsel. This letter, published in Thomas Birch's *Memoirs of the Reign of Queen Elizabeth*, holds several points of interest. Like Shakespeare's Sonnets 2 and 4, it addresses Southampton in terms of the parable of the talents (Matthew 25). It also contains the following passage, which confirms that on some previous occasion Essex eulogized Southampton: "What I think of your natural gifts... to give glory to God, and to win honour to yourself... I will not now tell you. It sufficeth, that when I was farthest of all times from dissembling, I spoke freely, and had witnesses enough."[1]

Southampton was Essex's right-hand man during the 1601 uprising, and they were tried and sentenced together; they kissed hands and embraced at the start of the trial, and Essex did what he could to protect Southampton. Both were adjudged to die, but Southampton was spared, though deprived of titles, estates, and liberty.

Second, Essex was rated a gifted poet by his contemporaries and was admired as a writer by Ben Jonson (who called him "noble and high") and as a critic by Gabriel Harvey. Essex's friend and sometime secretary Sir Henry Wotton wrote that it was "his common way . . . to evaporate his thoughts in a Sonnet." Essex wrote poems for specific occasions. Rather than out of any dedication to poetry, he penned his verses only for his own circle and the Queen, so little of his poetry survives. Thus the puzzling disappearance of the poems of Shakespeare's rival is quite understandable if Essex wrote them. Rival poems by a professional like Chapman should have survived.

Essex's verse is hardly in a class with Shakespeare's, nor is it close, but it is technically accomplished, sincere, and moving. It may be protested that Essex's talent was so slender that Shakespeare could not possibly have regarded him as a rival, but this objection ignores the fact that the rivalry lay in the eyes of Southampton and not in the views of literary critics. Any poetic praise from Essex was bound to make Southampton ecstatic, given his idolization of Essex. This is a sufficient answer to the objection, but two lesser points may be added. First, *Shakespeare's Sonnets* contain criticism that may not have been welcome to Southampton, e.g., "thou dost common grow" (69, 14). Next, Southampton was quite an active young man in the 1590s: a jouster, athlete, gambler, patron, womanizer, brawler, and above all, a would-be warrior who finally got his chance and distinguished himself on the Azores voyage. But Shakespeare's praise is all of passive qualities such as being fair and beauteous. His poetics may endlessly fascinate, but his subject matter can be tedious. Praise of Southampton's martial prowess by the great Essex might have been more agreeable.[2]

Third, the rival is said to be "learned" (78, 7); it is implied that he knew the art of rhetoric, a major academic subject in those days (82, 10), and he had a "polished form of well-refined pen" (85, 8). Essex received his MA from Cambridge in his mid-teens, maintained a lifelong interest in intellectual matters, and surrounded himself with educated men.

Fourth and fifth, the rival was "of tall building and of goodly pride" (80, 12), and his pride is further alluded to in Sonnet 86. Several contemporaries recorded that Essex was notably tall. His pride was inordinate even by the standards of Elizabethan nobility – it consumed and finally destroyed him.

Sixth, Shakespeare contrasts himself to his mighty rival with much nautical metaphor in Sonnets 80 and 86. Shakespeare is a "saucy bark" (80, 7), while the rival is "the proudest sail" (80, 6) whose "great verse" is called "the proud full sail" (86, 1). So we may suppose that the rival was something of a sailor. Essex distinguished himself on the Lisbon voyage of 1589, won further glory as co-commander of the 1596 Cadiz expedition, and was sole commander of the ill-managed Azores venture of 1597. (Essex unjustly placed the blame on his Rear Admiral, Sir Walter Raleigh).[3]

Seventh, Sonnet 86 says that the rival has an "affable familiar ghost/Which nightly gulls him with intelligence" (lines 9-10). Seekers of the rival poet always take this passage as indicating occult practices and try to show that their candidates were up to such activities. The task is not difficult, as almost everyone back then was more or less superstitious by modern standards, but a far more mundane explanation is available. Essex maintained his own international intelligence service as part of his rivalry with the Cecils, who commanded the official intelligence agency. It was Essex's aim to be better informed than the government and to be the first to tell the Queen of foreign events. Essex's chief of intelligence was the erudite Anthony Bacon, who had friends all over Europe and who lived in Essex's mansion in the Strand from 1595 to 1600.

Thus, without conjuring up necromancers and astrologers, we find the affable familiar ghost: an intelligence director whose greatest asset was his legion of overseas friends (hence, *affable*), and who lived as part of Essex's household (a *familiar* in the old-fashioned sense). *Ghost* is appropriate for a man who was active behind the scenes, but who suffered from so many ailments (dying in 1601) that he became a virtual recluse after moving to Essex House and was forced to decline invitations from the Queen to present himself at Court.

Eighth, the rival was a "spirit, by spirits taught to write" (86, 5), and had friends "giving him aid" (86, 8). Various people are believed to have assisted Essex with his writing, including his personal secretary Henry Cuffe, an occasional poet and former professor of Greek, Anthony Bacon, who is known to have written some sonnets, and Lord Henry Howard (later Earl of Northampton), a part-time consultant of Essex's. It is perfectly possible that Essex received aid from the professional poets he patronized, including George Chapman, in which case some of the other rival poet theories would be part right. But there is one poet who is known to have ghost-written serious essays and also a masque for Essex: Anthony Bacon's brother Francis.

Ninth, we can find support for the new theory of the Bacons as the rival poet's ghost writers by considering some word play in the passage, "affable familiar ghost/ Which nightly gulls him with intelligence." *Ghost* and *gulls* are linked by alliteration, but also by the superstition (prevalent then and now) that gulls are inhabited by the ghosts of drowned sailors. *Gulls* is thus a bridge between the two sets of imagery, nautical and ghostly, used in Sonnet 86. These words also harbor an appropriate Latin pun (all of the principals mentioned in this article were fluent in Latin), since the Latin for familiar ghost is *Lar* or *Lans*, usually encountered in its plural form *Lares*: the Latin for ghost or spectre is *larva*. The Latin for gull is *larus*; the modern scientific name for the gull family is *Laridae*. The Latin for bacon is variously *laridum, lardum*, or *larida*. It may be added that making puns, anagrams, and acrostics on names was a popular sport in that age.

Tenth comes the following passage on the rival: "He lends thee virtue, and he stole that word/From thy behavior" (79, 9-10). Essex's mottoes were Virtutis Com Invidia (literally *virtue with envy* or, more loosely *manliness draws envy*) and Basis Virtutum Constantia (*loyalty [is] the basis of virtue or manliness*).

The remaining items of evidence concern not only the identity of the rival, but also the question of the dates of the rival poet sonnets. My hypothesis is that Sonnets 78 to 86 were written soon after Essex and Southampton returned from the Azores in late October 1597.

Eleventh, despite objections by William Shakespeare, cosmetics were used by men as well as women in the Elizabethan Age. Judging by contemporary poetry, the fashionable complexion consisted of a face as white as lilies, a touch of roses in the cheeks, and lips like rubies (teeth were usually compared to pearls). Those not blessed by nature with such an appearance could paint their faces with white lead and redden their lips and cheeks with rouge. Sonnet 82 ("And their gross painting might be better used/Where cheeks need blood; in thee it is abus'd" lines 13-14) and Sonnet 83 ("I never saw that you did painting need" line 1) disparagingly associate the rival with the use of cosmetics.

There are two portraits of Essex in the National Portrait Gallery in London, both believed to have been painted around 1597. In any event, they are later than August 1596, as Essex is wearing the beard grown on the Cadiz voyage. One is a full-length portrait of Essex standing in the robes of a Knight of the Garter; it is reproduced in color in *National Portrait Gallery in Colour*, edited by Richard Ormond, who dates the portrait circa 1597. The other is a head and shoulders portrait of Essex in a white satin doublet (he wears the same garment in the standing portrait), with a ruff over a transparent collar over a wide blue ribbon that suspends his St. George medal. It is reproduced in color in *The Horizon Book of the Elizabethan World*, by Lacey Baldwin Smith and bears the date 1597. During the early part of that year, Essex would have had something of a tan left over from his several months at sea during the summer of 1596. During the latter part of 1597, Essex would have been bronzed by his voyage to the Azores. However, the standing portrait shows Essex with a ghastly pallor; his face has obviously been painted white and his lips have probably been carmined as well. The head and shoulders portrait shows him with lips of a bright, artificial red, unquestionably carmined, and a face that is not quite as pallid as in the other portrait, but that is far too pale for a man who had been making summer voyages to the latitude of southern Spain.

Yet Essex had another link to cosmetics at that time. At the beginning of 1598, the Queen gave him all of the available stock of cochineal, partly as an outright gift and partly by selling it to him at a reduced price. She then banned any further imports for two years; the total profit to Essex was reportedly the immense sum of £40,000. Cochineal is a bright red dye used then for textiles but also for painting the lips and cheeks. The two portraits of Essex are of around 1597, and the Elizabethan year 1597 was, by modern reckoning, April 4, 1597 to April 3, 1598, so the two portraits may show Essex wearing his own product. In short, Shakespeare simultaneously complains about the rival poet and face paint, while Essex used cosmetics and had a monopoly on rouge.

Twelfth is Shakespeare's assertion in the nautical Sonnet 80 (lines 3-4) that his rival "spends all his might/...speaking of your [Southampton's] fame." Hyperbolic praise was common in Elizabethan poetry, but the first incident in Southampton's career that would reasonably justify lauding his fame was his return from the Azores in late October 1597 with a knighthood and the spoils of one of the few prizes taken on that voyage.

We also know that Southampton's success was exaggerated. The prize that he looted and abandoned was quite small, but one courtier sent a friend the following information. "This morning my Lord Essex's letters came to court of his safe landing in Plymouth. He had unfortunately missed the (Spanish) King's own ships with the Indian Treasure but fell on the merchant fleet. Four of them he hath taken, and sunk many more, my Lord of Southampton fought with one of the King's great Men of War, and sunk her." So it appears that Essex was indeed puffing the fame of the fair youth.

Thirteenth, the theme of Sonnet 79 may be stated as follows: "You [the fair youth] owe the rival poet no thanks for his praise, because he is simply repaying his debt to you." A partisan of Southampton's who was resentful of Essex could very well make such an argument in the wake of the Azores expedition, in which the value of the loot was far less than the cost of the voyage. The five prizes taken kept the expedition from being a total failure, and one of them was seized by Southampton while his ship was detached from the fleet. So Shakespeare would feel justified in telling Southampton that Essex was simply giving him his due by knighting and praising him.

Fourteenth, and rather tenuously, we may note Shakespeare's remark in the same sonnet that "my sick Muse doth give another place" (79, 4). This line may be paraphrased in two ways, either "my sick Muse yields to another Muse," or "my sick Muse yields to another sick Muse." It is impossible to be certain as to whether the pronoun *another* includes the adjective *sick* as well as the noun *Muse*, but such a reference would be highly appropriate. When Essex returned from the Azores he found that the Queen blamed him for the expedition's failure and that two of his rivals at court had stolen marches on him during his absence. He responded by shutting himself up in his house for several weeks, claiming to be ill. So Shakespeare would be quite justified in implying that his rival's muse is sick.

Shakespeare's Sonnets describe a rival who was Southampton's friend, a poet, learned, tall, proud, probably a sailor, who had an affable familiar ghost who dealt in intelligence, who received assistance in his writing from friends, whose name makes a plausible Latin pun on Bacon, who was associated with the word *virtue* and with cosmetics, who boosted Southampton's fame while being in his debt, and who could be said to have a sick muse. This is quite a detailed portrait, and Essex matches it perfectly.

Notes

1. Thomas Birch, *Memoirs of the Reign of Queen Elizabeth*. London, A. Millar, 1754. p. 484.

2. The most recent and thorough analysis of Essex's surviving poems is in "The Poems of Edward DeVere, Seventeenth Earl of Oxford and of Robert Devereux, Second Earl of Essex," by Steven W. May, *Studies in Philology*, LXXVII, Early Winter 1980, No. 5.

3. If the arguments offered in this article in favor of Essex as the rival are applied one by one to Sir Walter Raleigh, it will be seen that a surprisingly strong case can be made for him as the rival poet. At any rate, the case for Raleigh is far superior to the arguments that have been offered in favor of Chapman, Marlowe, or any other professional poet. I mention this not to suggest Raleigh as a backup candidate behind Essex, but to underscore the dereliction of orthodox Shakespeare scholars. The courtier poets of the Elizabethan Age held high prestige, while the leading candidates for the role of Shakespeare's fair youth (Southampton and the Earl of Pembroke) were both courtiers. Yet it never occurred to the Shakespeare establishment that the rival poet might be a courtier.

The Rival Poet
in Shake-speare's Sonnets

by Hank Whittemore

The identity of the Rival Poet of the Shakespeare sonnets, who appears within the span of verses numbered 78 to 86, has seemed to elude Stratfordians and Oxfordians alike. The orthodox model has allowed us to view this series in just one way – that among the other poets there is one flesh-and-blood figure, towering above them all, who is stealing the attentions and affections of the Fair Youth,[1] who is generally regarded as Henry Wriothesley, third Earl of Southampton.[2]

When J. Thomas Looney expresses his agreement in *"Shakespeare" Identified* that the beloved younger man was Southampton, he points to the rival series (sonnets 78 to 86) as powerful evidence. First, he cites Sonnet 81: "Your name from hence immortal life shall have" and notes that this immortality would be achieved by means of the younger earl's unique association with William Shakespeare. Second, Looney cites the companion verse, Sonnet 82: "The dedicated words which writers use/ Of their fair subject, blessing every book" and notes that Oxford was referring to his own public dedications to Southampton of *Venus and Adonis* (1593) and *Lucrece* (1594) as by William Shakespeare (Looney, 440).

Given the premise that Southampton is the friend or fair youth, Stratfordians have postulated many rivals – Barnes, Chapman, Chaucer, Daniel, Davies, Davison, Drayton, Florio, Golding, Greene, Griffin, Harvey, Jonson, Kyd, Lyly, Markham, Marlowe, Marston, Nashe, Peele, Spenser, the Italian Tasso, and Watson. Oxfordians have come up with some overlaps, such as Chapman and Marlowe, while adding the likes of Raleigh and the Earl of Essex. In 1952, Dorothy and Charlton Ogburn Sr. thought the *rival,* a word never used in the Sonnets, was both Chapman and Marlowe (893-94). In 1984, their son Charlton Ogburn Jr. merely referred to "one other poet, whose identity I must leave to the contention of more confident minds" (328).

The late Peter Moore made a well-researched and detailed Oxfordian case for Essex, summing it up this way: "*Shake-speare's Sonnets* describes a rival who was Southampton's friend, a poet, learned, tall, proud, probably a sailor, who had an affable familiar ghost who dealt in intelligence, who received assistance in his writing from friends, who was associated with the word *virtue* and with cosmetics, and who boosted Southampton's fame while being in his debt. This is quite a detailed portrait, and Essex matches it perfectly" (Moore 10).

The Stratfordian view has required the rival poet to be some other individual who wrote poetry and publicly used Southampton's name. From the vantage point of the Oxfordian view, however, I have come to a much different – and even radical – solution to the other writer's identity.

To begin, the Oxfordian model opens the door to an entirely new way of looking at the nine sonnets in the rival series, resulting in the possibility that the rival poet was none of those individuals. In fact, this paper argues that the rival was not a *person* at all, but a *persona*. In other words, the rival series contains Oxford's own testimony about the authorship – a grand, poetic, profoundly emotional statement of his identity as the author being erased for all time and replaced by the printed name known since 1593 as William Shakespeare. In this context, the sonnets about a so-called rival refer not to Oxford's original use of the pseudonym in 1593, but rather to the need several years later for his real name – his authorship – to be permanently *buried* (Sonnet 72, line 11). In this, we don't need to be overly concerned about the nature of the relationship between de Vere and Wriothesley.[3]

The Stratfordian view provides no reason or motive to look for any kind of authorship statement anywhere, much less in the rival series. Oxfordians contend precisely that Oxford has split himself (metaphorically) into two separate entities. On the one hand, he's Edward de Vere, writing privately or secretly in the sonnets. On the other hand, he's Shakespeare, the name on the page.[4] According to the theory of Oxford as the author, he is pictured as deciding early on to write anonymously or under different names – that is, to hide behind fictitious names or the names of real persons. Meanwhile Oxfordians too, have been led by tradition to take it for granted that the rival must be some real individual. From Looney onward, supporters of the earl's authorship have pictured him as having created his own rival – of a quite different sort – in the form of a new pseudonym, on the 1593-94 dedications of *Venus and Adonis*

Hank Whittemore *is an actor, author, television writer, magazine journalist, and longtime Oxfordian. In addition to ten books published by major houses, he has self-published several Oxfordian books including* The Monument *(2005) and his current* 100 Reasons Why Oxford Was "Shakespeare" *(October 2016). Whittemore has also contributed many articles to Oxfordian publications and made numerous presentations at conferences. He has performed his one-man show* Shake-Speare's Treason, *co-written with director Ted Story, at venues across the US and in the UK and Canada, often discussing the authorship question with general-audience members as well as students. He continues writing entries for his online site* Hank Whittemore's Shakespeare Blog.

This essay is based on a presentation made at the 2013 Shakespeare Authorship Studies Conference at Concordia University in Portland, Oregon. It was first printed in the collection A Poet's Rage *(2013), edited by William Boyle. The argument set forth here – newly adapted and augmented for* The Oxfordian *– is part of the author's complete 900-page study of the Sonnets,* The Monument *(2005).*

and *Lucrece* to Southampton.

In the minds of Stratfordians, or readers with no knowledge or suspicion of a hidden author, that pen name can only take the form of a real person – as it certainly has over the past centuries. But is that necessary, or is it even logical, as part of the Oxfordian theory?

If not for automatically carrying old Stratfordian baggage, would Oxfordians postulate a flesh-and-blood rival within the Sonnets? If not pulled by the weight and force of tradition, would we not realize, or at least suspect, that the earl is referring to his secret identity as Shakespeare? After all, that's the name on those dedications to Southampton, which continued to appear in new editions of the narrative poems. It was the word *Shakespeare* that became publicly identified with Southampton, and, therefore, it was the name that received all public credit for making such a remarkable pledge to the young earl: "The love I dedicate to your Lordship is without end … What I have done is yours, what I have to do is yours, being part in all I have, devoted yours."[5]

The Monument

My take on the so-called rival began with Edward de Vere's authorship combined with the chronological context offered in my book *The Monument* (2005), which describes a macro theory of the language and structure of the 154 consecutively numbered sonnets as printed in 1609. The theory began with the premise that the entire sequence comprises a single, unified masterwork of related parts, each contributing to the whole "monument" of verse intended for posterity. The author tells Southampton in Sonnet 81, lines 9 and 10: "Your monument shall be my gentle verse / Which eyes not yet created shall o'er-read." In Sonnet 107, in lines 13 and 14, he uses this image again: "And thou in this shalt find thy monument / When tyrants' crests and tombs of brass are spent."

Shake-speare's Sonnets contains one hundred centrally-positioned sonnets – a century from #27 to #126 – that correspond with circumstances during 1601-03. Of those hundred, eighty sonnets (#27 to #106) were written about Southampton's imprisonment for his leadership role in the Essex Rebellion of February 8, 1601. There are also twenty sonnets (#107 to #126) that address Southampton. The first nineteen cover the nineteen days from his release on April 10, 1603 (#107) to Elizabeth's funeral procession on April 28, 1603 (#125). Finally, the twentieth sonnet (#126) serves as an envoi of farewell.

"The most startling aspect of the new picture," I wrote, "was the emergence of exactly eighty chronological sonnets – more than half the collection – addressed to Henry Wriothesley, third Earl of Southampton during the more than two years (1601-1603) he spent imprisoned in the Tower of London as a condemned traitor, after which, following the death of Queen Elizabeth, he was inexplicably released by the new monarch, James I of England" (Whittemore, xi).

In this context, Oxford agreed to sacrifice his identity as Shakespeare on a permanent basis in 1601, after Southampton was found guilty of high treason and sentenced to death. The younger earl's key role in the rebellion was his *crime* to which Oxford refers in sonnet 58: "…to you it doth belong / Yourself to pardon of self-doing crime" (11-12) and in sonnet 120: "To weigh how once I suffered in your crime" (8).

At some point in the development of the Monument theory, prior to publication, I realized that no contemporary writer was publicly addressing, much less praising, Southampton while he was legally "the late Earl" in the Tower.[6] It finally dawned on me that, during the two years and two months while he was facing, at first, execution and then, perpetual confinement, no rival poet could have been competing for his attention or affections. In the context of this chronology, there was no flesh-and-blood rival.

At the same time, however, the Shakespeare of those dedications was still prominently pledging his endless love and support for Southampton. Paradoxically, Oxford had created his own rival to be the poet known for his commitment to Southampton.

The Sacrifice

The testimony of Sonnets 78-86 is that Oxford's hope for being identified even posthumously as the one behind Shakespeare is fading away and that, once Oxford disappears "to all the world," he will also be replaced as the author permanently (so far as can be predicted) by the persona of Shakespeare.[7] In Sonnets 78 to 86 he is primarily speaking of his own invention or creation in the form of a pen name. By the end of this series, the writer de Vere is supplanted for all time by a "character" who writes and is published. The creation of such an *alter ego* would certainly be within the abilities of a dramatist who populated his plays with characters for the stage, as a matter of course.

In the sonnets immediately preceding the rival series, he appears to link the disappearance of his name to Southampton. In Sonnet 71, he pleads with the younger earl:

> When I perhaps compounded am with clay,
> Do not so much as *my poor name* rehearse.
> (10-11, emphasis added)

In Sonnet 72, he speaks of the death of his name and hints at its connection to Southampton:

> *My name* be buried where my body is,
> And live no more to shame nor me nor you.
>
> (11-12, emphasis added)

When the rival series begins with Sonnet 78, he appears to glance at other contemporary writers in lines 3-4: "As every *Alien* pen hath got my use / And under thee their poesy doth disperse."[8] *Every* in the first line above may represent Oxford identifying himself as *E. Ver.* The phrase *Alien pen* seems to refer to those other poets who have praised Southampton, such as Thomas Nashe, who dedicated his book *The Unfortunate Traveller, or the Life of Jack Wilton* to Wriothesley in 1593. But it is E. Ver's pen name (Shakespeare) that is alien, in the sense that it's not his real name. Of course, Oxford's secret identity or alter ego must have been very much part of his being, so it could not have been very much *alien* to him.

In the next sonnet he begins to lament his figurative loss of power. Anything written under his own identity is *decayed* and *sick* as it stands aside to make way for Shakespeare. In the process he is fainting and becoming tongue-tied.

> But now my gracious numbers are decayed,
> And my sick Muse doth give an other place.
>
> Sonnet 79, 3-4[9]

> O how I faint when I of you do write,
> Knowing a better spirit doth use your name,
> And in the praise thereof spends all his might
> To make me tongue-tied speaking of your fame.
>
> Sonnet 80, 1-4

In my view his *faint* in Sonnet 80 is a metaphor that describes the fading of de Vere's identity behind the new identity of Shakespeare, who has given Southampton fame by dedicating his work to him – and whose popularity serves to continue promoting the younger earl. Oxford is also feinting, or deceiving – and exercising the feint of a skilled fencer – by assuming an appearance or making a feint to conceal his real identity. He faints by becoming figuratively weaker, feebler – in other words – less visible, while Shakespeare takes his place. In fact, the final two words of sonnet 80 are *my decay*. Although this has nothing to do with losing his powers as a writer, it could be that the pen name gave him a renewed sense of power with the pen. As for calling his pen name *a better spirit*, I believe he's referring to his own mental and creative powers, which are being used – ghostlike – in the service of the Shakespeare works.

Back in Sonnet 66, at line 9 his art has been "made tongue-tied by authority." His work was being censored, suppressed, in the sense that he could not write openly and directly, as himself. The force keeping him silent is authority or officialdom, the government, as when he writes in *King John* of the monarch's "sovereign greatness and authority" (5.1.4). In Sonnet 80, he extends the same thought; it is the rival poet or Shakespeare that makes him "tongue-tied speaking of your fame." So Oxford's own pen name is now the unwilling agent of *authority* – the means by which he, the true author, is being silenced – not as a poet or dramatist per se, but in terms of his ability to write the truth directly.

This censorship would now obstruct his ability to tell what happened as a result of the failed rebellion in February 1601. In my view, he is aware that those who won the political struggle to control the succession and who will deliver the throne of England to a foreign king, will also get to write their version of history.[10] Therefore, he is attempting to tell some of his side of the story in the *Sonnets*, which will be attributed to "Shake-speare" on the title page.

"I, once gone, to all the world must die."

Here the door starts opening to a larger and more important story than merely Oxford disappearing forever – and doing so for no apparent reason. Again, back in Sonnet 66, Oxford cited "strength by limping sway disabled." The government, in the person of the figure who may be identified as limping, swaying – Robert Cecil, a hunchback – is using Oxford's pen name or persona Shakespeare as a weapon against him (Wilson 171).[11]

Oxford also comments in Sonnet 80, lines 7-8: "My saucy bark, inferior far to his / On your broad main doth willfully appear." Steven Booth writes that *willfully* "may have been chosen for its pun on the poet's name: the saucy bark is full of Will" (Booth, 274). It could just as easily be a pun on the poet's *pen* name. Now in Sonnet 81 come those two lines which for Oxfordians comprise clear evidence of an authorship question: "Your name from hence immortal life shall have / Though I (once gone) to all the world must die." Within the context suggested here, it's no accident that these lines appear within the rival poet sequence. Southampton's name will achieve immortal life, presumably because of the public dedications, which are the only such epistles the great author will ever offer to anyone. By the same token, also because of the pen name, the author's real name or identity will disappear from *all the world* for the foreseeable future.

In the next sonnet, number 82, Oxford makes apparent reference to the public dedications that Looney had identified:

> I grant thou wert not married to my Muse,
> And therefore mayst without attaint o'erlook
> The *dedicated words* which writers use
> Of their *fair subject*, blessing every *book*.
>
> (emphasis added)

My interpretation of the last two lines is: they refer to "the dedications I wrote under the Shakespeare name about the fair youth, Southampton, which are *blessing* the books *Venus and Adonis* and *Lucrece*." Sonnet 82 also contains a remarkable pair of lines in which Oxford appears to be playing upon his motto *Nothing Truer than Truth*, as if still insisting upon his own identity before any chance of it ever being revealed disappears completely:[12] "Thou truly fair wert truly sympathized / In true-plain words by thy true-telling friend."

By calling the younger man *fair*, he appears to link him to the *fair subject* of the dedications mentioned earlier in the same sonnet, and since we know for a fact that Southampton was the subject of those public epistles, we now have what appears to be strong confirmation within these lines that the younger earl is also the subject of the *Sonnets*. Oxford is *dumb* or *mute* in Sonnet 83, because he is unable to speak in public: "Which shall be most my glory, being *dumb* / For I impair not beauty, being *mute*" (emphasis added). As he ends sonnet 83, he refers to *both* poets writing to Southampton, that is, both himself and his pen name: "There lives more life in one of your fair eyes / Than both your poets can in praise devise."

In sonnet 84, he addresses the younger earl and appears to turn his alter ego (Shakespeare) into a fictional character by explaining how this other poet should write about him:

> Let him but copy what in you is writ,
> Not making worse what nature made so clear,
> And such a counterpart shall fame his wit,
> Making his style admired everywhere.

In sonnet 85 we read a further allusion to his personal silence: "Then others, for the breath of words respect / Me for my dumb thoughts, speaking in effect."

Sonnet 86, the final poem in the rival poet series, and therefore the most potentially important of them all, tells the whole story, beginning with the first quatrain:

> Was it the proud full sail of his great verse,[13]
> Bound for the prize of (all too precious) you,
> That did *my* ripe thoughts in *my* brain inhearse,
> Making their tomb the womb wherein they grew?
>   (emphasis added)

Clearly Oxford was well aware of the power and the popularity of the writing he had published under his pen name. "Bound for the prize of (all too precious) you" seems to be directed at Southampton, but the pen name is the means by which his own identity will be obliterated and his future public recognition denied. On the other hand, his real thoughts and feelings still live within these private sonnets, in which he refers to "my ripe thoughts in my brain."

In some sense the name Shakespeare conceals a disembodied "spirit" that might refer to Oxford's own creativity and genius, which infuses the literary and dramatic works with their extraordinary range of information, ideas and emotions. Again, in lines 5 and 6 of sonnet 86, the final one in the rival series:

> Was it his spirit, by spirits taught to write
> Above a mortal pitch, that struck *me* dead?
> (emphasis added)

Oxford knows his works soar above those of *mortal* poets and playwrights, and while "struck me dead" might sound like a reference to the killing of Christopher Marlowe in May 1593,[14] in this context it becomes a metaphorical death – a description of relinquishing any and all future claim to the authorship of his works. His only escape hatch, if you will, is that the Shakespeare works, because of the dedications, will always be linked uniquely to Southampton. Lines 7 through 12 of sonnet 86 seem to allude to both the Shakespeare name and Oxford's political enemies:

> No, neither he, nor his compeers by night
> Giving him aid, my verse astonished.
> He, nor that affable familiar ghost
> Which nightly gulls him with intelligence,
> As victors of my silence cannot boast;
> I was not sick of any fear from thence.

The "affable familiar ghost" is once again Oxford's own creative force and spirit, which "nightly" or secretly (as though in darkness, invisibly) crams "Shakespeare" with his substance, or perhaps literally with "intelligence," which sounds like the kind of information gathered by the secret service. It may also refer to sensitive information that Oxford is inserting within the lines of his plays as well. To "gull" is to cram full. Sonnet 86 ends thus: "But when your countenance filled up his line / Then lacked I matter, that enfeebled mine." The final couplet can be viewed as another statement of the authorship problem: as the pen name Shakespeare continues to gain fame in connection with Southampton, so Oxford fades away – as Touchstone in *As You Like It* tells William the country fellow: "Drink, being poured out of a cup into a glass, by filling the one doth empty the other" (5.1.41-43).

The rival series should be viewed as a separate piece within the larger structure of the 100-sonnet century. The central message of Sonnets 78-86 can perhaps be expressed in a line or two, but the sequence can also be seen as a much longer and more drawn-out pledge by Oxford to sacrifice himself for Southampton's life – that is, freedom from execution – and ultimate liberation from the Tower (if Robert Cecil succeeds in bringing James of Scotland to the throne).

The element of sacrifice had begun much earlier, for example in Sonnet 34:

> Though thou repent, yet I have still the loss;
> The offender's sorrow lends but weak relief
> To him that bears the strong offence's *loss*
> [emphasis added, usually emended to *cross*]¹⁵

Sacrifice is a theme in sonnet 36 as well: "So shall those blots that do with me remain / Without thy help, by me be borne alone." It appears in the Christian imagery of sonnet 42: "Lay on me this cross."

When the rival series begins with Sonnet 78, Oxford appears to confirm that he is attempting to "compile" the sonnets in a deliberate fashion, and in the same breath, he assures the younger man that the effort is all because of him (regardless of what their relationship has been or continues to be): "Yet be most proud of that which I compile / Whose influence is thine, and born of thee" (9-10).

I came to this view of the rival poet by first hypothesizing that the fair youth sonnets are in fact chronologically arranged from 1 to 126 – and that they lead up to and away from Sonnet 107, when Southampton is released from the Tower in April 1603 after having been "supposed as forfeit to a confined doom" (107, 4). That sonnet involves not only the liberation of Henry Wriothesley, third Earl of Southampton, but also the death of Queen Elizabeth, the succession of King James, and the end of the Tudor dynasty.[16] If the other sonnets have no relationship to that enormously serious, political subject matter, then Sonnet 107 must be one huge anomaly.

A simple question therefore becomes obvious. Given that Shakespeare is a masterful storyteller, and given that the high point of this story involves Southampton getting out of the Tower, it stands to reason that he must have marked the time when Southampton went into the Tower. Otherwise there is no chronological story at all and his liberation comes out of the blue, apropos of nothing. I moved back down the numbers from 107 and came to Sonnet 27 as marking that time on the night of February 8, 1601 when Southampton had entered the Tower expecting execution and being pictured by the author as languishing in the prison fortress (perhaps imagined or viewed from below, through a window) like "a Jewel hung in ghastly night." I tracked the sonnets that reflect those crucial days after the failed Essex rebellion until the moment of Southampton's reprieve from execution in March 1601. The rival series also corresponds with the younger earl's imprisonment – a time when, as already mentioned, no other poets could have been publicly praising him.

Also in this context it seems clear that Oxford made a deal with Robert Cecil involving a complete severance of the relationship between himself and Southampton, which he recorded for posterity in Sonnet 36 by telling the younger man: "I may not ever-more acknowledge thee." After coming to its conclusion with Sonnet 86, the rival series is followed immediately by Sonnet 87's first four lines, a declaration that their connection to each other has been severed:

> Farewell, thou art too dear for my possessing
> And like enough thou knowst thy estimate
> The charter of thy worth gives thee releasing
> My bonds in thee are all determinate.

The word *releasing* (above) may have multiple meanings, but it may also reflect the final stage of a deal to guarantee Southampton's release from prison, if James eventually succeeds Elizabeth. Adopting the pen name in 1593 had been Oxford's way of calling public attention to Southampton and, we can infer, of lending public support to him and his political-military future as a peer and rising star of the realm. At that point, Oxford probably expected posthumous recognition of his authorship of the Shakespeare works (as in the case of Philip Sidney and his writings). But now, eight years later in 1601, it appears that – to save the younger earl's life, and to gain his eventual freedom – he agreed to allow the pen name to become permanent. It was a trade-off and from that point on, even four centuries after his death, the rest is silence.

In conclusion, Oxford's statement in Sonnet 81 that "I (once gone) to all the world must die" within the rival poet series rather brazenly advertises the presence of a Shakespeare authorship problem. That is, we should observe the presence of a writer with a divided self. For the traditionally-perceived author to claim that upon his death he would have to disappear to all the world was quite obviously untrue, given the popularity of the Shakespearean works in his own time. The only way such a claim makes any sense is if the "I" of the Sonnets, the true author, was hiding behind a pen name. He could write those apparently heartfelt words of Sonnet 81 only if he knew the identity standing behind Shakespeare was never going to be revealed.

Shake-speare's Sonnets became the vehicle by which Edward de Vere chose to communicate this knowledge – concealing yet simultaneously revealing himself, within the lines of magnificent poetry capable of communicating on different levels – to those of us living in the future. As he testifies with utter confidence in the power of his lines to endure: "Not marble nor the gilded monuments/ Of Princes shall outlive this powerful rhyme" (55, 1-2). Here in the *monument* of the *Sonnets*, we have always had the answer to the authorship question, straight from the pen of the author himself.

Works Cited

Adams, J.Q. *A Life of Shakespeare*. Houghton Mifflin, 1925.

Akrigg, G.P.V. *Shakespeare and the Earl of Southampton*, Harvard UP, 1968.

Booth, Stephen. *Shakespeare's Sonnets*, Yale UP, 1977.

Duncan-Jones, Katherine. *Shakespeare's Sonnets – Arden Edition*. Edinburgh, Nelson and Sons, 1997.

Looney, J. Thomas. *"Shakespeare" Identified in Edward de Vere, the Seventeenth Earl of Oxford*. London, Cecil Palmer, 1920.

Moore, Peter. *The Lame Storyteller, Poor and Despised.* Special Issue 1 of *Neues Shakespeare Journal*. Buchholz, Germany, Verlag Uwe Laugwitz, 2009.

Ogburn Jr., Charlton. *The Mysterious William Shakespeare*. New York, Dodd-Mead, 1984. Reprinted, EPM Publications, McLean, VA. (1992).

Ogburn, Dorothy & Charlton Sr. *This Star of England*. New York, Coward-McCann, 1952.

Rowse, A.L. *Shakespeare's Sonnets: The Problems Solved*, London and New York, Harper & Row, 1964.

Rowse, A.L. *Shakespeare's Southampton*. London, McMillan, 1965.

Whittemore, Hank. *The Monument*. Marshfield Hills, MA, Meadow Geese Press, 2005.

Wilson, Dover. *Shakespeare's Sonnets: An Introduction for Historians and Others*, Cambridge University Press. 1963.

Notes

1. For example, Katherine Duncan-Jones, p. 270. Re: Sonnet 80, line 2. Duncan-Jones writes of "a better spirit doth use your name" – that it suggests "both a superior being and a more inspired writer" than the author.

2. Southampton was identified first in 1817 by Nathan Drake in *Shakespeare and His Times*; since then many scholars have followed, for example, Rowse, xiv: "The Sonnets were written to and for the obvious person, Shakespeare's patron, the young Earl of Southampton…"

3. The continuing controversy among Oxfordians over the connection between Oxford and Southampton has tended to obscure my conviction (and evidence) that the proposed time frame and circumstances of the central 100 sonnets is correct no matter what the nature of their relationship was. Although I continue to believe the so-called Prince Tudor theory that Southampton was Oxford's natural son by the queen, that theory is not necessary in order to see the structure and chronology proposed for Sonnets 27-126, which are placed between two smaller sequences of twenty-six sonnets apiece.

4. On the first page of *Life of Shakespeare* (1923), J.Q. Adams indicates that "Shakespeare" evoked "the shaking of the spear," referring to warrior-like chivalry.

5. Those words are part of the dedication of *Lucrece* in 1594. I have been baffled by attempts to view any statements in the public dedications as less than genuine, that is, to see them as fatuous or insincere in some other way. I take Oxford at his word when, as "Shakespeare," he tells Southampton that his love for him is "without end" and that "what I have to do is yours." Those are huge, straightforward commitments, made for all the world to witness and the younger earl's predicament in the Tower occurred just seven years later.

6. Rowse, in *Shakespeare's Southampton*: "…so long as the Queen lived, Southampton remained a close prisoner in the Tower. He was a condemned man, a dead man in the law – the documents refer to him as 'the late Earl' " (164).

7. In this essay, I do not refer to the man from Stratford-upon-Avon, because it has not been established just when that individual became attached to the name of the poet-dramatist William Shakespeare. I see no record of that linkage during his lifetime. (Nor do I see any possible way that he could have been accepted by anyone, during his lifetime, as the great author.)

8. To date there has been no coherent theory as to why various words of the 1609 *Sonnets* are capitalized and/or italicized and I have no explanation for either ele-

ment of formatting in the case of *Alien*.

9 In the Quarto of 1609 the word "another" is printed as "an other," making it more specific. The "other" would be a reference to the pseudonym, which will take his place from here on.

10 The victor was clearly Robert Cecil, who had the queen's confidence while simultaneously, behind her back, he conducted a secret correspondence with James VI of Scotland about how to ensure his succession upon her death. The cruel irony is that Oxford, to gain Southampton's eventual liberation with a royal pardon, must go along in support of this secret communication, in which he may be the unidentified "40" who works with "10" or Cecil.

11 Wilson also comments on sonnet 66, line 9: "It is tempting to suspect a glance at the control of the State, including vigorous military men like Raleigh and Essex, by the limping Robert Cecil."

12 In 1593, when Oxford adopted the Shakespeare name under which to publish his revised works, he expected to be recognized posthumously. But during 1601-03, he agreed to allow that recognition to be prevented – and, eventually, if need be, given falsely to some other real individual.

13 Let no one say de Vere didn't have an ego he could access whenever he wanted to.

14 Commentators have often cited Touchstone's comment in (3.3) of *As You Like It* as a reference to Marlowe's death: "When a man's verses cannot be understood, nor a man's good wit seconded with the forward child understanding, it strikes a man more dead than a great reckoning in a little room." There is no proof of this, however, and it may not refer to that event in any way.

15 Booth inserts *cross* in his modern-English text alongside the 1609 reprint (page 32). In his commentary for line 12 of Sonnet 34 on p. 188, he writes that *cross* is "the almost universally accepted emendation for Q's *losse*," adding that *bears* suggests bearing the cross. He also notes that "in a Christ-like manner" is implied.

16 In his Southampton biography, Akrigg (254) cites "the mass of evidence which has firmly established the dating of this sonnet [107]" as the spring of 1603, following Southampton's release from the Tower by King James in April 1603. Sonnet 107 "is what Shakespeare had to say to Southampton upon his release from imprisonment."

A Psychiatrist's View of Shakespeare's Sonnets

by Eliot Slater

Editor's Note: *In 1969 Eliot Slater published a substantial article on the Shakespeare Authorship Question in the journal of psychiatry* Anais Portugueses de Psiquiatria. *The first half of the article is available on the website http://eliotslater.org. The second half of the article, in which Slater focuses on the Sonnets and in particular what he – as an eminent psychiatrist – sees in them, has never been reprinted. The text below picks up where Slater is summarizing the reasons why he finds the Stratfordian position unconvincing.*

[. . .]

The Stratfordian case has persisted largely by default, just because it is so generally adhered to. It has not been my purpose to prove that William of Stratford did not write the works of Shakespeare but merely to show that it is possible that he did not – that there are rational grounds for doubt – and above all, that in view of the arguments that can be raised on both sides, the only appropriate attitude is an open-minded one. If we wish, as we should, to make a scientific approach to the range of problems with which Shakespeare and his works confront us, we must not assume a certainty of the authorship as our basic premise. This is a question that has to be solved by research, not first answered by an act of faith and then used as an axiom to guide or to misguide.

In scientific work, hypotheses are valued according to their heuristic potentialities. The Stratfordian hypothesis has been very fully exploited; it has led to solutions of some questions of a varying degree of satisfactoriness, and it has proved incapable of providing any acceptable solution of some other questions. In contrast, the hypothesis that Shakespeare was not William of Stratford, but an unknown to be identified, has received hardly any attention. The proponents of non-Stratfordian hypotheses practically always start with another identification as a basic premise, and then see how well the facts can be fitted, though it is true that J. Thomas Looney began his work on the basis of an unknown anonymous author, and then proceeded by literary detective work to identify the unknown with Edward de Vere.

In the discussion that now follows I wish to make no identification at all – not even to exclude William of Stratford – but to see where we are led if we approach the

Sonnets without any preconceptions at all.

The Poet's Age

Shake-speare's Sonnets were first published in 1609, but modern authorities are agreed they were written very much earlier. They are mentioned as having been in circulation in a pamphlet published in 1598 and two of them were published in 1599 in an anthology of mixed authorship. Most scholars think the sonnets were started in 1593-4 and they connect the earlier ones with *Venus and Adonis* (published 1593) and *The Rape of Lucrece* (published 1594). Again, most scholars think they continued to be written until 1603, since sonnet 107 is thought to refer to the death of Queen Elizabeth, the accession of King James, and the release of the Earl of Southampton from the Tower of London; all these events occurred in that year in quick succession. The Earl of Southampton was the subject of the dedications by Shakespeare of both poems. The dedication of *Lucrece* is in warm, intimate terms, breathing a devotion which the poet seems to feel sure is acceptable and accepted.[1]

It seems therefore probable, if not certain, that the aristocratic and beautiful young man to whom the sonnets are addressed was this same young nobleman who fits the empty place in the jigsaw very well. Nevertheless, there are other possibilities and Dover Wilson prefers another still younger man, William Herbert, Earl of Pembroke.

There are in all 154 sonnets. The first 126 are addressed to this youth, whoever he may have been, the remainder being a rather miscellaneous group of doubtful dating, of which the most interesting are those concerned with or addressed to the "Dark Lady of the Sonnets." The first 17 sonnets urge the young man to marry in order that he may immortalize himself in his posterity. In 1590 the Earl of Southampton was aged 17 and from 1590 to 1594 negotiations were going on, though ultimately to break down, to make a match between him and Elizabeth, the daughter of Edward de Vere, 17th Earl of Oxford (1550-1604) whom some believe to have been Shake-

---

Eliot Slater *was a British psychiatrist and a pioneer in the field of the genetics of mental disorders. He held senior posts at the National Hospital for Nervous Diseases, Queen Square, London, and at the Institute of Psychiatry at the Maudsley Hospital. He was the author of some 150 scientific papers, co-author of several books on psychiatric topics, and for many years he co-edited* Clinical Psychiatry, *the leading textbook for psychiatric trainees. He had wide interests including chess (he published a statistical investigation of chess openings), music (he studied and published on the pathography of Schumann and other composers), poetry (he published a book of his own, poetry* The Ebbless Sea), *and the statistical study of literature. He was awarded a PhD from London University at the age of 77 for a statistical word study of the play* Edward III, *which provided evidence that the play was by Shakespeare. He died in 1983. This article has been reprinted with the consent of Eliot Slater's heirs.*

speare. After sonnet 17 these appeals cease, but the sonnets continue, now in terms of increasing tenderness and devotion – "affectionate admiration – perhaps adoration at times would not be too strong a term – of a man of mature years for another man much younger than himself, in this case perhaps fifteen to seventeen years younger."[2] It may be that this is an underestimate of the difference which could be, say, twenty-three years.

Sonnet 2 begins:

> When forty winters shall besiege thy brow
> And dig deep trenches in thy beauty's field,
> Thy youth's proud livery so gazed on now,
> Will be a tattered weed of small worth held

The first *thy* carries a stress that draws the contrast between the speaker and the youth. The time will come when the latter too, will be over the age of forty, with wrinkled forehead and "deep sunken eyes" (line 7). The same gap of a generation is implied less directly in sonnet 3:

> Thou art thy mother's glass and she in thee
> Calls back the lovely April of her prime

which tells us that Southampton's mother was a beauty in days of youth when Shakespeare knew her. In sonnet 22, we read:

> My glass shall not persuade me I am old,
> So long as youth and thou are of one date,
> But when in thee time's furrows I behold,
> Then look I death my days should expiate.

That is, it will be time in every sense for me to die, when you are as old as I am now – and I am, say sixty? Similarly sonnet 37 ("As a decrepit father takes delight, / To see his active child do deeds of youth") implies a difference in ages of not less than twenty years. In sonnet 62 the poet bitterly reproaches himself for self-love, even love of his own person, until the moment:

> But when my glass shows me myself indeed,
> Beated and chopped with tanned antiquity.

Everyone who believes the speaker was William of Stratford who at the time, say 1596 or so, would have been about 32 years old, exclaims against this ludicrous self-description. Even for a man in his mid-forties it would seem to be excessive, but not so if he were either depressed or physically ill, a possibility which is discussed later. The theme is developed at length in sonnet 63:

> Against my love shall be as I am now
> With Time's injurious hand crushed and o'erworn,
> When hours have drained his blood and filled his brow
> With lines and wrinkles, when his youthful morn
> Hath travelled on to age's steepy night,
> And all those beauties wherof now he's king
> Are vanishing, or vanished out of sight,
> Stealing away the treasure of his spring:

Once more we see the contrast between the Poet and his beloved: "as I am now... When hours have drained *his* blood." Finally we have a wonderful description of the age of involution as seen from within in sonnet 73:

> That time of year thou mayst in me behold,
> When yellow leaves, or none, or few do hang
> Upon those boughs which shake against cold,
> Bare ruined choirs, where late the sweet birds sang.
> In me thou seest the twilight of such day,
> As after sunset fadeth in the west,
> Which by and by black night doth take away,
> Death's second self that seals up all in rest.
> In me thou seest the glowing of such fire,
> That on the ashes of his youth doth lie,
> As the death-bed, whereon it must expire,
> Consumed with that which it was nourished by.
>   This thou perceiv'st, which makes thy love more strong
>   To love that well, which thou must leave ere long.

The picture is of intense depression, and carries a strong hint of bodily illness and death not far away.

It is very relevant to a consideration of the probable age of the Poet that he is so much with death and with the ineluctable passage of time. The ravages of Time are a main theme of sonnets 1, 2, 3, 5, 7, 11, 12, 15, 16, 17, 18, 19, 22, 30, 33, 55, 60, 63, 64, 65, 77, 104, 107, 123, 126, and 146. In sonnets 12, 15, 19, 55, 60, 63, 64, 65 and 77 the theme dominates the sonnet completely and is very powerfully expressed. In sonnet 12:

> When I do count the clock that tells the time,
> And see the brave day sunk in hideous night,
> When I behold the violet past prime,
> And sable curls all silvered o'er with white:
> When lofty trees I see barren of leaves,

> Which erst from heat did canopy the herd
> And summer's green all girded up in sheaves
> Borne on the bier with white and bristly beard:
> Then of thy beauty do I question make
> That thou among the wastes of time must go

Against this terrible deity, the Poet lifts up, as a shield over the head of the beloved youth, a tremendous incantation in sonnet 55:

> Not marble, nor the gilded monuments
> Of princes shall outlive this powerful rhyme,
> But you shall shine more bright . . .
> 'Gainst death, and all-oblivious enmity
> Shall you pace forth, your praise shall still find room,
> Even in the eyes of all posterity
> That wear this world out to the ending doom.[3]

Nevertheless Time remains, from start to finish of the sonnet sequence, the inveterate enemy with whom no reconciliation is possible: *Wasteful Time, this bloody tyrant Time, devouring Time, swift-footed Time, Time's injurious hand, Time's fell hand, Time's thievish progress to eternity, Time's spoils, Time's hate, the fools of Time, Time's fickle glass.* From sonnet 1 to 126, Time figures 51 times in 33 sonnets. But the poet achieves no equanimity, no philosophical acceptance of the inevitable. Time is opposed again and again to Love, but after all vicissitudes, in the end there is only such despair as speaks in the heart-rending answer of sonnet 64:

> When I have seen such interchange of state,
> Or state itself confounded to decay,
> Ruin hath taught me thus to ruminate
> That Time will come and take my love away.
> This thought is as a death which cannot choose
> But weep to have, that which it fears to lose.

Considering the progress of Time, the Poet finds himself looking ever and again in the face of death. *Death, deaths, dead, die, dies, diest, dying, died* come 53 times in 41 sonnets and receive the stress and prominence of rhyming syllables 16 times. In addition are many synonyms: perish, end, decease, expire, mortality, and many references to graves, tombs, monuments, and sepulchers. No better than to Time can the poet reconcile himself to Death, least of all to the death of his beloved, but not even to his own death though he feels it as the end to mortal sickness: "To be death's conquest and make worms thine heir," "And barren rage of death's eternal cold," "When that churl death my bones with dust shall cover." The death theme is dealt with at full length in sonnets 71 to 74 and again in sonnet 81 – death with all its panoply of worms and corruption.

Rendall, in *Shakespeare's Sonnets and Edward de Vere*, has pointed out that Shakespeare nowhere hints at any belief in life after death, and that in the Sonnets the only hope of immortality he expresses is that his verse shall live to enshrine the name of his beloved (who is nowhere mentioned by name). He seems to believe that even these sonnets will not immortalize his own name, and writes as if his authorship was covered by anonymity:

> My name be buried where my body is. (72)

> Why write I still all one, ever the same,
> And keep invention in a noted weed,
> That every word doth almost tell my name. (76)

> Though I (once gone) to all world must die,
> The earth can yield me but a common grave . . .
> Your monument shall be my gentle verse . . .
> You still shall live, (such virtue hath my pen)
> Where breath most breathes, even in the mouths of men. (81)

> I'll live in this poor rhyme. (103)

The Poet's Melancholia

Shakespeare's preoccupation with his own aging, a physical decay destined to end in death, gives by itself an impression of such melancholy that we are bound to consider whether he may have had a depressive illness. Scholars have repeatedly emphasized the world-weariness, the despair of human kind and the self-contempt that inspire so much of the poetry and the action of such plays as *Hamlet*, *King Lear*, and *Timon of Athens*; and some (Chambers, for instance) think of the possibility of a nervous breakdown. *The Sonnets* are a record which can help us to a partial answer of whether the Poet was ever in worse case than merely very miserable, or whether, in fact, he had a mental illness.

The illness that comes in question is an endogenous depression,[4] and there is much to suggest that it did actually occur. During the course of the sonnets we see signs, first of its appearance from nowhere, then a progressive worsening to a state that is unmistakably morbid, and then its gradual passing off in a grumbling diminuendo. As is the way with an endogenous depression, when it is at its worst, psychic powers are slowed down, perhaps to a halt. Sonnets 85, 86, 100, and 101 suggest invention completely dried up for a time; in sonnets 76, 103, and 105 the Poet complains of its sameness and monotony.

All is well until sonnet 27. In sonnet 26, Shakespeare has made a formal acknowledgement of his beloved's suzerainty as in feudal days of yore:

> Lord of my love, to whom in vassalage
> Thy merit hath my duty strongly knit;
> To thee I send this written embassage
> To witness duty, not to show my wit.

In the next sonnet, abruptly, and for the first time, we are told of an intractable insomnia, very commonly the first symptom of an involutional depression.[5] The insomnia persists, and comes out again even more strongly in sonnet 28:

> How can I then return in happy plight
> That am debarred the benefit of rest?
> When day's oppression is not eased by night,
> But day by night and night by day oppressed,
> And each (though enemies to either's reign)
> Do in consent shake hands to torture me.

In the next sonnet, 29, with equal abruptness, the note of a bitter self-reproach is struck for the first time, to recur later again and again:

> When in disgrace with Fortune and men's eyes,
> I all alone beweep my outcast state,
> And trouble deaf heaven with my bootless cries,
> And look upon my self and curse my fate . . .
> . . . in these thoughts my self almost despising.

Depiction of depression of the involutional type continues in sonnets 33, 34, 36 ("my bewailed guilt"), 37, 43 (insomnia again), and in 44, 45, 49, 50, 61, 62, 66, 71, 72 and 74.

In sonnet 45 two elements, "Slight air and purging fire," have left him, and "My life, being made of four, with two alone / Sinks down to death, oppressed with melancholy." In sonnet 49, he looks forward to the time when "thou shalt strangely pass, / And scarcely greet me with that sun, thine eye." Sonnet 50 gives almost a classic account of that feeling of heaviness, like a cold weight in the chest, which we know as one of Schneider's first-rank symptoms of depression. The poet on a journey, away from his beloved, is one with his horse, each carrying a dead weight ("The beast that bears me, tired with my woe, / Plods dully on, to bear that weight in me"). In sonnet

61 comes more insomnia, and in the night the thought of "shames and idle hours." More self-reproach is the theme of sonnet 62:

> Sin of self-love possesseth all mine eye,
> And all my soul, and all my every part;
> And for this Sin there is no remedy,
> It is so grounded inward in my heart.

Sonnet 66 begins "Tired with all these for restful death I cry," and follows with a list of human follies and villainies which bear a strong resemblance to the list in Hamlet's soliloquy (*Hamlet*, 3, 1). In sonnet 71 we reach at last the nadir, the pit of despair, with a total self-abnegation which would yet seek to spare the beloved some pain:

> No longer mourn for me when I am dead,
> Than you shall hear the surly sullen bell
> Give warning to the world that I am fled
> From this vile world with vilest worms to dwell:
> Nay if you read this line, remember not
> The hand that writ it, for I love you so,
> That I in your sweet thoughts would be forgot,
> If thinking on me then should make you woe.
> O if (I say) you look upon this verse,
> When I (perhaps) compounded am with clay,
> Do not so much as my poor name rehearse;
> But let your love even with my life decay.
> Lest the wise world should look into your moan,
> And mock you with me after I am gone.

Sonnet 72 continues the same theme; his friend must forget him when he is gone: "After my death (dear love) forget me quite, / For you in me can nothing worthy prove . . . My name be buried where my body is, / And live no more to shame nor me, nor you." In sonnet 74 again he is "Too base of thee to be remembered."

After this, the depth of the depression lessens, but it comes back and back in later sonnets to interrupt or to tinge reflections of another kind with an inky hue in sonnets 76, 79 ("my sick muse"), 81, 89, 90, 92, 93, 95, 110, 111, 112, 119. In the last of these the Dark Lady has entered on the scene, to bring the poet tortures of another kind.

However, before the depressive mood has petered out it has provoked some exhibitions of a paranoid tendency. He suspects his friend of hating him and wishing him ill, even as the world itself has had a spite against him:

> Then hate me when thou wilt, if ever, now,
> Now while the world is bent my deeds to cross,
> Join with the spite of fortune, make me bow,
> And do not drop in for an after-loss. (90)

This is the first of four sonnets handling the same theme. Sonnet 91 imagines his friend deserting him completely; sonnet 92 begins by defying him to "do thy worst thyself to steal thyself away," and ends "Thou mayst be false, and yet I know it not." Sonnet 93 continues with "So shall I live, supposing thou art true, / Like a deceived husband," and with imaginings of the evil thoughts, the false heart behind the face of sweet love. This suspicion, morbid one would think, leads directly into an outright attack on the friend, which comes up for discussion in the next section.

In Summary, the *Sonnets* provide very suggestive evidence that during the time they were being written Shakespeare passed through a severe but temporary depression. After the worst of the storm was over, a melancholic groundswell persisted for some time. But temporary the depressive illness must have been. The later sonnets show an improved mental state and reconciliation to his friend and to his fate. We can be sure, despite uncertainties of dating, that energetic play-production continued after *Troilus* and *Lear* and *Timon*, with the equable and serene *Tempest* as the last play of all.

The Poet's Homosexuality

Most lovers of Shakespeare, particularly the orthodox scholars of an earlier academic generation, are so affronted by the suggestion that Shakespeare was "homosexual" that they reject it out of hand and do not stop to consider just what is implied. The hypothesis that is advanced here is not one to impute moral infamy of even the slightest degree, but it is one which should be of great help in understanding Shakespeare's attitude to sexuality. The hypothesis can be based solely on the evidence of the *Sonnets*, which permits us to use the plays as an independent check. The hypothesis proposed is that Shakespeare had a basically homosexual (or perhaps better "homoerotic") orientation, which laid him open to a passionate and romantic attachment to one of his own sex and made it impossible for him to develop a normally tender, protective, and fully erotic love for a woman. While it is suggested that Shakespeare was "in love" with the young man he addresses in the *Sonnets*, it is not suggested that the love relationship ever took on an overtly sexual character. Let us first examine the evidence for the negative part of this formulation.

Sonnets 1-126 cover several years (at least three)[6] and show a series of stages of development. After the initial courtly overtures and an increasing attachment, there came periods of separation, periods of regular, perhaps daily contact,[7] estrangement and reconciliation. It is almost unthinkable that if the relationship between the two men had had an overtly sexual aspect, there should have been no echo of it in the poems of love and adoration that poured out in such profusion. Love-making of its essence involves bodily contact; and those who love one another, and who have made love, are bound in times of absence or frustration to call to mind the solace that such bodily contacts provided. In all his sonnets to his friend, Shakespeare never makes mention of a bodily touch. There is no word about the soft texture of skin, the resilience of muscles, the suppleness of limbs, the firmness of an embrace – in fact no imagery at all drawn from tactile, hot and cold, deep pressure and kinaesthetic senses.[8] In fact, one can be nearly certain, not only that physical love-making never took place between the two friends, but that the imagining of such a physical relationship played no significant part in the Poet's emotional enslavement.

That being granted, we still have to concede that the nature of Shakespeare's attachment was much more one of love than friendship. Relationships of these two kinds differ not only in the level and intensity but even in the psychic dimension in which they manifest. The love relationship, calling on energies of profounder origin in subcortical centers arising in fact from brain systems involved in sexuality, provides a much more potent and enduring source of driving emotion than any unsexualized feelings of friendship. It was emotions of great depth and power and constancy that drove the Poet on, over the course of years, to produce these sonnets of elation and despair, of self-dedication, self-abasement and self-torture, of violent jealousy and savage reprisal.

Shakespeare's feeling for the beloved youth is an infatuation – not love in any temperate sense – and, as is the nature of an infatuation in contrast to a love that is returned, it thrived on neglect, humiliation, and equally casual acceptance and rejection.[9] Shakespeare's love has been likened to the love of a doting father, and he does indeed choose for himself the role of 'father' in sonnet 37, but also that of 'husband' in sonnet 93, to define his attitude, and to the love of Socrates for Alcibiades. But, to the present writer, it calls to mind more readily the infatuation of Oscar Wilde for Lord Alfred Douglas. There is little to show that the mental characteristics of the beloved youth, his wit or wisdom or graces of the mind, or his tenderness or affection played any real part in his allure. To be sure, in sonnet 69 we read of "the beauty of thy mind," and in sonnet 82 the Poet says "Thou art as fair in knowledge as in hue." In sonnet 105 he calls him "fair, kind and true," and begs for a welcome, "even to thy pure and most loving breast" in sonnet 110. But these are quite isolated instances, and apart from them, the talk is all of "bright eyes," "sweet self," "your sweet semblance," "my love's fair brow," "thy lovely grace," "my love's sweet face," and in sonnet after sonnet it is the word *beauty* signifying particularly the beauty of the eyes and face that comes to his mind, as he attempts to pin down, like a captured butterfly, the perfections of his lovely boy. A number of sonnets (18, 20, 24, 53, 54, 99, 104, and 106) are devoted exclusively to hymning the beauty of the youth. Shakespeare, in fact, made for himself an idealized image before which to prostrate himself, and that he could go on loving, even when the real man was treating him with carelessness and, perhaps, cruelty.

The only idea that springs up in the poet's mind more constantly than this physical beauty is the overmastering obsession of his own love. The statement of this love is at its most powerful when it is least covered in conceits, and is presented naked, in the simplest possible language: "Thou . . . hast all the all of me" (31), "thou art all the better part of me" (39), "Thou best of dearest, and mine only care" (48), "My spirit is thine, the better part of me" (74), "You are my all the world" (112).

To these many more could be added, but the following must suffice:

> Haply I think on thee, and then my state
> (Like to the lark at break of day arising
> From sullen earth) sings hymns at heaven's gate.
> (Sonnet 29)

> Take all my loves, my love, yea take them all,
> What hast thou then more than thou hadst before?
> No love, my love, that thou mayst true love call
> All mine was thine, before thou hadst this more:
> (Sonnet 40)

> Tired with all these, from these I would be gone,
> Save that to die, I leave my love alone.
> (Sonnet 66)

> No longer mourn for me when I am dead…
> Nay if you read this line, remember not
> The hand that writ it, for I love you so,
> That I in your sweet thoughts would be forgot,
> If thinking on me then should make you woe.
> (Sonnet 71)

> For nothing in this wide universe I call
> Save thou my rose, in it thou art my all.
> (Sonnet 109)

In sonnet 75, the Poet indicates how his love has become an obsession ("So are you to my thoughts as food to life"). He compares himself to a miser with his wealth:

> Now proud as an enjoyer, and anon
> Doubting the filching age will steal his treasure,
> Now counting best to be with you alone,

> Then bettered that the world may see my pleasure,
> Sometime all full with feasting on your sight,
> And by and by clean starved for a look,
> Possessing or pursuing no delight
> Save what is had, or must from you be took.

The development of the poet's passion shows up in the succession of sonnets, as each follows the one before. After the first seventeen beseeching the youth to marry, with their flowery but restrained expressions of admiration, there comes something more fervent in the eighteenth: ("Shall I compare thee to a summer's day? / Thou art more lovely and more temperate"). Sonnet 20 describes in all detail what gave the youth his magical attractions. This sonnet has been the cornerstone of the arguments for and against an attribution of homosexual inclinations to the Poet, since it allows of two deductions which appear to be in contradiction:

> A woman's face with nature's own hand painted
> Hast thou, the master-mistress of my passion;
> A woman's gentle heart, but not acquainted
> With shifting change as is false women's fashion;
> An eye more bright than theirs, less false in rolling,
> Gilding the object whereupon it gazeth;
> A man in hue, all hues in his controlling,
> Which steals men's eyes and women's souls amazeth.
> And for a woman wert thou first created,
> Till nature as she wrought thee fell a-doting,
> And by addition me of thee defeated,
> By adding one thing to my purpose nothing.
> But since she pricked thee out for women's pleasure,
> Mine be thy love and thy love's use their treasure.
> (Sonnet 20)

The double interpretation arises from the double entendre *pricked* in line 13. This does indeed state quite clearly that when nature made the youth a man, the Poet was 'defeated,' that is, prevented from consummating his love. This is in line with the hypothesis proposed earlier, that this love for the beautiful boy was 'platonic.' But at the same time the double entendre tells us what kind of love it was that could be so defeated. These were such feelings as might have led – if they had been aroused by a girl – not to 'defeat' but to 'conquest.' The last four lines define explicitly what is implicit in the rest of the poem, the romantic and erotic tone of the emotional pressures under which the Poet was writing. The boy was an object of sexual love, even if he was a forbidden object. One might go further and say it was the very feature which made him a forbidden object which potentiated his attraction. Though he had all and more of a woman's charms, he was not a member of that dangerous sex, not one of those "false women."

From sonnet 20 on, the love story takes an uneventful course for some time. His love is one of few solaces to which recourse is possible when Shakespeare is troubled by insomnia and depression. Then with sonnets 33-35 we hear that the young man has "disgraced" himself, has done a deed of "shame," by which Shakespeare has been sorely hurt. Sonnets 40-42 make it clear that the offence was in having an affair with Shakespeare's own mistress. In sonnets 133 and 134, when Shakespeare bitterly reproaches the Dark Lady, we get the other half of the picture. Shakespeare's attitude to the two unfaithful ones is very partial: the youth is quickly forgiven, but the woman is not. She is condemned outright.

At this point something happens which is very strange indeed. Shakespeare finds some consolation by identifying himself with the other two lovers, to be present as it were, at their lovemaking. This comes out in sonnet 133 and even more so in sonnet 42, below.

> But here's the joy, my friend and I are one;
> Sweet flattery! Then she loves but me alone.

Of Sonnet 42, the psychoanalyst Bronson Feldman (1953) has written: "The repressed homosexuality of Shakespeare becomes painfully manifest here. It is obvious that his imagination rioted in fantasies of the woman yielding herself to the man in whom he saw the mirror of his own youth. Unknown to his infinitely clever ego was the fantasy beneath these thoughts, the fantasy of taking the woman's place."

If such mechanisms did indeed play a part in Shakespeare's unconscious, it would help us to understand how he could empathize himself into the personalities of some of the women of his plays. Such fictional women would in any case not have for the hypersensitive homosexual, the terrifying qualities of women of flesh and blood, and would be additionally idealized by being represented on the stage by boys.

In sonnet 42, Shakespeare tells us what it was that wounded him when the third side of the triangle was completed: "That thou hast her it is not all my grief . . . That she hath thee is of my wailing chief." This was, to be compelled, by a female, to share the possession of his beloved boy. The whole of Shakespeare's affections were monopolized by the boy, and he would have wished to monopolize him in turn. The bargain proposed in sonnet 20 ("Mine be thy love and thy love's use their treasure."), that the young man was to be allowed his heterosexual liaisons, proves in the end to be beyond Shakespeare's powers of fulfillment.

After the rather feeble rebukes of sonnets 33 and 34, in the attempt somehow to retain his hold, Shakespeare turns his rage upon himself and ends by groveling in a pit of self-humiliation (sonnets 35, 40, and 42). Such a point is reached in sonnet 57 that

Dover Wilson thinks he is speaking ironically, but alas, one fears that Shakespeare did actually reach this abyss:

> Being your slave, what should I do but tend
> Upon the hours and times of your desire?
> I have no precious time at all to spend,
> Nor services to do, till you require;
> Nor dare I chide the world-without-end hour
> Whilst I (my sovereign) watch the clock for you,
> Nor think the bitterness of absence sour
> When you have bid your servant once adieu.
> Nor dare I question with my jealous thought
> Where you may be, of your affairs suppose,
> But like a sad slave, stay and think of naught,
> Save where you are, how happy you make those.
> So true a fool is love, that in your will
> (Though you do anything) he thinks no ill.

Sonnets 58, 71 (painfully sincere), and 72 (more melancholic than masochistic) continue the theme, to end with the triple gush of sonnets 88, 89, and 90.

After this there is a sudden revulsion, and Shakespeare turns on the friend who has caused him such pain, and rends him. We see his character analyzed in sonnet 94:

> They that have power to hurt, and will do none,
> That do not do the thing they most do show,
> Who moving others are themselves as stone,
> Unmoved, cold, and to temptation slow

and his "sins" and "vices" are sternly pointed out in sonnets 95 and 96.

Only after all these storms have passed over is Shakespeare able to settle into the comparatively quiet mood of the later sonnets.

Important evidence bearing on Shakespeare's homoerotic orientation is to be gathered from his attitude to women. It seems that, while women were to be tolerated as long as they no constituted no threat to him, a desirous, sexually aroused woman was for him an object at once terrifying and disgusting. While he was at times able to observe his own reactions in a tolerant spirit (151), this seems to have been but rarely the case. As a rule, feelings of lust in himself were abominable, and to give way to them was a degradation. The passionate outburst in sonnet 129 ("Th' expense of spirit in a waste of shame / Is lust in action;") is too well known to need quotation in full. This cry of self-hatred and self-contempt is (to my knowledge) unique in English literature, and shows a pathological attitude to sex, and an incapacity to reconcile sexual drives with the rest of his nature.

It has been maintained by J. Dover Wilson that Shakespeare only developed an attitude of rejection towards the normal physical relations of the sexes in his later plays.[10] But this is a mistaken view. Dislike and disgust for human sexuality are shown from the very beginning. *Venus and Adonis*[11] depicts the queen of love as a ravening bird of prey, and *The Rape of Lucrece* gives a correspondingly shocked and shocking picture of the lustful male in the role of the ruthless ravisher. One of the earliest plays, *The Comedy of Errors*, gives an anatomical analysis of the human female which is at once ludicrous and revolting. And another, *Love's Labour's Lost*, presents Berowne (the dramatist's spokesman) exclaiming against contemptible Dan Cupid, "Dread Prince of Plackets, King of Codpieces," and angrily resenting his enslavement to:

> A whitely wanton with a velvet brow,
> With two pitch-balls stuck in her face for eyes,
> Ay and, by heaven, one that will do the deed,
> Though Argus were her eunuch and her guard!
> And I to sigh for her, to watch for her,
> To pray for her, go to: it is a plague
> That Cupid will impose for my neglect
> Of his almighty dreadful little might.
>
> (*LLL*, 3, 1, 191-198)

No, we must accept the fact that Shakespeare never did have a normal attitude either to women or to sexuality, that his deficiency showed itself from the beginning of his writing life, and that it stayed with him (apart from a few sunnier hours) all through it to the end.

However, he was entrapped into a sexual relationship with a woman, as he states specifically in sonnets 138 and 151. In a more tolerant mood (151), it seems to have been momentarily a source of wonder to him, rather than guilt; one supposes that he had feared he would prove impotent (an anxiety which would have been only too natural in his case) and was correspondingly relieved when the reverse proved true in the event. However, "she who makes me sin, awards me pain" (141), and the magical effect the lady had upon him also caused him to torture himself, to rebel against his infatuation – "thou proud heart's slave and vassal wretch to be" – and to do all he could to destroy her utterly in his mind and annihilate her attraction.

Psychologically naive commentators have taken Shakespeare's complaints of his mistress at face value, despite the fact that the charges he brings against her are monstrous and, obviously, inapposite ("the bay where all men ride," "the wide world's common place," sonnet 137, and see also 147 below.) One does not accuse a common prostitute of being a common prostitute, and against anyone else the accusation, though frequently made by enraged lovers, is merely so much abuse intended to relieve the feelings of the one and hurt the feelings of the other. In the same spirit, Shakespeare disparages the lady's physical charms. The famous sonnet 130, ("My mistress' eyes are nothing like the sun") is, to be sure, a skit on the extravagances of other sonneteers, but shows a morbid hostility in the grossness and insult to which it descends ("And in some perfumes is there more delight, / Than in the breath that from my mistress reeks.") The physical attack on the enchantress is repeated again and again, in the effort, one supposes, to annul her magic:

> In faith, I do not love thee with mine eyes,
> For they in thee a thousand errors note;
> But 'tis my heart that loves what they despise,
> Who, in despite of view, is pleased to dote.
> Nor are mine ears with thy tongue's tune delighted;
> Nor tender feeling to base touches prone.
> Nor taste, nor smell, desire to be invited
> To any sensual feast with thee alone:
> But my five wits, nor my five senses can
> Dissuade one foolish heart from serving thee,
> Who leaves unswayed the likeness of a man,
> Thy proud heart's slave and vassal wretch to be:
> Only my plague thus far I count my gain,
> That she that makes me sin awards me pain.
>
> (Sonnet 141)

The attack on her person is paralleled by the attack on her character: "In nothing art thou black save in thy deeds" (131), "thy cruel eye," "thy steel bosom" (133), "thou art covetous" (134), "I know she lies" (138), "my female evil," "her foul pride" (144), "thy foul faults" (148), etc. Not a shadow of a cause is shown why she should be thought so ill of, and what we listen to is the hatred and abuse that is wrung from a self-tortured spirit. The reason for his malignity was not in her, but in him. The extremity in which he found himself provides an amply sufficient explanation:

> My love is as a fever longing still,
> For that which longer nurseth the disease,
> Feeding on that which doth persevere the ill,
> The uncertain sickly appetite to please . . . .
> Past cure I am, now reason is past cure,
> And frantic-mad with evermore unrest,
> My thoughts and my discourse as mad men's are,
> At random from the truth vainly expressed,

> For I have sworn thee fair, and thought thee bright,
> Who art as black as hell, as dark as night.
> 							(Sonnet 147)

Perhaps the only sonnet which shows the Poet in a mood of some tenderness is 143, in which he imagines himself "thy babe," and begs her to "play the mother's part, kiss me, be kind."

The sonnets to the man and the sonnets to the woman throw light on Shakespeare's sexual nature from opposite sides, and enable us to see it in depth. Sexuality was the element in his nature with which he was never able to cope successfully. The love he felt for the young man had no conscious sexual component (though a powerfully homoerotic element at an unconscious level), and, despite the suffering it brought him, he felt it to be a healthful, altruistic self-dedication, that ennobled both him and the beloved boy. On the other hand, the enslavement to the sexually active female, which held him for a time, ran, he felt, against the truest inclinations of his nature, and debased both him and her:

> Two loves I have of comfort and despair,
> Which like two spirits do suggest me still,
> The better angel is a man right fair:
> The worser spirit a woman coloured ill.
> 							(Sonnet 144)

When one reads in these poems, in which there is so much more of despair than of comfort, of the frantic efforts Shakespeare made to come to terms with his own nature, and somehow or other to achieve a rewarding relationship with the one sex and with the other, one is wrung with pity, not only to see such a great spirit brought to such depths of suffering and humiliation, but to know that his struggles were foredoomed. There was, in fact, nothing to be hoped for from the young man, held off from a loving relationship by his own superficial nature as well as community of sex. Who knows but the woman might have been able to return his love, if only he had been able to give it to her?

Works Cited

Chambers, E.K. *William Shakespeare: A Study of Facts and Problems Vol. 1*. London, Oxford University Press, 1966.

Chambers, E.K. *Shakespeare: A Survey*. London, Sidgwick and Jackson, 1925.

Feldman, Bronson. "The Confessions of William Shakespeare" *The American Imago #10* (p. 113-166). 1953.

Greenwood, G.G. *The Shakespeare Problem Restated*. London, John Lane The Bodley Head, 1916.

Johnson, Edward D. *The Shakespeare Quiz*. London, George Lapworth, 1950.

Knight, G. Wilson. *The Mutual Flame*. London, Methuen, 1955.

Levin, Harry. *The Question of Hamlet*. New York, Oxford University Press, 1959.

Looney, J. Thomas. *"Shakespeare" Identified in Edward de Vere, the Seventeenth Earl of Oxford*, London, Cecil Palmer, 1920.

Nicol, Allardyce. *Shakespeare*. London, Oxford University Press, 1952.

Rendall, Gerald H. *Shakespeare Sonnets and Edward de Vere*. London, John Murray, 1930.

Rendall, Gerald H. *Personal Clues in Shakespeare's Poems and Sonnets*. John Lane the Bodley Head, 1934.

Rowse, A.L. *Shakespeare's Sonnets*. Edited with an Introduction and Notes. London, Macmillan, 1964.

Tucker, T.G. *The Sonnets of Shakespeare, Edited from the Quarto of 1609* with Introduction and Commentary. Cambridge University Press, 1924.

Wilson, John Dover, *The Works of Shakespeare*. Cambridge University Press, reprinted 1969.

Wilson, John Dover, *The Essential Shakespeare: A Biographical Adventure*. Cambridge University Press, 1932.

Notes

1 "The love I dedicate to your Lordship is without end... The warrant I have of your honorable disposition... makes it [i.e., this pamphlet] assured of acceptance. What I have done is yours; what I have to do is yours; being part in all I have, devoted yours..." (*The Rape of Lucrece*, dedication.)

2 *The Sonnets: Preface and Text* (edited by John Dover Wilson).

3 In this we hear what the poet thought of his own poetry; there is no lack of awareness of success, when his powers of verbal magic captured the immortal phrase.

4 A mood disorder caused by internal cognition, a biological stressor.

5 A melancholia related to aging.

6 > To me fair friend you never can be old,
  > For as you were when first your eye I eyed,
  > Such seems your beauty still: three winters cold
  > Have from the forests shook three summers' pride,
  > Three beauteous springs to yellow autumn turned,
  > In process of the seasons I have seen.
  > Three April perfumes in three hot Junes burned
  > Since first I saw you fresh which yet are green
  > (Sonnet 104)

7 Sonnets 36, 49, and 89 imply that the two men were liable to run into one another in the course of daily life; sonnets 75 and 85 (and others) imply a common social world they both inhabited. Sonnets 57 and 58 depict a personal association that was for a time, very close. Sonnet 113 begins, "Since I left you..."

8 Such images do appear in the sonnets concerned with the dark lady. However the imagery that ran riot in Shakespeare's mind, and finds expression in the Sonnets was very largely visual. Many sonnets show that the capacity for visual imagery was strong, and the images very vivid. Not only could he call up an image of the beloved youth at will, but such images came unbidden both by night (27, 43, 61) and by day (113). Apart from visual imagery, the other sense in which spontaneous images seem to have come relatively freely is the olfactory.

9 Rendall in *Personal Clues* writes: "To the author it was all in all... From

the other side . . . the overtures and professions of affection were welcomed, tolerated, or ignored, as occasion or self-interest suggested; from sonnet 34 onwards, there is nothing to suggest that they elicited much warmth of response, and this is quite in keeping with the Southampton disposition."

10. "Another personal clue . . . is the strain of sex nausea which runs through almost everything he wrote after 1600. The 'sweet desire' of *Venus and Adonis* has turned sour . . . possibly due to the general morbidity of the age . . . That it is not the mere trick of a practicing dramatist is proved by its presence in the ravings of Lear, where there is no dramatic reason for it at all." A total of nine plays are then discussed. "Collect these passages together, face them as they should be faced, and the conclusion is inescapable that the defiled imagination of which Shakespeare writes so often, and depicts in metaphor so nakedly material, must be his own." J. Dover Wilson, *The Essential Shakespeare*, pp. 118-119.

11.
> Even as an empty eagle, sharp by fast,
> Tires with her beak on feathers, flesh and bone,
> Shaking her wings, devouring all in haste,
> Till either gorge be stuffed or prey be gone;
> Even so she kissed his brow, his cheek, his chin,
> And where she ends she doth anew begin.
> (*Venus & Adonis*, 55-60)

See also lines 553-558. In lines 793-804, Adonis contrasts love and lust in identically the same spirit as sonnet 129. Precisely the same picture of lust is presented in *The Rape of Lucrece* (ll. 687-714). For the passage in *The Comedy of Errors* see 3, 2, 109-138; and for the passage in *Love's Labour's Lost*, see 3, 1, 172-204.

Quentin Skinner's Forensic Shakespeare

Reviewed by Richard M. Waugaman

Published by Oxford University Press in 2014, *Forensic Shakespeare* will interest Oxfordians for several reasons. New discoveries about Shakespeare often expose further weaknesses in the traditional authorship theory, and inadvertently lend support to de Vere as the real "Shake-speare." That is the case with this book. Quentin Skinner is not primarily a Shakespeare scholar. Those who come to Shakespeare from other disciplines often make fresh observations, since they are less constrained by the groupthink of mainstream Shakespeare scholars. Skinner significantly expands Shakespeare's literary sources, which undermines the false Stratfordian notion that Shakespeare was relatively unlearned. This review will focus especially on Skinner's discovery that the Roman rhetorician Quintilian (c. 35-c.100 CE) had a crucial influence on how Shakespeare structured several of his works. Further study of Quintilian reveals numerous passages that may have inspired de Vere.

Skinner is an intellectual historian who serves as Professor of Humanities at Queen Mary University in London. He spent four years at the prestigious Institute for Advanced Study in Princeton in the 1970s. This is his first book on Shakespeare. One of his previous books explored the rediscovery of ancient Roman rhetoric and its impact on Renaissance Italy. Most of his previous books are on early modern political history. His *The Foundations of Modern Political Thought* (1978) was named by the Times Literary Supplement as one of the 100 most influential books since World War II.

Since the anonymous *Arte of English Poesie* (1589) – which was probably written by de Vere – was only the sixth book in Early English Books Online (EEBO) to cite Quintilian,[1] Skinner's findings help support de Vere's authorship of that influential Elizabethan book on rhetoric.[2] In a forthcoming article, I will outline my reasons for thinking that de Vere also translated Johann Sturm's 1549 treatise on rhetoric as *A Ritch Storehouse or Treasurie for Nobilitye and Gentlemen* (1570).

Before going any further, I would like to cite previous reviews of Skinner's book, in order to establish that many of his conclusions have been accepted by Stratfordians. Andrew Hadfield, former editor of *Renaissance Studies*, calls Skinner's book "powerful and important." He adds that "some might wish that Skinner had attempted to explain why Shakespeare paid such close attention to rhetorical techniques and argument…" (review in online *Irish Times*, March 7, 2015). Hadfield would not find this surprising if he shared my assumption that de Vere wrote or translated two books on rhetoric. Another reviewer, Richard Hull, in *The Review of English Studies* (vol. 66, 777-778, 2015), acknowledges that Skinner's book "adds up to a remarkable account of Shakespeare's engagement with classical rhetoric."

Brian Vickers, in his review, calls Shakespeare "the greatest practitioner of rhetoric in English literature" (*Common Knowledge* 22:322-323, May, 2016). Vickers does not end his sentence, though, before hastily adding that Shakespeare learned about rhetoric in the Stratford grammar school. (We respectfully disagree.) David Wooton, in the *New York Review of Books* (December, 2014), faults Skinner for emphasizing judicial rhetoric at the expense of early modern legal history. Yet Stratfordians themselves are forced to conjecture that Shakespeare knew so much about law because he was a party to so many lawsuits; or even that he "must" have worked as a law clerk during his Christ-like "lost years."

Skinner's book is organized around the various stages of a judicial argument: beginnings, judicial narrative, confirmation, refutation, and the peroration, or rhetorical conclusion. As a result, somewhat confusingly, the same plays are discussed in several chapters.

Skinner maintains that the structure of the *Rape of Lucrece* and seven of Shakespeare's plays are heavily influenced by principles of judicial rhetoric, as spelled out in both classical and Renaissance treatises. Whether or not Shakespeare's audience and readers recognized these sources, Skinner believes they still helped Shakespeare "get his imagination on the move"(2). Skinner names Cicero, the anonymous author of *Rhetorica ad Herennium* (c. 80 BCE) and Thomas Wilson, author of *Arte of Rhetorique* (1553) as crucial sources for Shakespeare's approach to rhetoric. The book also has dozens of references to Quintilian's *Institutio Oratoria*. Skinner is adding significantly to our still inadequate understanding of Shakespeare's immense literary sources.

Richard Waugaman, M.D. *is Clinical Professor of Psychiatry, and 2012-2016 Faculty Expert on Shakespeare for Media Contacts at Georgetown University. He is also Training and Supervising Analyst, Emeritus at the Washington Psychoanalytic Institute. His 160 publications include some 60 works on Shake-speare. His two ebooks are* Newly Discovered works by "William Shake-Speare," a.k.a. Edward de Vere *and* It's Time to Re-Vere the Works of "William Shake-Speare": A Psychoanalyst Reads the Works of Edward de Vere, Earl of Oxford. *He is indebted to Roger Stritmatter's research on de Vere's Geneva Bible for interesting him in Oxfordian research. He has two websites:* www.oxfreudian.com *and* explore.georgetown.edu/people/waugamar/. *The full texts of most of his Shake-speare publications are accessible on the latter website.*

The most recent compilation of these literary sources, Stuart Gillespie's *Shakespeare's Books* (London, Continuum, 2001) fails to include either Wilson or Quintilian.

Despite Skinner's focus on judicial rhetoric, he seems poorly informed about Shakespeare's legal knowledge. He fails to cite George Greenwood's classic studies on this topic (e.g., *Shakespeare's Law*, 1920). So he claims that some scholarship on this topic has tended to "exaggerate the extent of Shakespeare's legal competence" (7). Most Stratfordians must instead underestimate his legal knowledge, or undermine the credibility of their authorship theory. Skinner is aware that he risks incurring the wrath of the Stratfordians if he implies a degree of learning in the author that seems inconsistent with the legendary authorship theory. He tries to "forestall egregious questions about how the classical learning I attribute to [Shakespeare] could possibly have been attained by a mere grammar school boy." His preemptive answer? With Stanley Wells-like tortured syntax, he asserts that "there is nothing in the erudition displayed in any of the plays I discuss that could not readily have been acquired from an education of precisely the kind that Shakespeare would have received" at the Stratford grammar school (10). Again, we respectfully disagree.

Skinner makes the plausible case that Renaissance thinkers "were prepared to treat the rhetorical . . . texts of classical antiquity as if they were contemporary documents . . . [There was] an extraordinarily strong sense of cultural continuity with which the humanists confronted their classical authorities" (26). By asserting that Shakespeare was indeed a Renaissance humanist, Skinner gives the lie to a core Stratfordian misconception. As stated by Stanley Wells, it holds that Shakespeare "was not all that learned" (interview in documentary film Last Will. and Testament), so his alleged grammar school education and supposed inborn genius would have sufficed.

Skinner notes that, as early as *Lucrece*, Shakespeare "became deeply interested in exploring . . . problems about guilt and responsibility" (51). It was in *Hamlet* that he showed a "deeper preoccupation with the theory of forensic eloquence" (55). We are accustomed to linking Horatio with Oxford's cousin Horace de Vere. Skinner has a different theory, although it does not contradict ours. He reminds us that Cicero holds that two qualities allow us to speak persuasively: ratio (reason) and oratio (powerful speech). Horatio's name, combining both, is for Skinner one of the reasons Hamlet chooses him to tell his story in the future. Polonius appears so ridiculous partly because he comically manages to botch the rules of rhetoric; he is "a model of technical incompetence" (189). De Vere is especially inventive when it comes to skewering his father-in-law. *All's Well*, as it weaves together three narrative strands of forensic argument, "must count as Shakespeare's most spectacular use of judicial rhetoric for dramatic purposes" (63).

Skinner makes a fascinating observation about Shakespeare's typical endings. Rhetoricians all agreed with Quintilian that the *peroratio*, or ending, is when "we are allowed to open up the full flood of our eloquence" (291). By contrast, Skinner notes that "some of [Shakespeare's] most intensely forensic scenes come to an end without any such *peroratio*" (302). Further, when Shakespeare does imitate a more conventional rhetorical ending, he does so in a way that undermines rather than strengthens the points being made. For example, Hamlet, in Act 3, Sc. 2 makes what seems like a "deliberately anti-climactic" *peroratio* (303). Shakespeare always resists resolving complexity with simplistic solutions. As Skinner puts it, "It often seems that Shakespeare has a constitutional antipathy towards the conclusive…" (311). Helen Vendler made a similar observation about Shakespeare's *Sonnets* – when a given sonnet ends with a couplet that sounds proverbial, it suggests that Shakespeare is giving up on trying to solve the problems posed by that sonnet.[3]

Colin Burrow's superb book *Shakespeare and Classical Antiquity* (Oxford University Press, 2013) persuasively expands our awareness of Shakespeare's crucial Latin sources. Skinner describes his book as a supplement to Burrow on the influence of ancient Roman literature on Shakespeare – especially since Burrow does not discuss works of rhetoric. In fact, Burrow alarmed some Stratfordians with his efforts to document Shakespeare's intimate familiarity with many Latin classics – not only their content, but even their style, which had an important influence on him. Burrow and I have corresponded about the likelihood that Shakespeare, in choosing his words, was always mindful of their Latin etymology, adding deeper levels of complexity to his language. Burrow agreed (July 21, 2014) that "maturity" in Sonnet 60, line 6, might allude to the Latin meaning of "maturare" as "hasten," and that "saucy" in Sonnet 80, line 7 might allude to the Latin "saucium" as "wounded." However, Burrow, like Skinner, makes major concessions to the traditional authorship theory. They both want Shakespeare to have learned most of what he knew about the Latin classics in the Stratford grammar school. Refreshingly, though, in a lecture at Washington and Lee University (April 4, 2016), Skinner admitted that he doubts Quintilian was studied in the Stratford Grammar School.

What about Quintilian? Skinner spends so much of his book showing Shakespeare's familiarity with Quintilian that I soon found myself reading this ancient Roman author. Oxfordians have a plausible explanation for de Vere's fascination with Quintilian's contributions to judicial rhetoric: de Vere was trained in law at the Inns of Court. Everything he read – including law – contributed to his artistic creativity. Although Quintilian mentions poets, plays, and actors in passing, his sustained focus is on the education of the ideal orator, who could use his skills in arguing legal cases. Nevertheless, de Vere discerned that Quintilian's insights about how to influence judges to accept the orator's arguments could often be adapted to play-writing, with other characters and the audience in the role of the judges.

Let me now turn to some further observations about passages in Quintilian's *Institutio Oratoria* (*Institutes of Oratory*, c. CE 95) that I believe may have influenced de Vere's literary works. Quintilian repeatedly returns to the emotions of the audience as the primary target of the orator. Modern literary theory tries to sever the close connection between the author's life experiences and her literary works. Quintilian, by contrast, would have expected de Vere to draw on his personal experiences in his creative works: "The prime essential for stirring the emotions of others is . . . first to feel those emotions oneself" (location 35442,[4] quoted by Skinner). Quintilian links the role of figures of speech with appealing to the emotions of the audience: "there is no more effective method of exciting emotions than an apt use of figures" (loc. 40883).

Although he did not know that the emotional center of our brain, our limbic system, sends more neurons to our neocortex than it receives from it, Quintilian did know that our reason is often ruled by our emotions: "the appeal to the emotions [of the judges] will do more, for it will make them *wish* our case to be the better. *And what they wish, they will also believe*" (loc. 35279, emphasis added). Long before Freud, Quintilian knew about our penchant for wish fulfillment. Stratfordians, of course, are expert in appealing to the widespread wish that a lowly commoner wrote the greatest literary works in English. *Anyone* can win that lottery, as it were.

Music has a mysteriously powerful effect on our emotions. Scholars have noted the importance of music in Shakespeare's works. Every play includes music, or references to musical terminology. So de Vere probably resonated with Quintilian's remarks on music – "poetry is song and poets claim to be singers" (loc. 25177); "the art of letters and that of music were once united" (loc. 25453).

One of the most shocking scenes in Shakespeare is Richard III wooing Lady Anne, just after he has killed her husband. Richard's chutzpah here illustrates Quintilian's assertion that "there are some acts which require to be defended with no less boldness than was required for their commission" (loc. 35095). We think of Richard III's several comments made directly to the audience, when Quintilian writes, "We may confer with our audience, admitting them as it were into our deliberations…a device which is one of the greatest embellishments of oratory and specially adapted to win over the feelings [of the audience], as also frequently to excite them" (loc. 40954).

Puck addresses the audience in the final two lines of *MND*. He says, "Give me your *hands*, if we be *friends*,/ And Robin shall restore amends" (5.1.423-24). The King speaks the epilogue to the audience at the end of *All's Well*, "Your gentle *hands* lend us, and take our hearts" (5.Epilogue.6). Similarly, Quintilian writes, "it is at the close of our drama that we must really stir the theatre, when we have reached the place for the phrase with which the old tragedies and comedies used to end, '*Friends*, give us your *applause*' " (loc. 35221, emphasis added in each quotation).

EEBO shows no instances of "mind's eye" before its two occurrences in *Hamlet*. Quintilian wrote "quae non vidistis oculis, animis cernere potestis," or, in English translation, "you can see it with the mind's eye" (more literally, "which you don't see with your eyes, but you can see with your mind") (loc. 41387). One thinks of Hamlet's advice to the players when Quintilian writes that "the orator . . . must rigorously avoid staginess and all extravagance of facial expression, gesture and gait" (25664).

Mark Antony, in his funeral speech, holds up Caesar's mantle before the crowd, showing the bloody holes made by the assassins' daggers: "behold/ Our Caesar's vesture wounded? Look you here,/ Here is himself" (*Julius Caesar* 3.2.195-97). De Vere may have been inspired by Quintilian's comment that "The impression produced by such exhibitions is generally enormous, since they seem to bring the spectators face to face with the cruel facts. For example, the sight of the bloodstains on the purple-bordered toga of…Caesar…aroused the Roman people to fury…his garment, still wet with his blood, brought such a vivid image of the crime before their minds, that Caesar seemed…to be being murdered before their very eyes" (loc. 35078, cited by Skinner).

Skinner observes that Iago, more than any other Shakespeare character, shows that an evil person can misuse rhetorical skills to persuade someone that a malicious falsehood is the truth. Iago manipulates Othello by pretending to want to protect him from his worst suspicions of Desdemona. Iago feigns unwillingness to answer Othello's growingly insistent questions about Iago's ostensible suspicions that Desdemona is unfaithful. Quintilian explains this strategy – "The facts themselves must be allowed to excite the suspicions of the judge…words broken by silences [are] most effective. For thus the judge will be led to seek out the secret which he would not perhaps believe if he heard it openly stated, and to believe in that which he thinks he has found out for himself" (loc. 41636).

As I mentioned earlier, one of the many reasons that I find Skinner's book so fascinating is that it dovetails with the likelihood that de Vere wrote the 1589 *Arte of English Poesie*. As Skinner points out, its third part deals extensively with rhetoric, especially figures of speech. By the way, Angel Day's *The English Secretorie* (1586), dedicated to de Vere, included marginal glosses highlighting rhetorical figures.[5] It is noteworthy that Day uses the word "coined" in the sense that de Vere seems to have coined it in 1570:[6] "Such odd coyned tearmes," referring to an example of a "preposterous and confused kind of writing"(39). Further, in 1592 Day seems to have been the second author, after de Vere in the *Arte*, to use the term "hendiadys" in English. In his 1592 edition, Day included a new section on rhetorical figures.

The hypothesis that de Vere wrote *The Arte of English Poesie* gains support from the connections between Quintilian and the Shakespeare canon, because the *Arte* twice mentions Quintilian by name. Recall that the *Arte* is only the sixth book in EEBO to cite Quintilian. In the second chapter of Book 3, de Vere recommends the use of figures of speech. In that context, he says, "I have come to the Lord Keeper Sir Nicholas Bacon, & found him sitting in his gallery alone with the works of Quintilian before him, in deede he was a most eloquent man, and of rare learning and wisedome, as ever I knew England to breed" (224).[7] And, in chapter 9 of Book 3, the author says that "the learned orators and good grammarians among the Romans, as Cicero, Varro, Quintilian, and others, strained themselves to give the Greek words [for figures of speech] Latin names" (241). Further, according to editors Whigham and Rebhorn, the *Arte* uses some seventy of Quintilian's terms for figures of speech.

Yet another example of Quintilian's likely influence on the *Arte* was the latter's focus on dissembling and dissimulation. Chapter 18 of Book 3 repeatedly connects figures of speech with dissembling, dissimulation, and duplicity. The title of chapter 23 of Book 3 begins, "That the good poet or maker ought to dissemble his art" (378). De Vere adds that the role of the courtier "is, in plain terms, cunningly to be able to dissemble" (379). Quintilian may have shaped de Vere's emphasis here by his statement that "There is also available the device of dissimulation, when we say one thing and mean another, *the most effective of all means of stealing into the minds of men* and a most attractive device" (loc. 40946, emphasis added).

Skinner helps us better understand just how Shakespeare steals into our minds so effectively. I am delighted by Skinner's book, and I recommend it highly. Skinner accomplished what he set out to do – and so much more.

Notes

1. Only 19 books published before the 1616 death of Shakspere cite Quintilian. In sharp contrast, more than 600 books before 1589 referred to Cicero.

2. See "The Arte of English Poesie: The Case for Edward de Vere's Authorship." *Brief Chronicles: The Interdisciplinary Journal of the Shakespeare Fellowship* 2:121-141 (2010) and also see "The Arte of Overturning Tradition: Did E.K. – a.k.a. E.O. – Write The Arte of English Poesie?" *Brief Chronicles: The Interdisciplinary Journal of the Shakespeare Fellowship* 2:260-266 (2010).

3. *The Art of Shakespeare's Sonnets*. Cambridge, MA, The Belknap Press, 1997.

4. My citations from Quintilian are to the Kindle version of his *Complete* [surviving] *Works*. Delphi Classics, 2015.

5. See Robert Sean Brazil. *Angel Day: The English Secretary and Edward de Vere, Seventeenth Earl of Oxford*. Seattle, Cortical Output, 2013.

6. In his English translation of Johann Sturm's *A Ritch Storehouse*.

7. Edited by Frank Whigham and Wayne A. Rebhorn. Ithaca: Cornell University Press, 2007.

Robert Bearman's Shakespeare's Money

Reviewed by Richard M. Waugaman

At the conference on "Shakespeare and the Problem of Biography" at the Folger Shakespeare Library in the spring of 2014, Lena Orlin thought she had an explanation for Shakspere's great business success. It was Anne Hathaway. Yes, the Executive Director of the Shakespeare Association of America, and English Professor at Georgetown University, seriously claimed that Anne must have run the family business. No, she offered no evidence whatsoever. But no evidence seems to be needed when defending the True Bard from us heretics.

So, why did Orlin feel the need to defend Shakspere from the charge of having earned too much money from his Stratford business dealings? She was probably reacting to a widely publicized paper delivered nearly a year earlier, that characterized him as a wealthy but unscrupulous businessman. An article in the online March 31, 2013 *Telegraph* states:

> As well as writing many of the world's greatest plays, he [Shakspere] was a successful businessman and major landowner in his native Warwickshire who retired an extremely wealthy man. However, a new study has found that he was repeatedly prosecuted and fined for illegally hoarding food, and threatened with jail for failing to pay his taxes ... Court and tax records show that over a 15-year period Shakespeare purchased grain, malt and barley to store and resell for inflated prices, according to a paper by Aberystwyth University academics Dr Jayne Archer, Professor Richard Marggraf Turley and Professor Howard Thomas. The study notes: 'By combining both illegal and legal activities, Shakespeare was able to retire in 1613 as the largest property owner in his home town, Stratford-upon-Avon. His profits - minus a few fines for illegal hoarding and tax evasion - meant he had a working life of just 24 years."

The same day, the online *Daily Mail* reported that Jonathan Bate said of these findings that the scholars "had performed a valuable service in setting Shakespeare's work in the context of the famines...of the period."

Robert Bearman's book *Shakespeare's Money: How Much Did He Make and What Did This Mean?* (Oxford University Press, 2016) disputes nearly all of these assertions. The hagiographic mirror image of Alan Nelson's character assassination of de Vere,

Bearman tries at every turn to rescue Shakspere's reputation from such insinuations. For example, Bearman claims that Shakspere "may be acquitted of any charge of deliberate hoarding" of grain (99). Bearman feels certain Shakspere was simply trying to provide for his family. Bearman, former Head of Archives at the Shakespeare Birthplace Trust, seems to have divided loyalties to the truth and to the Shakspere authorship myth. To his credit, Bearman writes that "David Ellis has recently and entertainingly drawn our attention to the limited value of much … so-called biographical work" (5).

Bearman is unable to explain convincingly why Shakspere, as a presumably excellent grammar school student, was not sent to university, when promising but indigent students such as Marlowe were. Bearman discovered that Shakspere's marriage at eighteen was unusual in Stratford. He was "one of only three known teenage bridegrooms from Stratford marrying during the years 1570-1640" (27).

Most of what is written about the Merchant of Stratford is tendentious in the extreme, forcing the facts of his life to fit the misguided if traditional authorship theory. One of many reasons that Bearman's book is so welcome is that he chooses to avoid that route to the exploration of Shakspere's life. Here is one of his central conclusions: "Deservedly renowned though his career as a writer . . . in financial terms he achieved only modest success. More importantly, this fundamental issue in any assessment of his life is derived from those very documents which are barely considered as relevant by many Shakespeare biographers who prefer not to see their subject engaged in the more practical issue of making a living and providing for his family . . ." (175). Lena Orlin, who is currently writing yet another biography of Shakspere, clearly fits this description.

Although Shakspere died "a man of considerable means" (174), the picture is more complicated than a steady upward trajectory. "His purchases came to a virtual end in 1605 . . ." (174). That is, just one year after the death of Edward de Vere. "[H]is theatre income . . . may well have come to a virtual end when, in or soon after 1612,

---

Richard Waugaman, M.D. *is Clinical Professor of Psychiatry and 2012-2016 Faculty Expert on Shakespeare for Media Contacts at Georgetown University. He is also Training and Supervising Analyst, Emeritus at the Washington Psychoanalytic Institute. His 160 publications include some 60 works on Shake-speare. His two ebooks are* Newly Discovered Works by "William Shake-Speare," a.k.a. Edward de Vere *and* It's Time to Re-Vere the Works of "William Shake-Speare": A Psychoanalyst Reads the Works of Edward de Vere, Earl of Oxford. *He is indebted to Roger Stritmatter's research on de Vere's Geneva Bible for interesting him in Oxfordian research. He has two websites:* www.oxfreudian.com *and* explore.georgetown.edu/people/waugamar/. *The full texts of most of his Shake-speare publications are accessible on the latter website.*

he surrendered his company shares." Bearman finds it likely that "his stepping back from full-time theatrical work was something more or less forced upon him . . ." (175). Bearman further believes that Shakspere's "careful husbanding of his resources" after 1612 is consistent with a forced retirement. Not realizing that Shakspere's services as a front man were no longer needed, Bearman speculates that exhaustion or poor health was the reason for his retirement. Shakspere's father had a sharp decline in his fortunes in the 1580s, when his credit was withdrawn, leading him to mortgage, then lose some of his landholdings.

Despite his father's financial reversals, and despite the financial problems of contemporaries such as Thomas Dekker, who was imprisoned for debt, "almost miraculously it now seems, Shakspere appears to have steered his way though these troubled waters with no surviving evidence to indicate that he ever got into serious [financial] difficulties, albeit that problems of debt surface from time to time in his writings" (177).

In defending the traditional theory, Bearman claims that "there is no record of his ever having seriously [sic] run afoul of the law" (2). Bearman claims Shakspere only twice was in trouble with the authorities, in 1597 and 1598, for failure to pay his taxes. Bearman thus ignores the evidence from Aberystwyth researchers. Tellingly, Bearman calls Shakspere "a man who rarely emerges from the shadows" (2). Bearman makes the fascinating observation that there is more archival evidence of Shakspere's father than of the alleged Bard himself. Surprisingly, Bearman asserts that Shakspere "was hardly ever involved in legal proceedings" (3). This appears to be an attempt to put a Stratfordian spin on the actual record.

Bearman concludes that "it was from his involvement as a sharer in the profits of his acting company that he derived the major portion of his income" (5-6). But he then admits, "an almost total lack of material evidence requires us simply to hazard estimates of what this [sharer income] might have been" (6). And Shakespere's income as a writer "remains undefined" (6). The only supposed record of his earning money for writing was his receiving payment in 1613 for devising a motto for the impresa for the earl of Rutland. But it seems to have been a John Shakspere who designed impresas. The vast majority of surviving records are from Shakspere's affairs in Stratford, not in London – casting doubt on the assumption that he spent much of his life in London. It becomes apparent that, despite Bearman's goal of sticking to the archival evidence, his interpretation of it is constantly distorted by his assumption that Shakspere was the author.

Bearman never admits we have no record of Shakspere ever being paid for his plays. But he does acknowledge that there is no record of Shakspere acting after 1603. He also admits Shakspere's alleged literary productivity dropped after 1605. However, "Alongside this evidence of a dwindling [literary] output is Shakspere's surprising decision to part with his shares in both the [theatrical] company and its playhouses"

(151). These shares are not mentioned in his will. Bearman speculates he sold them in 1613. Bearman speculates that Shakspere's fellow sharers may have pressured him to withdraw. A central enigma for Bearman is why Shakspere gave up an estimated £200 pounds as sharer of the theatrical company and of the Globe, when his other income was only about £70.

How does this narrative of Shakspere's rising, then falling fortunes possibly relate to de Vere's life? We know he spelled his pen name "Shakespeare" in 1593 and 1594, when he first published his two long poems. But he used that pen name for a *play* for the first time in 1598. Uniquely for an undisputed work, he spelled his name "Shakespere" (without the final "a") for his 1598 *Loves Labours Lost*. (The 1612 third edition of *Passionate Pilgrim* attributed all its poems to "Shakespeare" until protests led the publisher to remove this name). Thus, de Vere's first use of the pen name for a *play* suggests an effort to make it resemble the name of the Merchant of Stratford. Perhaps de Vere rewarded Shakspere with shares in the theatrical company for playing along as de Vere's front man.

The hyphenated pen name "Shake-speare" appeared with only the next three plays, after *Love's Labours Lost*. Subsequently, the notorious, winking hyphen may have been suppressed under pressure from Robert Cecil or Queen Elizabeth. With King James' accession in 1603, the hyphen reappeared in many publications during the ensuing decades, including Jon Benson's 1640 edition of the *Sonnets*. Since hyphenated last names were fairly rare in early modern England, I read the "Shake-speare" spelling as toying with a form of transparent pseudonymity. So Shakspere's peak years financially may roughly correspond with the period during which the strictest form of authorial anonymity was imposed on de Vere. Oxford's own preference seemed to be one of sprezzatura-like nonchalance about his pseudonym being recognized as such.

When people ask me the inevitable question, "What was de Vere's relationship with Shakspere of Stratford?" I usually say we can only speculate. But reading Bearman's book makes more plausible for me the conjecture that Shakspere was chosen as something of a front man for de Vere during his lifetime. Consider what Bearman says about the year following de Vere's death as a "turning point" in Shakspere's life. "The year 1605 [i.e., one year after Oxford's death] marks something of a turning point in Shakspere's financial dealings." During the previous eight years, he purchased some £900 of property in Stratford. "Thereafter, he made only one further, and rather odd addition to his portfolio" – the Blackfriars Gatehouse, in 1613 (122). Bearman suspects that purchase may have been part of a compromise with his fellow sharers when Shakspere sold his own shares. The purchase was designed so the Gatehouse would pass to its trustees on Shakspere's death, rather than to his family.

Once again, a book by a Stratfordian fails to support their authorship theory, but is instead consistent with Oxford's authorship. The timing of Shakspere's greatest financial success is also consistent with his having been paid to serve as Oxford's front man.

"Written with wit, humor, erudition and the instincts of a real working actor ... Bristles with humanity ... A truly original approach ... Well worth the attention of academics and non-academics alike." - **Don Rubin, editor of *The World Encyclopedia of Contemporary Theatre* and former chair of the Department of Theatre at York University, Toronto.**

"An exceptionally lucid and thorough exploration of the arguments supporting the controversial theory that the true Shakespeare was the Earl of Oxford. Masterfully organized." – **Roger Stritmatter, associate Professor of Humanities at Coppin State University.**

"If Stratfordians could assemble even a handful of arguments this powerful and this persuasive, they'd say, 'Game over. We've proved our case.'" – **Mark Anderson, author of *"Shakespeare" by Another Name*.**

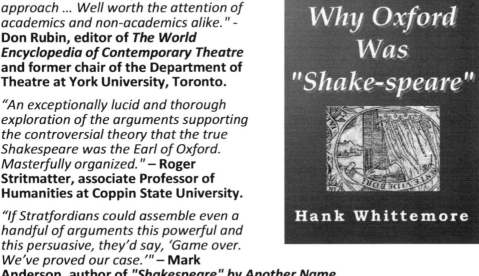

"Unlocks the door to a rich garden of truth about William Shakespeare from whence no serious lover of his poems and plays will ever wish to return." – **Alexander Waugh, author, scholar, Chairman of the De Vere Society, President of the Shakespeare Authorship Coalition.**

"We now have an indisputable claimant for the answer to the question: What is the first book to read about the Shakespeare authorship question? Answer: Hank Whittemore's 100 Reasons Why Oxford Was 'Shake-speare'." – **Linda Theil, editor of the *Oberon Shakespeare Study Group Weblog***

"Read this book before you decide who wrote Shakespeare ... We've all been sold a defective Avon product, folks. It's time to return it for a full refund!" – **Richard M. Waugaman, M.D., Professor of Psychiatry, Georgetown University School of Medicine.**

Available now on amazon.com

$19.95

Forever Press
www.foreverpress.org

Made in the USA
San Bernardino,
CA